TELOS MOVIE CLASSICS # 2

THE MAKING OF *CASINO ROYALE* (1967)

TELOS MOVIE CLASSICS # 2

THE MAKING OF
CASINO ROYALE (1967)

Michael Richardson

First published in 2015 by Telos Publishing Ltd
5A Church Road, Shortlands, Bromley, Kent BR2 0HP,
United Kingdom
www.telos.co.uk

Telos Publishing Ltd values feedback. Please e-mail us with any comments you may have about this book to:
feedback@telos.co.uk

ISBN: 978-1-84583-932-1

Telos Movie Classics # 2

The Making of Casino Royale *(1967)* © 2015 Michael Richardson

Index by Ian Pritchard

The moral right of the author has been asserted.

British Library Cataloguing in Publication Data.
A catalogue record for this book is available from the British Library.

This book is sold subject to the condition that it shall not by way of trade or otherwise, be lent, resold, hired out or otherwise circulated without the publisher's prior written consent in any form of binding or cover other than that in which it is published and without a similar condition including this condition being imposed on the subsequent purchaser.

Dedication

Dedicated to Val Guest

Acknowledgements

I have to express extreme gratitude to the following, as without their endless enthusiasm and devotion, this project would have been much more difficult to achieve. Their support, assistance and encouragement pushed me forward to research further and make this volume more detailed than I ever could have imagined when I began writing.

Proof-reader: Annette Hill

Chris Bentley, Simon Coward, Sam Denham, Geoff Dodd, Jennifer Evans of the British Board of Film Classification, Alan Field, Val Guest, Alan Hayes, Gerald Lovell, Anthony McKay, Frank Morgan, Simon Mills, Andrew Pixley, Martin Randall, Robert Banks Stewart, Tony Sullivan, Kevin Wilkinson and Dave Wright.

I would also like to thank for their invaluable assistance certain patrons of the Britmovie: British Film Forum, who can be identified only by their usernames: Cully, Euryale, Ghughesarch, Philly and Wee Sonny MacGregor.

CONTENTS

INTRODUCTION	9
PART ONE: PRODUCTION HISTORY	11
Chapter One: The Original James Bond	13
Chapter Two: Development Hell	31
Chapter Three: The Impressionist Meets the Magician	55
Chapter Four: Torture of the Mind	79
Chapter Five: The Spy Chick Affair	101
Chapter Six: Psychedelic Cinema	121
Chapter Seven: The Cold War in Borehamwood	151
Chapter Eight: The Fun Movement	173
PART TWO: BIOGRAPHIES	185
APPENDIX ONE: PRODUCTION DETAILS	213
APPENDIX TWO: MISSING SCENES AND FOOTAGE	221
APPENDIX THREE: PRODUCTION SCHEDULE	227
APPENDIX FOUR: RECORDINGS – UK RELEASES	229
INDEX	232
ABOUT THE AUTHOR	238

Introduction

I had watched producer Charles K Feldman's James Bond feature film *Casino Royale* (1967) on television many times before a friend of mine, Andrew Pixley, furthered my interest in the production by pointing out the different plotlines within it and the disjointed nature of the screenplay. Over the years, I both researched and came across much more information about the haphazard manner in which *Casino Royale* was assembled, which only wetted my appetite to learn as much as I possibly could about this film that had somehow managed to get out of control.

My fascination with this craziest Bond film of all eventually brought about, during the summer of 2004 and early 2005, an exchange of faxes with one of its directors, Val Guest, who was living in California at the time. When Guest made a flying visit to London for Christmas 2005, I telephoned him at his London home in Belgravia just before the New Year. Unfortunately, he was returning to the US the following day, but he suggested that the next time he was in London I should pay him a visit and conduct the ultimate interview regarding *Casino Royale*.

Sadly, Guest never did return to London, as he passed away five months later in Palm Springs, California. Sometime later I was reading an interview that he had given to the magazine *SFX*, published in March 2003, where he was quoted as saying, 'There's a whole film to be made about the making of *Casino Royale!*' This made me think. Making a film was beyond my abilities and resources, but writing a book that covered both the development and the production of *Casino Royale* was certainly something I could do. The end result is the volume you now see before you.

INTRODUCTION

Feldman, a self-made millionaire, first became interested in producing a cinema version of author Ian Fleming's debut James Bond novel *Casino Royale* in 1960. The launch a couple of years later of the successful Eon Productions series of 007 movies, beginning with *Dr. No* (1962), made him believe initially that he required the services of their star, Sean Connery, to make his project viable. From 1963 to mid-1965, he and later his financial backer Columbia Pictures had intermittent discussions with Eon Productions and their distributor United Artists regarding a possible co-production. Ultimately it proved impossible to reach an agreement that satisfied all parties; but Feldman remained determined to proceed with his project regardless, even without Connery. This led to the production of the most complicated and intricately-assembled big budget feature film ever made, boasting seven directors, numerous scriptwriters and footage filmed at three major British studios.

Casino Royale is a complex combination of spoof, style and storylines amalgamated within one feature film of truly epic proportions. Almost fifty years after its production, the elements that were originally thought to work against it, such as the lack of a coherent plot and the sending up of James Bond, are now considered to work in its favour, and have assisted in making it a cult slice of '60s psychedelia.

Michael Richardson
August 2015

Part One
Production History

Chapter One
The Original James Bond

Fleming creates Bond

Ian Fleming wrote his initial James Bond novel *Casino Royale* during February/March 1952, while at his Jamaican home Goldeneye, submitting his typed manuscript upon his return to London to Jonathan Cape Ltd, who accepted it for publication in October of the same year. The first hardback edition of *Casino Royale* became available in booksellers on 13 April 1953, though by May the print run of 4,750 copies had completely sold out, prompting a second printing, shortly followed by a third. Meanwhile, the novel was doing the rounds of American book publishers, and the New York-based Al Hart of the Macmillan Publishing Company was sufficiently impressed to offer Fleming a contract, which saw a first stateside edition published in March 1954.[1]

Television adaptation

Sometime later, Fleming was approached by the American CBS network and accepted $1,000 for the television rights to *Casino Royale*, which allowed them to adapt it as an instalment of their anthology series *Climax!*. This fifty-minute presentation of the story was transmitted live from Stage 43 at CBS Television City studios, based on Beverly Boulevard in Los Angeles, on the evening of 21 October 1954. Obviously with the aim of making

---

[1] *The James Bond Bedside Companion*, Raymond Benson, Boxtree, September 1988.

Bond more identifiable to the US audience, the producers decided that he and his associate Felix Leiter, an American CIA agent in the novel, should exchange nationalities. Hence, Bond became an American agent working for Combined Intelligence, while Leiter became a British Station S operative called Clarence (whose surname was misspelt on the closing credits as 'Letter').

Barry Nelson starred as secret agent James Bond, with Hungarian-born actor Peter Lorre playing the communist paymaster Le Chiffre, and the screenplay revolved around their confrontation in a high-stakes baccarat game. Linda Christian co-starred as Le Chiffre's girlfriend Valerie Mathis, an undercover agent for the French Deuxième Bureau, who was an amalgamation of two characters from the novel: Bond's secret service colleague Vesper Lynd and his French ally René Mathis. Australian actor Michael Pate brought Leiter to life as a quintessential Englishman, and the *Climax!* series host, actor William Lundigan, spoke a short and ironic introduction warning about the dangers of gambling.

Scriptwriters Charles Bennett and Anthony Ellis were responsible for adapting Fleming's work to the visual medium, but due to the restrictive fifty-minute format for the hour timeslot, several elements of the plotline were omitted. Bennett was a longstanding film and television writer, who had collaborated with Alfred Hitchcock on some classic mystery thrillers such as *The Man Who Knew Too Much* (1934) and *The 39 Steps* (1935), but Ellis's credits were confined to television screenplays. As this version of *Casino Royale* went out live, it was thought for a long time that the production was lost forever, until airline executive and television historian Jim Schoenberger located a telerecording (kinescope) in a film can in 1981.

You Asked For It

The first hardback edition of Fleming's second James Bond adventure, *Live and Let Die*, was published in the UK by Jonathan Cape in April 1954 and in the States by Macmillan in

January 1955. American sales of both Bond books were however disappointing by comparison with UK sales, so when the Popular Library imprint came to publish the first stateside paperback edition of *Casino Royale* in April 1955 – at the same time as Pan published the first UK paperback edition – they gave it what they considered to be a more commercial title, *You Asked For It*, and also changed the lead character's name to Jimmy Bond.[2] However, later American editions from different publishers would revert to the original title and reinstate the James Bond name.

Film rights

Despite the relatively weak early American sales of the book, Russian-born actor/film producer Gregory Ratoff saw plenty of potential in *Casino Royale*, and in March 1955 he acquired the film rights from Ian Fleming for a modest fee of $6,000. Having become somewhat discouraged by the Bond books' reception in the US, Fleming accepted Ratoff's offer without negotiating, and quickly purchased an American Ford Thunderbird car with the proceeds.[3] Ratoff had borrowed the money for the deal from two old friends, the film producer Charles K Feldman and Darryl Zanuck, who was then the President of 20th Century Fox.[4]

Screenplays

By January 1956, Ratoff and fellow film producer Michael Garrison (who would later create the television series *The Wild Wild West*) had formed a production company, intending to shoot *Casino Royale* as a feature film with backing from 20th

---

[2] *The James Bond Bedside Companion*, Raymond Benson, Boxtree, September 1988.
[3] *The James Bond Bedside Companion*, Raymond Benson, Boxtree, September 1988.
[4] Dr Shatterhand's Botanical Garden website, *It's a Mad, Mad, Mad, Mad Royale*, Stuart Basinger, retrieved July 2013.

Century Fox. According to an article in the *New York Times*, a mid-summer shooting schedule had been arranged, which included not only filming in England, but also location work planned to be undertaken in San Remo, Italy and Estoril, Portugal.[5]

The approach made by Ratoff and Garrison to 20th Century Fox proved to be unsuccessful, however, as the studio failed to share the producers' enthusiasm for the project, ultimately turning down their proposal.[6] Despite this setback, Ratoff developed a screenplay together with Lorenzo Semple Jr, though the twist in this storyline was that Bond would be a woman; should the project have reached production, she would have been portrayed by actress Susan Oliver.[7]

Screenwriter and novelist Ben Hecht, famous for contributing to movies such as *Scarface* (1932), *Gone With the Wind* (1939) and *Notorious* (1946), also penned a *Casino Royale* adaptation for Ratoff at some point during 1957. However, this did not actually feature James Bond, but substituted him with a wealthy and smart-mouthed American gangster called Lucky Fortunato, who was also a skilled cardsharp. Although nothing came of this at the time, Hecht would become involved with *Casino Royale* again several years down the line, when he would devote more time to story outlines and screenplays for the enterprise.[8]

The *Daily Express* comic strip

Also during 1957, Fleming was approached by the British *Daily Express* newspaper, who wanted the rights to take James Bond

---

[5] The *Telegraph* website, Casino Royale: *60 Years Old*, Jeremy Duns, retrieved April 2013.
[6] *The James Bond Films: A Behind the Scenes History*, Steven Jay Rubin, Random House, September 1983.
[7] The *Telegraph* website, Casino Royale: *60 Years Old*, Jeremy Duns, retrieved April 2013.
[8] The *Telegraph* website, Casino Royale: *60 Years Old*, Jeremy Duns, retrieved April 2013.

into a totally different medium, that of the black-and-white comic strip. An agreement was reached whereby the Bond strip would become a regular daily feature, beginning with *Casino Royale*. The story was adapted by Anthony Hern, who had previously been responsible for prose serialisations of the fourth and fifth Bond novels, *Diamonds Are Forever* and *From Russia, with Love*, for the same newspaper. Artwork was handled by Scotsman John McLusky, who had served as a scenic artist with Bomber Command during World War Two before turning freelance illustrator, and he visualised Bond as a rough-looking and muscular individual.[9]

Proposed Bond television series

Sometime after April 1958, CBS contacted Fleming with what appeared to be a generous offer regarding a James Bond television series, wanting the author to provide scripts for 32 episodes over a period of two years. With the exception of Fleming developing several story outlines, this concept unfortunately failed to progress, but later the author would recycle some of the outlines into his eighth Bond book, *For Your Eyes Only* (1960), which was a collection of short stories.

Kevin McClory

Around this time there was another attempt to mount a James Bond feature film. This came about after Fleming's childhood friend Ivar Bryce introduced him to an Irish scriptwriter/director called Kevin McClory.[10] During the winter of 1958, Fleming reviewed a rough-cut of McClory's recent movie *The Boy and the Bridge*, which he generally appreciated, and this led to discussions between them about bringing James

---

[9] MI6: The Home of James Bond 007 website, *James Bond 007 Comics*, retrieved July 2013.
[10] *The James Bond Bedside Companion*, Raymond Benson, Boxtree, September 1988.

Bond to the cinema screen. Rather than adapt one of Fleming's Bond novels, it was decided to construct a completely original screenplay, and McClory suggested the Bahamas as a setting, adding that the then novelty of underwater filming could be utilised. Another of Fleming's close friends, Ernest Cuneo, who had initially met the Bond creator during his time with British Intelligence in World War Two, was recruited, penning the first draft script for the proposed film. This screenplay was then submitted to Bryce and McClory, whose production company, Xanadu Productions, were lined up to actually make the picture. They in turn passed it on to Fleming, who then assembled a second draft.[11]

Eventually Fleming, McClory, Bryce and Cuneo collaborated on, wrote and rewrote various scripts, treatments and outlines for the proposed film, under a number of different titles including *James Bond of the Secret Service*, *SPECTRE* and *Longitude 78 West*. However, when *The Boy and the Bridge* opened in July 1959, it failed to generate the anticipated audience or monetary returns that could have been invested into the Bond project. Fleming realised that any Bond movie would be an expensive proposition, and on speaking with the film company MCA, he was advised that bringing a seasoned director on board could attract the required funding. Although McClory had been pencilled in for this job, it was suggested that he instead concentrate on producing the movie. Stepping aside, the Irishman recommended Alfred Hitchcock as a replacement director. However, when approached, the famed British auteur declined.[12]

During October 1959, Fleming's attention was more focused on his day job with *The Sunday Times*, which press baron Lord Thomson had recently acquired from the Kemsley Newspaper Group. He did however find time to approve McClory's request

---

[11] *The James Bond Bedside Companion*, Raymond Benson, Boxtree, September 1988.
[12] *The James Bond Bedside Companion*, Raymond Benson, Boxtree, September 1988.

to bring an experienced scriptwriter onto the project. This writer was Jack Whittingham, who had been involved in scripting feature films for twenty years. Whittingham and McClory together refined the Bond screenplay and, after further discussions, mailed Fleming a new draft under the *Longitude 78 West* title. Fleming was happy with how things were progressing, but decided that a much punchier title was needed, so he renamed it *Thunderball*.[13]

Sometime during January 1960, McClory visited Fleming at Goldeneye for an update on the film project, but he received mixed messages from the author, who was apparently having second thoughts regarding the deal. Fleming spoke about offering the screenplay to MCA for their evaluation, with McClory as a component of the package as the producer. However, he warned McClory that should MCA reject the proposal because of his involvement, then he ought to leave the project or be prepared to risk court action. Understandably, this statement left McClory feeling confused and angry, and he departed Goldeneye shortly after his arrival. The Xanadu Productions Bond movie proposal then fizzled out over the next couple of months.[14]

Patrick McGoohan

Later in 1960, Scottish scriptwriter Robert Banks Stewart (credited as Robert Stewart at the time) was commissioned by 20th Century Fox to adapt *Casino Royale* for the big screen, and he spent three months writing a screenplay. This situation came about after a recommendation by Stewart's agent to Darryl Zanuck, fuelled by the writer's involvement with the half-hour episodes of the ITC-produced television series *Danger Man*, starring Patrick McGoohan as British spy John Drake, which

---

[13] *The James Bond Bedside Companion*, Raymond Benson, Boxtree, September 1988.
[14] *The James Bond Bedside Companion*, Raymond Benson, Boxtree, September 1988.

under the title *Secret Agent* had begun transmissions on the CBS network in the States during April. Stewart, who had previously written episodes of Granada Television's *Knight Errant '60* and *Knight Errant Limited*, plus ITC's *Interpol Calling*, turned in what he described as a 'straight adaptation' of the *Casino Royale* novel. When later interviewed on the subject, he also recalled who was lined up to play the lead: 'It was to star Patrick McGoohan.'[15] However, in view of his strong moral and religious convictions, it appears highly unlikely that McGoohan would actually have accepted the James Bond role. (He was apparently offered it again in the autumn of 1961. On the latter occasion, producer Harry Saltzman approached the actor, on the strength of his *Danger Man* role, to become the leading man for the initial Bond film, *Dr. No*. However, Saltzman and his business partner Albert R Broccoli were disappointed when McGoohan refused, later stating, 'It wasn't a part for me.'[16])

Charles K Feldman

In July 1960, Gregory Ratoff once again announced that pre-production planning was under way to film *Casino Royale*, presumably from Stewart's screenplay, in the UK, with backing from 20th Century Fox, starring Peter Finch as Bond and Robert Morley as his MI6 boss M.[17] Ratoff's acting schedule brought him to Europe for a couple of months in 1960 to play a role in a movie entitled *The Big Gamble* (1961), but upon its completion, production on *Casino Royale* still failed to get under way. Sadly Ratoff was diagnosed with leukaemia, and he died on 14 December that year. Sorting out his estate, his ex-wife Eugenie Leontovich and Michael Garrison found that Charles K Feldman was one of his creditors. Instead of reimbursing Feldman what he was owed, the estate reached an agreement

---

[15] E-mail from Robert Banks Stewart to Michael Richardson, January 2013.
[16] Her Majesty's Secret Servant website, *A Prisoner in Bondage*, Mike Vincitore, retrieved August 2013.
[17] *Variety: Weekly*, Reed Business Information, 13 July 1960.

with him whereby he received the *Casino Royale* film rights.[18] This change of ownership prompted Fleming to try to reacquire the rights, instructing his film agent Bob Fenn to make a substantial offer for them. However, believing that he now held something of great value, Feldman refused.[19]

Legal action

Other parties were becoming interested in seeing James Bond at the movies, and one of these was Canadian producer Harry Saltzman, who in December 1960 managed to scrape together enough money to secure a six month option on Fleming's novels, except for *Casino Royale*. Several months later, Fleming's popularity was given a boost in the US when President John F Kennedy's top ten favourite books were announced in *Life* magazine dated 17 March 1961, and they included *From Russia, with Love*. However, Fleming was confronted with a major problem the same month, when Kevin McClory read an advance copy of the ninth Bond novel, *Thunderball*, and was incensed to discover that it included long passages lifted from the *Longitude 78 West* screenplay. McClory immediately instigated legal action, alleging plagiarism, but the initial hearing on 24 March went Fleming's way and the novel, which had already been distributed to retail outlets, was allowed to be sold. However, the door was left open for McClory to continue proceedings, which he did, and this possibly contributed toward the ailing Fleming suffering a heart attack the following month.[20]

---

[18] Dr. Shatterhand's Botanical Garden website, *It's a Mad, Mad, Mad, Mad Royale*, Stuart Basinger, retrieved July 2013.
[19] *The James Bond Films: A Behind the Scenes History*, Steven Jay Rubin, Random House, September 1983.
[20] *The James Bond Bedside Companion*, Raymond Benson, Boxtree, September 1988.

Albert R Broccoli and Harry Saltzman

Fleming recuperated for a month at the London Clinic, Devonshire Place, London, although by this time another major development had occurred. Saltzman's option was rapidly running out, and he had so far been unable to interest any major film company in backing the idea of a James Bond film. Then, during May 1961, he was introduced by a mutual friend, scriptwriter Wolf Mankowitz, to American producer Albert R Broccoli, aka Cubby Broccoli, who was also interested in getting a Bond movie under way. Saltzman and Broccoli decided to pool their resources, forming the production company Eon Productions. Then, after being turned down by Columbia Pictures, they had a meeting with United Artists on 21 June, where they arranged a deal to produce six Bond films.[21]

Dr. No

Saltzman and Broccoli wanted to film *Thunderball* as their initial Bond picture, but due to the ongoing legal proceedings this idea went on the backburner, and they decided to forge ahead by instead adapting Fleming's sixth Bond novel, *Dr. No*. While the film was in pre-production, a number of directors were considered, including Ken Hughes and Val Guest, who was given three Bond novels by Saltzman and Broccoli in order to familiarise himself with 007. Guest was very enthusiastic about the original idea of making *Thunderball*, but was disappointed when the producers explained the litigation wrangles surrounding the book and told him they had decided to go with *Dr. No* instead.[22] Some years later, Ken Hughes, Val Guest and Wolf Mankowitz would all play major parts in the production of *Casino Royale*.

---

[21] *The James Bond Bedside Companion*, Raymond Benson, Boxtree, September 1988.
[22] *SFX* No. 102, *Honoured Guest*, Steve O'Brien, Future Publishing, March 2003.

With Scottish actor Sean Connery cast as Bond, *Dr. No* entered principal photography on Tuesday 16 January 1962. Terence Young had the director's chair, as Guest was already committed to the murder mystery *Jigsaw* (1962), which started filming on location in Brighton on Monday 26 February.[23] Just over a month later, filming on *Dr. No* had been completed, although the movie would not premiere until Friday 5 October 1962, at the London Pavilion cinema.

During the same year, Charles K Feldman had at least one serious discussion with his old friend, noted producer/director Howard Hawks, regarding a possible production of *Casino Royale*. This resulted in a consultation with scriptwriter Leigh Brackett, who had co-written the acclaimed Hawks-directed films *The Big Sleep* (1946), *Rio Bravo* (1959) and *Hatari!* (1962), amongst others. Speculation suggests that Cary Grant would have been offered the lead, should the film proposal have advanced further, though any plans were abruptly dropped after Hawks saw an American preview copy of *Dr. No* in March 1963.[24]

From Russia with Love

After their successful debut with *Dr. No*, Eon Productions pressed ahead with their second Bond film, *From Russia with Love*, which began shooting on Monday 1 April 1963 and completed principal photography on Friday 23 August. The film premiered at the Odeon cinema, Leicester Square, London, on Thursday 10 October, going on to achieve box office takings surpassing those of any other feature film in the UK that year.

During the second half of 1963, Charles K Feldman opened negotiations with both United Artists and Eon Productions, attempting to obtain the services of Sean Connery for his proposed production of *Casino Royale*.[25] Feldman and Cubby

---

[23] *Variety: Weekly*, Reed Business Information, 26 February 1962.
[24] Her Majesty's Secret Servant website, *Howard Hawks' Casino Royale*, Bill Koenig, retrieved June 2005.

Broccoli were no strangers, the latter having worked in Hollywood after World War Two for the former's Famous Artists acting agency, before becoming a film producer. An announcement in November stated that *Casino Royale* would be in production within ninety days, with Connery reprising his role as Bond, and that Feldman hoped United Artists would distribute the picture. However, it appears that talks either broke down after this press release was issued, or that this was an early example of Feldman leaking inaccurate material to the newspapers in order to create publicity.[26]

Thunderball film rights go to McClory

The *Thunderball* court case began in earnest during the third week of November 1963, having become more complicated as not only was Kevin McClory suing Fleming over copyright infringement, but he had also begun legal proceedings against Ivar Bryce over problems arising from the winding up of Xanadu Productions. Due to financial difficulties, Jack Whittingham declined to take any action against Fleming himself – but then, having sold all his interests in *Longitude 78 West* and *Thunderball* to McClory, he gave testimony on the latter's behalf.

Despite his ill health and McClory's strong case, Fleming was disinclined to settle the case. However, Bryce persuaded him that this would be the best option, and in December a settlement was agreed. Future editions of the *Thunderball* novel would include a byline stating, 'Based on a screen treatment by Kevin McClory, Jack Whittingham and Ian Fleming', though the author would retain his sole credit on the cover. More importantly, though, McClory secured the film rights to *Thunderball*, along with the rights to all the scripts and outlines that he and Whittingham had contributed to the unmade Bond

---

[25] *Bondage* No. 15, *The Forgotten Bond*, Leonard Thomason, The James Bond 007 International Fan Club, May 1987.
[26] *Variety: Daily*, Reed Business Information, 8 November 1963.

film project.[27]

Ben Hecht

Charles K Feldman had meanwhile enlisted the assistance of Oscar-nominated screenwriter Ben Hecht, who had obviously become enthralled with *Casino Royale* as a feature film concept, as he invested himself heavily in writing material for it. A three-page story outline dated 17 December 1963 had a more international flavour than the novel, including scenes set in Algiers in Algeria, Baghdad in Iraq and Naples in Italy, eventually culminating in an assault upon a castle in Germany. Later, Hecht delivered forty pages of a screenplay dated 20 February 1964 that replaced Bond with an unknown American agent who had been drafted in by M to assume the identity of 007 after the death of the original. As a measure to confuse the opposition, MI6 renamed several agents James Bond 007 – an element of Hecht's writing that would actually make it through into the finished film. This aspect of the screenplay would seem to have been designed to get around the fact that the film would be made without the involvement of Sean Connery, allowing for another actor to play the unnamed American agent.[28]

The storyline involved this new Bond being assigned the mission of taking down Chiffre (not Le Chiffre as in the novel), the head of the criminal organisation SPECTRE – which stood for Special Executive for Counter-intelligence, Terrorism, Revenge and Extortion. SPECTRE had first appeared in the *Thunderball* novel three years earlier, hence this aspect of the screenplay would have needed altering, as it was outside Feldman's ownership of *Casino Royale*. Besides Chiffre, Bond's allies Felix Leiter and Vesper Lynd were both included in a screenplay that was extremely graphic in terms of both sex and

---

[27] *The James Bond Bedside Companion*, Raymond Benson, Boxtree, September 1988.
[28] The *Telegraph* website, *Casino Royale: 60 Years On*, Jeremy Duns, retrieved April 2013.

violence. Hecht also introduced some new characters of his own, including Bond's former lover Lili Wing – an attractive Eurasian woman who suffered from drug abuse – and her girlfriend Georgie – who was inseparable from a pet black kitten. This screenplay also catered for action enthusiasts by including a car chase through the red light district of Hamburg, which concluded with the intriguing plot element of Bond disguising himself as a lesbian mud-wrestler![29]

Woody Allen

During February and March 1964, stand-up comedian Woody Allen had a five week residency at the Blue Angel nightclub in New York, where one night the actress Shirley MacLaine attended to watch his innovative act.[30] MacLaine was accompanied by Charles K Feldman, who was extremely impressed with the comedian and his self-written material, feeling that his fresh approach of anecdotal humour appealed to a young audience. Having witnessed the appreciative reaction of the nightclub's clientele, Feldman was convinced that this writer/comedian could achieve the same success with a screenplay – and by chance the producer had just such a project in mind. Allen was contracted through his agents to construct a contemporary script based on the play *Lot's Wife* by Czech writer Ladislaus Bus-Fekete. This was another property Feldman had acquired years earlier, hoping to arrange a film adaptation starring Cary Grant. However, despite commissioning scripts from various different scriptwriters, he had never been entirely happy with the end results.[31] Allen's agents agreed on a sum of \$35,000 for their charge to provide the screenplay for what would become *What's New Pussycat?* (1965). Feldman had secured Allen's services quite

---

[29] The *Telegraph* website, *Casino Royale: 60 Years On*, Jeremy Duns, retrieved April 2013.
[30] *Variety: Weekly*, Reed Business Information, 12, 19 and 26 February, 4 and 11 March 1964.
[31] *Woody Allen: A Biography*, Eric Lax, Jonathan Cape, August 1991.

inexpensively – he later admitted that he had been willing to invest considerably more in the script – but Allen compensated for the shortfall by writing himself an acting role in the picture, thus earning an additional fee. This enterprise was originally intended as a madcap comedy vehicle for MacLaine's brother Warren Beatty, titled after the way he frequently answered the telephone to his girlfriends, but later the lead was recast and Peter O'Toole took over.[32] The working relationship between Feldman and Allen would bear further fruit later on, on *Casino Royale*.

Peter Sellers

Sometime during early spring 1964, Feldman made the first of what would eventually be many approaches to famed comic actor Peter Sellers, hoping to recruit him to star in *Casino Royale*. At this early stage, Feldman apparently had no intentions of producing a comedy film – which prompts the question, did he believe that Sellers, a master mimic, could actually impersonate Sean Connery? Whatever his motivation, it initially seemed this would come to nothing, as the actor at first completely dismissed the offer. Later, however, Sellers warmed to the thought of playing Bond, but felt that he needed to get physically fit before exploring the idea further.[33]

At the time, Sellers was working in Hollywood on the Billy Wilder-directed romantic comedy *Kiss Me, Stupid* (1964), but with Bond in mind, he engaged a personal trainer. The trainer devised a rigorous routine of bodybuilding exercises, which the actor went through after completing each exhausting day's filming. Sellers also associated Bond with large jungle cats, thus he perfected what he called a 'panther-like' walk as another element of getting into character.

Sellers had admired Wilder's abilities before becoming

---

[32] *Woody Allen: A Biography*, Eric Lax, Jonathan Cape, August 1991.
[33] *Peter Sellers: The Authorised Biography*, Alexander Walker, Weidenfeld & Nicolson, January 1981.

involved with *Kiss Me, Stupid*, but the director's policy of having a totally open set was causing him problems.[34] Finding himself constantly distracted by the huge number of people visiting the set, Sellers was struggling to give a performance he was happy with, and most days he returned to his rented Beverley Hills home feeling frustrated. These stresses and other factors, reportedly including Sellers' use of a stimulant drug to boost his sexual performance with his new young wife Britt Ekland, culminated on the night of Sunday 5 April 1964 with the actor suffering severe chest pains. Cardiologist Dr Rex Kennamer attended him, and initially assured him that he was not in a serious condition and that several weeks' rest would cure the symptoms. Two days later, however, the actor suffered a heart attack, and Kennamer had to perform cardiac massage to revive him. Sellers was then speedily admitted to intensive care at what is now Cedars-Sinai Medical Centre in Los Angeles.[35] Unwilling to wait for Sellers to recuperate, Wilder brought in Ray Walston to replace him on *Kiss Me, Stupid*, reshooting all the scenes he had already filmed.

More *Casino Royale* scripts and outlines

Meanwhile, Ben Hecht was still diligently working away on successive drafts of his *Casino Royale* script. The latest version introduced Chiffre's beautiful wife Gita, who featured prominently in two drafts dated 8 and 14 April 1964 respectively. The first of these, running to 84 pages, covered most of the plotline from the February script, while the second, totalling 49 pages, consisted of additional material. When amalgamated, the two formed a complete feature film screenplay.

The 8 April material had 007 back as the original James Bond

---

[34] *Peter Sellers: The Authorised Biography*, Alexander Walker, Weidenfeld & Nicolson, January 1981.
[35] *Peter Sellers: The Authorised Biography*, Alexander Walker, Weidenfeld & Nicolson, January 1981.

and contained elements indicating that both Feldman and Hecht had watched *Dr. No,* as it had the character flirting with M's secretary Miss Moneypenny and exhibiting other personality traits similar to Connery's celluloid 007. This approach was short-lived, however, as the pages produced the following week reverted to the concept of the replacement Bond.

The new material involved Bond and Vesper Lynd tracking down incriminating filmed evidence that Chiffre had obtained on various diplomats, which was *en route* to him from Hamburg. This time, the aforementioned car chase sequence concluded with Lili Wing being crushed to death in the mechanism of a refuse truck, then Bond being forced to use Gita as a human shield in a gunfight with Chiffre's henchmen.[36]

Another car chase sequence ensued after Bond hijacked the van containing Chiffre's evidence, resulting in the vehicle careering off a cliff in the Swiss Alps and exploding upon impact below, though 007 narrowly escaped. With his blackmail operation now in tatters, Chiffre travelled to Casino Royale in France, intending to win replacement funds, only to be confronted by Bond across the baccarat table, resulting in him losing a large amount of money.

Later, this screenplay included an infamous torture scene from the novel, in which Bond is tied to a chair while Le Chiffre attacks a sensitive part of his naked anatomy with a carpet-beater. However, in Hecht's screenplay version it was Gita Chiffre who administered the beating, as revenge for her face being horribly disfigured during the earlier shoot-out. Further to this, her larynx had been removed due to gunshot damage, and she was forced to speak through a metal tube inserted in her throat.[37] Although suffering agonising pain, Bond refused to talk, prompting Chiffre to expand his repertoire of torture by waterboarding the agent, with the unusual twist of using

---

[36] The *Telegraph* website, Casino Royale: *60 Years Old*, Jeremy Duns, retrieved April 2013.

[37] The *Telegraph* website, Casino Royale: *60 Years Old*, Jeremy Duns, retrieved April 2013.

whisky rather than water. With his demise seemingly a certainty, Bond was rescued by the arrival of SPECTRE assassins, who killed Chiffre for losing valuable resources; as they had no instructions to harm 007, the assassins simply scarred the back of his hand to allow their colleagues to recognise him in future operations. This scenario was lifted intact from Fleming's novel, where plastic surgery would hide the scar.

Hecht was obviously enjoying himself working on *Casino Royale*, and at one point he informed Feldman in writing, 'Never had more fun writing a movie.'[38] Without doubt the April 1964 drafts exhibited the strongest James Bond drama ever written; stronger in both style and content than Ian Fleming's novels and considerably more potent than anything contained in an Eon Productions film. Bubbling with enthusiasm for the project, Hecht contacted Feldman by letter dated Thursday 16 April, promising to provide a written analysis of his latest screenplay by the following Monday and going on to describe Bond as cinema's first 'gentleman superman'. However, fate intervened, and Hecht died suddenly from a heart attack while reading at his home on Saturday 18 April.

Following Hecht's death, Feldman brought in Billy Wilder to work on the script, and the famous Austrian-born writer/director/producer rewrote virtually all of Hecht's material.[39]

Paperwork exists showing that toward the conclusion of 1964, the American writer/director Norman Foster also wrote some *Casino Royale* material and collaborated with Italian scriptwriter Alberto Lattuado. It is believed highly unlikely that any of this combined work was later incorporated into the actual film.

---

[38] The *Telegraph* website, Casino Royale: *60 Years Old*, Jeremy Duns, retrieved April 2013.
[39] The *Telegraph* website, Casino Royale: *60 Years Old*, Jeremy Duns, retrieved April 2013.

Chapter Two
Development Hell

Terence Cooper

During the spring of 1964, Charles K Feldman continued with his plan to bring Ian Fleming's debut James Bond novel to the big screen. It was around this time that he first encountered Ulster-born actor Terence Cooper in a nightclub and instantly began considering him as a potential Bond. As a tall, square-jawed and traditional-looking hero type, Cooper was perhaps more suitable than Peter Sellers. However, Feldman's initial approach to the actor in the nightclub was met with open hostility, as Cooper thought his two female companions were the only reason that the middle-aged American had engaged him in conversation, claiming to be a film producer. With this misunderstanding addressed, Feldman explained the situation and subsequently placed Cooper on a £200-a-week retainer in readiness for production to begin on the film. One of the conditions of the contract was that Cooper should remain free to become involved in *Casino Royale* at short notice, meaning that he was unable to accept any other acting work whatsoever in the meantime. Uncharacteristically, Feldman insisted on a complete publicity blackout regarding Cooper's involvement, as he wanted the new 007 casting to be a total surprise to the public when eventually revealed.[40]

Cooper insisted that this was nothing new, as in the late '50s

---

[40] *Park City Daily News*, John Pipes Gaines, 7 April 1966.

he had been approached by Kevin McClory about portraying Bond in the proposed feature film project that later formed the basis for the *Thunderball* novel. When he was finally allowed to give an interview on the subject, Cooper courted controversy by asserting that in his opinion Sean Connery played Bond completely out of character when compared with the depiction in Ian Fleming's books.[41]

Roger Moore

It appears that Feldman was already thinking along the lines of multiple Bonds for *Casino Royale*, as during June 1964 contact was also established with well-known actor Roger Moore regarding the role of 007. This pre-dated by seven years Moore's eventual casting in Eon Productions' *Live and Let Die*, but at the time, the actor's ongoing contract with ITC for the television series *The Saint* prevented him from becoming involved.[42]

Goldfinger

Meanwhile, Eon Production's third Bond movie, *Goldfinger*, based on Fleming's seventh novel, was undergoing principal filming, though the producers' initial choice of Orson Welles to play the villain Auric Goldfinger had been scuppered due to the actor's unaffordable fee. German actor Gert Fröbe had been hired as a replacement, although in addition to his salary he had also attempted to negotiate himself a ten percent bonus from the film's profits, making Saltzman and Broccoli wonder if Welles would have been more a cost effective option after all. Although Welles had narrowly missed out on portraying a Bond villain, any disappointment he might have felt with regard to the situation would be rectified several years later.[43]

---

[41] Our Man from Bond Street website, *Terence Cooper: The Perfect Bond?* Tony Crawley, retrieved March 2010.
[42] *Daily Mirror*, Trinity Mirror Group, 27 June 1964.
[43] MI6: The Home of James Bond 007 website, *Trivia – Goldfinger*, retrieved July 2013.

Ursula Andress

Having spent time looking at possible lead actors, Feldman now began considering casting options for *Casino Royale*'s lead actress, and his initial choice was Ursula Andress, who had become the first Bond girl when she co-starred in *Dr. No*. However, Andress would be otherwise employed from late August to October 1964 playing the lead character Ayesha (She Who Must be Obeyed) in Hammer Films' *She* (1965), adapted from H Rider Haggard's novel of the same title, and at this time there was no confirmation regarding her possible involvement in *Casino Royale*.[44] Later, other actresses would also be considered for the role.

What's New Pussycat?

Wanting to employ London-born director Clive Donner, whose work he admired, Feldman offered him a choice between several possible projects, including the Ben Hecht-scripted *Casino Royale*. However, the production Donner chose to become involved with was *What's New Pussycat?*. This decision resulted in Donner working alongside Woody Allen for six weeks in New York, where together they developed and refined the screenplay until Feldman was overjoyed with it. The central role of psychiatrist Dr Fritz Fassbender was written with Groucho Marx in mind, but upon Donner's urging, Feldman agreed to cast Peter Sellers, who had now recovered from his heart attack earlier in the year. However, this caused problems with the film's financiers, United Artists, who refused to insure the production, fearing that a relapse in Sellers' health would suspend filming and cause spiralling costs.[45] Stepping into the breach, Feldman put up $350,000 from his personal account, covering the eventuality of Sellers falling ill again by underwriting the liability himself, figuring that the Fassbender

---

[44] *Variety: Daily*, Reed Business Information, 28 August 1964.
[45] *Woody: Movies from Manhattan*, Julian Fox, Batsford, May 1996.

role was a relatively small one and that all of Sellers' scenes could be filmed within 16 days.[46, 47]

The cast and crew of *What's New Pussycat?* assembled in Rome on Wednesday 29 September 1964, allowing Feldman to speak with Sellers again regarding *Casino Royale*, but nothing could be agreed. Ever the eccentric, Feldman then decided on a change of location, and moved the entire production to what was Billancourt Studios in the Hauts-de-Seine area of Paris – which pleased Woody Allen, as his screenplay had originally been set in the French capital. Shooting commenced in late October, though it did not progress entirely as planned, as Peter Sellers was allowed to ad-lib, and spontaneous improvisation became the order of the day. Scenes set in Fassbender's office featuring Sellers and Peter O'Toole became longer and longer, resulting in material having to be taken out elsewhere; hence Allen's role as Victor Shakapopolis was reduced.[48]

Allen would later describe his arrival in the movie business as 'a nightmarish experience in many ways,' as the ad-libbing led to Sellers, with the assistance of O'Toole, not only rewriting existing scenes but also writing completely new ones on an almost daily basis.[49] With the addition of Ursula Andress to the cast, what had originally looked like a small romantic comedy movie had suddenly been transformed into a large slice of swinging '60s entertainment. As Allen observed, 'Everything was big and jazzy.'[50] Clive Donner was unable to interfere, as his authority was undermined by Feldman, who had United Artists' executives closely watching the proceedings. Allen, who had also been forced to make various changes to the screenplay himself, was obviously dismayed at the situation, and he

---

[46] *Peter Sellers: A Film History*, Michael Starr, Robert Hale, December 1991.
[47] *Peter Sellers: The Mask Behind the Mask*, Peter Evans, Frewin, September 1969.
[48] *Woody Allen: A Biography*, John Baxter, HarperCollins, November 1998.
[49] *Woody: Movies from Manhattan*, Julian Fox, Batsford, May 1996.
[50] *Woody Allen: A Biography*, Eric Lax, Jonathan Cape, August 1991.

arranged for his agents to contact Feldman requesting that his screenplay credit be dropped, further to which he refused to carry out any more rewrites. In fact, Allen was all for walking away from the project altogether, but, his agents pointed out the enormous benefits that could accrue to him down the line from his involvement, so he agreed to see it through to its conclusion.

More negotiations with Eon Productions

While *What's New Pussycat?* was in production, Feldman went through a second round of negotiations with Eon Productions, in which he once again enquired about borrowing Sean Connery for *Casino Royale*.[51] However, Harry Saltzman and Cubby Broccoli had since September been finalising a deal with Kevin McClory to film *Thunderball* as a Connery-starring co-production, and with agreement now reached, principal photography would begin on Tuesday 16 February 1965. Finding himself passed over in favour of this other Bond property, Feldman then attempted to broker an independent agreement with United Artists to finance *Casino Royale*, but this fell through when Eon Productions learnt about it and threatened to take their films to another distributor.

Wolf Mankowitz

It was around this time that Feldman brought scriptwriter Wolf Mankowitz onto the project, possibly because he had written an uncredited treatment for *Dr. No* and had also contributed to the screenplay for *Goldfinger*. Mankowitz, who was a successful playwright, novelist and screenwriter, also ran the Wedgewood chinaware shop based in Piccadilly Arcade, London, with his sister Barbara.

Mankowitz proceeded to assemble yet another script for *Casino Royale*.[52] In the third week in January 1965, the American

---

[51] *Variety: Weekly*, Reed Business Information, 11 November 1964.
[52] *Kiss Kiss Bang! Bang!: The Unofficial James Bond Companion*, Alan

trade press carried a story claiming that Feldman had secured a co-production deal with Harry Saltzman and Cubby Broccoli for the movie, but this statement was completely untrue.[53]

Columbia Pictures

There was good news for Feldman in February 1965 when, having evaluated the project, Columbia Pictures saw it in a positive light and, despite Sean Connery's lack of involvement, decided to provide funding for the film.[54] Feldman's production company, Famous Artists Productions Ltd, took out a full page advertisement in *The Daily Cinema* trade publication, announcing that shooting on *Casino Royale* would commence on 29 March.[55]

Pre-production

Having lost out on Connery, Feldman again tried to interest Peter Sellers in starring as James Bond, hoping that their working relationship built up while making *What's New Pussycat?* would influence the outcome. However, Sellers was extremely indecisive regarding the part, and although Feldman almost persuaded him to accept, ultimately he rejected it again.[56] Meanwhile, Famous Artists had acquired 16 South Audley Street, London, to serve as a pre-production base for the film, and John C Shepridge, who had served as executive producer on *What's New Pussycat?*, began planning a production schedule. Shepridge was joined by casting director Maude Spencer, who began auditioning performers for roles in the film, but the 29 March start-of-filming date was cancelled.[57]

Barnes and Marcus Hearn, Overlook Press, October 1998.
[53] *Variety: Daily*, Reed Business Information, 21 January 1965.
[54] *Variety: Daily*, Reed Business Information, 10 February 1965.
[55] *The Daily Cinema*, Cinema Press Ltd, 24 February 1965.
[56] *Mr Strangelove: A Biography of Peter Sellers*, Ed Sikov, Sidgwick & Jackson, September 2002.

A rival James Bond film

The situation surrounding *Casino Royale* had changed as, with Columbia having agreed to finance it, the project had taken an important step forward. Harry Saltzman and Cubby Broccoli realised that a rival to their own 007 movies was now a strong possibility. Hence, this time around, Feldman was the one who found himself being courted, as he was offered $500,000 together with a percentage of profits if he would make the film in conjunction with Saltzman and Broccoli for United Artists. Feldman, though, had already invested $550,000 in pre-production, and with funding in place and the embargo on revealing Terence Cooper's involvement now lifted, an Easter 1966 premiere seemed eminently achievable. Therefore he completely dismissed the offer.[58]

Despite this, during May 1965 lengthy discussions took place between Columbia and United Artists, again exploring the possibility of *Casino Royale* being made as a co-production. This inevitably drew in Saltzman and Broccoli. Apparently, at this point, Feldman would still have accepted a co-production deal that included Sean Connery playing the lead and *Casino Royale* entering production after *Thunderball* as the fifth Bond film.[59] However, as *Thunderball* itself was also a co-production, Saltzman and Broccoli were against entering into another one straightaway, and they would make *You Only Live Twice* next in the series.[60] This would push *Casino Royale* back to Bond film number six, meaning that principal photography could not begin until late 1968 at the earliest. Feldman rejected this idea as totally unacceptable, despite being offered a 50/50 split of the profits. Decades later, Cubby Broccoli would assert that the main reason *Casino Royale* never progressed into being a co-

---

[57] *The Stage and Television Today*, The Stage Newspaper Limited, 4 March 1965.
[58] *Variety: Weekly*, Reed Business Information, 31 March 1965.
[59] *Variety: Daily*, Reed Business Information, 12 May 1965.
[60] *Variety: Weekly*, Reed Business Information, 29 June 1965.

production with Eon Productions was that Feldman always wanted too big a share of the profits.[61]

Changing tactics, Columbia Pictures then went on the offensive, unsuccessfully attempting to buy out Eon Productions' film rights to all the other Bond novels.[62] Meanwhile, Feldman continued to develop the *Casino Royale* screenplay by having novelist Joseph Heller polish up some scenes. At the time, Heller had very little film or television writing experience, although several years earlier he had been responsible for the bestselling novel *Catch-22* (1961). Heller worked on the project for a couple of weeks before departing, though none of his material would actually feature on screen.[63] Further to this, it appears that between other film-making assignments, all-rounder Billy Wilder was still finding time to be involved with both writing and developing the screenplay.[64] In June 1965, both Wilder and director/scriptwriter Blake Edwards were reported to have been working on the script, as a result of their old friend Feldman calling in favours; but neither would receive an on-screen credit.[65]

Michael Sayers

Irishman Michael Sayers was another writer brought onto the scripting team, and he would eventually be one of only three screenwriters to actually receive a credit on the film. Having worked as both a journalist and an author during the '30s and '40s, he had emigrated to the US after World War Two and managed a small amount of television writing in the '50s. However, his communist sympathies had been brought to the

---

[61] *When the Snow Melts: The Autobiography of Cubby Broccoli*, Cubby Broccoli & Donald Zec, Boxtree, September 1998.
[62] *Kiss Kiss Bang! Bang!: The Unofficial James Bond Companion*, Alan Barnes and Marcus Hearn, Overlook Press, October 1998.
[63] *Woody Allen: A Biography*, John Baxter, HarperCollins, November 1998.
[64] *Variety: Weekly*, Reed Business Information, 12 May 1965.
[65] *Variety: Weekly*, Reed Business Information, 16 June 1965.

attention of the House Committee on Un-American Activities, who had blacklisted him, after which he had found it impossible to obtain writing work in the States.

Returning to Ireland, Sayers assumed the pseudonym Michael Connor and began contributing scripts to various British television series such as *The Adventures of Robin Hood*, *Sword of Freedom* and *Interpol Calling*. His American passport had been revoked during the '50s, but was finally reinstated in 1965 when Feldman hired him, thus allowing him to travel to Hollywood and contribute toward *Casino Royale*.[66] With shooting now expected to get under way in August 1965, 15 June saw Columbia announce a large budget for the film of between $4½ and $6 million, adding that the company was searching for a star name to play James Bond.[67] This statement obviously gave rise to speculation as to what exactly Terence Cooper's role would now be in the film.

Feldman chases Sellers

What's New Pussycat? opened in the US the following week and, when rated on box office takings, eventually became the highest-grossing comedy film up to that point. In the process, it increased both Sellers' and Feldman's stock in the marketplace, and this boded well for the prospects of them collaborating again in the future. Feldman appeared to be thinking along the same lines when, in an interview for the American industry publication *Variety*, he heaped praise on Sellers for his huge contribution to *What's New Pussycat?*, disclosing that his involvement had gone far beyond the requirements of his contract.

This latest attempt to attract Sellers to *Casino Royale* continued with Feldman describing him as, 'The most talented

---

[66] The *Independent* website, *Michael Sayers: Writer Whose Career Never Recovered from Being Blacklisted in the United States*, Gordon Bowker, retrieved July 2010.
[67] *Variety: Daily*, Reed Business Information, 16 June 1965.

guy I ever worked with,' then stating that the British comedy actor could virtually demand whatever salary he desired, and as a bonus could both write and direct the picture as well. Although he stated categorically that he had no intentions of beginning court action, Feldman suggested that owning the rights to *Casino Royale* possibly entitled him to be the legal copyright-holder of both the James Bond name and the character. Figuring that this statement was nothing more than self-publicity on Feldman's part, Eon Productions and United Artists refrained from rising to the bait, and by not responding they deprived him of further press coverage.[68]

Potential directors

During June 1965 the first indications surfaced that Feldman was abandoning plans to produce a straight James Bond adventure, when the potential *Casino Royale* was described in *Variety* as being a high comedy incorporating gaudy sets and '60s psychedelia.[69] Peter Sellers was still undecided about appearing in the film, but meanwhile Feldman was attempting to entice director Bryan Forbes to the production by showering him with gifts such as theatre tickets and expensive silk scarves. Attempting to influence Forbes' decision, Feldman also offered him the chance to write some of the screenplay, which by this point was planned to include five James Bonds and an all-star international cast.[70] Eventually these tactics bore fruit, and Forbes was convinced and ready to sign a contract. However, the enormous sum he demanded by way of remuneration precluded his involvement, causing Columbia executives to brand him 'a blackmailing whore.'[71]

Searching for a competent replacement to helm the

---

[68] *Variety: Daily*, Reed Business Information, 16 June 1965.
[69] *Variety: Daily*, Reed Business Information, 16 June 1965.
[70] The *Sabotage Times* website, *A Cocktail Recipe for Disaster*, Richard Luck, retrieved June 2013.
[71] *Mr Strangelove: A Biography of Peter Sellers*, Ed Sikov, Sidgwick & Jackson, September 2002.

production, Feldman returned to Clive Donner. However, Donner was obviously aware of the producer's interest in recruiting Peter Sellers for the film, and this apparently turned him against the idea. After his unhappy experience on *What's New Pussycat?*, where in his opinion Sellers had ruthlessly hijacked the production, Donner was against any further involvement with the actor, and ruled himself out of contention.[72]

Eventually, sometime during August 1965, Sellers gave Feldman a verbal agreement that he would star in *Casino Royale* for a $750,000 fee plus $10,000 expenses, though he insisted on director approval and suggested Sophia Loren as his co-star.[73] As a result, Wolf Mankowitz performed a major rewrite of the screenplay, giving Sellers the new role of casino croupier Nigel Force and taking a completely novel approach that avoided the actor having to play the lead part anything like Sean Connery.[74]

Sellers-Mankowitz Productions

However, Mankowitz held deep misgivings where Sellers was concerned, warning Feldman that his leading man could be both temperamental and unpredictable and that under no circumstances should he trust him.[75] Mankowitz's attitude stemmed from a bad experience in early 1960. He and Sellers had agreed to form a production company, Sellers-Mankowitz Productions, to make the kind of movies they both passionately wanted to produce, but Sellers had never quite got around to making the partnership official, despite the pair seeking financial backing for him to play the lead in Mankowitz's screenplay *The Memoirs of a Cross-Eyed Man*. On the morning of

---

[72] *Woody Allen: A Biography*, John Baxter, HarperCollins, November 1998.
[73] *Mr Strangelove: A Biography of Peter Sellers*, Ed Sikov, Sidgwick & Jackson, September 2002.
[74] *Peter Sellers: The Authorized Biography*, Alexander Walker, Weidenfeld & Nicholson, January 1981.
[75] *Mr Strangelove: A Biography of Peter Sellers*, Ed Sikov, Sidgwick & Jackson, September 2002.

a meeting with financiers who were prepared to invest a six-figure sum in the project, Mankowitz received a handwritten letter from Sellers explaining that he had decided against going through with their plans, preferring to concentrate on his acting career. Taking the letter, Mankowitz faced the financiers alone to explain the situation, which brought about the demise of both the potential film and Sellers-Mankowitz Productions.[76]

Joe McGrath

Sellers insisted that Feldman hire Scotsman Joseph McGrath to direct *Casino Royale*. McGrath possessed no feature film directing experience whatsoever, but Sellers had great faith in him, despite the fact that they had worked together only twice before. Their initial meeting had come about by accident in December 1957, when McGrath had attended a premiere screening of the Sellers-starring comedy film *The Naked Truth*. Sellers was also present, but keeping out of everybody's way so that he could gauge the audience's reaction as they departed the cinema. McGrath however boldly walked up to him and cracked a mildly amusing joke about recognising him. They then retired to a coffee bar.[77] Their first professional collaboration occurred sometime during the late '50s, when McGrath directed Sellers in the role of the Scottish poet William McGonagall for ABC Television's arts programme *Tempo*.[78] The second occurred on an edition of the Peter Cook and Dudley Moore comedy sketch series *Not Only ... But Also*, transmitted on BBC2 on Saturday 20 March 1965, which was directed by McGrath and featured Sellers as a guest star.

Feldman's acquiescence to the stipulation that McGrath be hired as director of *Casino Royale* shows just how desperate he was to enlist Sellers' services for the film, in that he was

---

[76] *Peter Sellers: The Mask Behind the Mask*, Peter Evans, Frewin, September 1969.
[77] *Peter Sellers: The Authorized Biography*, Alexander Walker, Weidenfeld & Nicholson, January 1981.
[78] *The Life and Death of Peter Sellers*, Roger Lewis, Century, April 1994.

prepared to stand back and allow a television director, whose prior experience was confined to videotape productions, to take control of a multimillion-dollar picture.

Burt Bacharach

Having been pleasantly surprised by the chart success of the *What's New Pussycat?* theme song, sung by Tom Jones, which had been written by Burt Bacharach and Hal David, Feldman had no hesitation in asking the two songwriters to perform the same task on *Casino Royale*. Bacharach would also repeat his scoring duties, eventually creating an impressive soundtrack for the film. Feldman's paperwork indicates that the composer was entrusted with a copy of the screenplay on Saturday 21 August 1965; however, exactly which draft he received, of the many different ones written so far, has never been revealed. In the event, there would be many further script changes even after filming began, so Bacharach's job would certainly be far from straightforward.[79]

Twelve writers?

Shortly after this, Columbia Pictures confirmed a budget of $6 million for the film, the action of which would feature none of the kind of gimmicks or gadgets that had recently invaded the Eon Productions Bond films such as *Goldfinger* and *Thunderball*. Wolf Mankowitz, described in print as the latest of 12 writers to have contributed toward the screenplay (though there is no documentation to confirm this figure), was at this point still engrossed in rewriting. The movie was to be UK based, but location filming was also planned for Spain, Germany and France. Feldman was reported as being in negotiations to secure the involvement of big-name stars Jack Lemmon and Sophia Loren. However, Loren and her agent were both unimpressed

---

[79] *The Music of James Bond*, Jon Burlingame, Oxford University Press, October 2012.

by Joseph McGrath's installation as director, thinking that a blockbuster like *Casino Royale* needed someone well seasoned to command the action.[80] Hence Loren declined to become involved; and although her name would again be linked to the movie some time later, when it was suggested that she might make a cameo appearance, this also failed to occur.[81]

At the beginning of September 1965, the *Daily Express* newspaper devoted column inches to *Casino Royale*, claiming that the screenplay was faithful to the original Ian Fleming novel – though this statement was only partly true, and then only in respect of the card game sequence. The principal cast members were named as Peter Sellers, Shirley MacLaine and Terence Cooper.[82] Sellers and Cooper already knew each other, having met through their mutual friend, actress Sue Lloyd. Having a joint interest in keep-fit and bodybuilding they got along extremely well, although they would not share any scenes in the film.[83]

Script development

In early September 1965, Feldman, McGrath and Mankowitz all discussed arrangements for the movie in a pre-production meeting with Sellers in Rome, where the actor was involved in making the comedy film *After the Fox* (1966). Several days later, Feldman accompanied Shirley MacLaine to the Trader Vic's restaurant in Los Angeles, from where they telephoned Sellers long distance for half an hour to clarify matters regarding their respective roles. Some sources indicate that MacLaine was going to portray Bond's illegitimate daughter Mata Bond, with the actress's background as a dancer being utilised within the storyline, resulting in Mankowitz undertaking another rewrite

---

[80] *Variety: Daily*, Reed Business Information, 30 August 1965.
[81] *Mr Strangelove: A Biography of Peter Sellers*, Ed Sikov, Sidgwick & Jackson, September 2002.
[82] *Daily Express*, Northern & Shell Media, 1 September 1965.
[83] *It Seemed Like a Good Idea at the Time*, Sue Lloyd and Linda Dearsley, Quartet, October 1998.

to gain her approval.[84]

The following day, a worried Sellers contacted Feldman. Fearing that Mankowitz was failing to develop the screenplay to his satisfaction, the actor requested that screenwriter Terry Southern be brought onto the production and placed on the payroll. Southern, who had co-scripted *Dr. Strangelove* (1964), for which Sellers had received an Oscar nomination for Best Actor, was hired for the exclusive purpose of supplying Sellers' dialogue in *Casino Royale*, or in other words giving him all the funny lines.[85] He was paid $25,000 and was provided with accommodation at the exclusive Dorchester Hotel in Park Lane, London, though while associated with the film he frequently flew between Los Angeles and the UK, writing most of Sellers' lines during the flights.[86]

Throughout September, the casting and crew news was recycled in several publications, with the screenplay now credited to Wolf Mankowitz and Michael Sayers and shooting said to be scheduled to begin on 15 November.[87] However, mystery still surrounded the contents of the film, as strange rumours began filtering through regarding plans to kill off James Bond. It was also stated that Peter Sellers would not portray Bond but would play the completely different character Nigel Force, and that Orson Welles and Trevor Howard had now been added to the cast list. The latter part of this statement was untrue, as Howard had merely been approached regarding the possibility of him taking the Sir James Bond role; but Feldman's self-publicity machine had put his name out to the popular press and, eager for news, they had printed it without checking the facts.[88]

---

[84] *Mr Strangelove: A Biography of Peter Sellers*, Ed Sikov, Sidgwick & Jackson, September 2002.
[85] *Mr Strangelove: A Biography of Peter Sellers*, Ed Sikov, Sidgwick & Jackson, September 2002.
[86] *A Grand Guy: The Art and Life of Terry Southern*, Lee Hill, Harper, February 2001.
[87] *Variety: Daily*, Reed Business Information, 28 September 1965.
[88] *Variety: Weekly*, Reed Business Information, 29 September 1965.

Orson Welles

Feldman had known Orson Welles for almost twenty years, since they had co-produced together in Hollywood a feature film adaptation of William Shakespeare's *Macbeth* (1948). Having become disenchanted with the Hollywood system of film-making, Welles had now settled in Europe, appearing in films and financing his own productions – including the ambitious *Don Quixote*, which had undergone various bouts of principal filming since 1957 but would never be completed.[89] Welles chose some acting roles simply for the large fee they gained him, which he promptly channelled back into his own projects. His agreement to appear in *Casino Royale* in the part of Le Chiffre (the character having regained his original name in the latest screenplay drafts) is thought to have been one such instance. There would later be a publicity statement issued that described the Sellers/Welles casting as 'The explosive casting chemistry of 1966', although due to subsequent developments this would be quickly withdrawn.[90]

Shirley MacLaine walks out

The production faced a major setback during the first week of October 1965 when Shirley MacLaine checked out of the Hilton Hotel in London, where she had been staying at Feldman's expense, and returned to the USA without informing him. Up to that point, things had been progressing so well that the start of filming had been brought forward to the second week of October, allowing MacLaine about seven days to settle into her new surroundings before commencing work. Feldman ruled out taking any legal proceedings against the actress, describing

---

[89] *Rosebud: The Story of Orson Welles*, David Thomson, Alfred A. Knopf Inc, September 1996.
[90] *007 Magazine* No. 40, *Casino Royale*, The James Bond 007 International Fan Club, Michael Richardson and Graham Rye, January 2002.

her as a friend; but his questionable business practice of not getting principal cast members to sign contracts until after filming began, as on *What's New Pussycat?*, suggests that in any case he had nothing more than a verbal agreement with her at the time.[91]

One possible explanation for MacLaine's behaviour is that she never really intended to appear in *Casino Royale* at all, despite being promised $1 million by Columbia's head of production Mike Frankovich. The theory goes that, as her contract with Universal Pictures was close to renewal, she used Feldman's casting of her in *Casino Royale* as a bargaining tool, manipulating Universal's executives into thinking she was about jump ship to another major Hollywood studio.[92]

Sometime later, Joan Collins was given the opportunity of assuming the female lead on the picture when Feldman offered her the Vesper role, but due to her being pregnant, she was unable to accept.[93]

Take the Money and Run

Meanwhile, having originally signed a three picture deal with Feldman, Woody Allen presented him with a screenplay he had written called *Take the Money and Run*, which the producer thought could be filmed on a budget of between $600,000 and $700,000. However, after the bad experience of having his *What's New Pussycat?* script constantly rewritten, Allen wanted to have complete control of his future movie productions, so not only would he star in *Take the Money and Run*, but he also intended to produce and direct it. Feldman knew that attracting backing to the project would prove difficult, because Allen had never directed before. In the meantime, while finance was being arranged, he asked Allen if he would consider contributing

---

[91] *Daily Express*, Northern & Shell Media, 7 October 1965.
[92] *Woody Allen: A Biography*, John Baxter, HarperCollins, November 1998.
[93] The *Telegraph* website, *Joan Collins: The Day I Said No to James Bond*, Joan Collins, retrieved May 2008.

toward the *Casino Royale* screenplay. Allen agreed to become involved, but knew exactly what he was getting himself into, understanding that any script he assembled for the Bond movie could and probably would be heavily rewritten. Allen's contract included the provision that he would not receive an on-screen scriptwriter credit for *Casino Royale* and that Feldman would also provide a signed letter to that effect.[94, 95]

Production rescheduled

While casting for a new female lead got under way, the start of filming on *Casino Royale* was rescheduled back to 8 December 1965. Information meanwhile emerged suggesting that Sellers' character Nigel Force would not appear until forty minutes into the action. With all the speculation surrounding the number of writers who had contributed to the script, *Variety* asked Wolf Mankowitz who would actually receive the screenplay credit, to which he jokingly replied, 'Wolf Mankowitz and friends.' Reports indicated that principal photography would take between 24 and 26 weeks to complete, with the film being shot in the widescreen format, but not on the Cinerama system as some publicity material had previously advised.[96]

Despite having his attention focused on *Casino Royale*, Feldman found time to negotiate a long-term agreement to oversee the production of 15 feature films for United Artists, the first of which was expected to be Woody Allen's *Take the Money and Run*. However, with Allen occupied on scripting duties for *Casino Royale*, it was estimated that the earliest *Take the Money and Run* could enter production would be spring 1966 – though in the event it would actually be considerably later, due partly to the fact that Allen would find himself drawn more and more into the intricate filming process of *Casino Royale*, which would monopolise his time during the spring and summer of 1966.[97]

---

[94] *The Coryphaeus*, University of Waterloo, Ontario, 21 October 1965.
[95] *Variety: Daily*, Reed Business Information, 10 November 1965.
[96] *Variety: Weekly*, Reed Business Information, 10 November 1965.

Val Guest

During November 1965, the head of the William Morris agency in London, John Mather, received an enquiry regarding the possibility of his charge Val Guest directing on *Casino Royale*, back to back with the highly respected John Huston. This would not be the last instance of Feldman name-dropping to attract others to the project, and on this occasion it worked extremely well, as Guest was a great admirer of Huston's work. Feldman explained that *Casino Royale* was made up of several different segments, and that Guest and Huston would direct one each. Guest was initially informed that he would be required for seven to eight weeks sometime during 1966 to direct his portion. However, he was then recruited to work on the screenplay as well, which led to him concocting some of the film's conclusion in conjunction with Woody Allen. Eventually, Guest would take on a huge amount of responsibility for the narrative, coordinating some of the various shoots, and would end up devoting almost a year to the film.[98]

Guest found Feldman to be instantly likable, a true eccentric, but extremely indecisive, jumping from one idea to another and thinking nothing of phoning people up in the early hours of the morning to talk about some fantastic concept he had thought up. Arriving on the production, Guest found that the current version of the screenplay was in a state of flux, as some portions were nothing more than an outline, with Feldman indicating that the dialogue would be created in part by the leads and directors during filming.[99] However, Feldman also possessed several earlier, complete versions – apparently including one by Eon Productions Bond scriptwriter Richard Maibaum, although

---

[97] *So You Want to Be in Pictures: The Autobiography of Val Guest*, Val Guest, Reynolds & Hearn, May 2001.
[98] Telephone conversation between Val Guest and Michael Richardson, December 2005.
[99] *So You Want to Be in Pictures: The Autobiography of Val Guest*, Val Guest, Reynolds & Hearn, May 2001.

this has never been substantiated – which he passed across to Guest with the instruction that he should write a new draft that incorporated elements of them all. Later, Guest returned and offered his resignation (which Feldman declined), having found it impossible to make sense of all the various versions, let alone amalgamate them into one.[100]

Guest hoped for inspiration from the novel, but *Casino Royale* was Ian Fleming's shortest Bond adventure and did not offer an extensive plotline. One incident in which two Bulgarian agents are blown up by their own bomb while attempting to kill 007 would be omitted from the finished film, as would the torture scene involving the carpet-beater, which was obviously considered too sadistic for inclusion.

The *Daily Express* interviews Sellers

Having recently recorded versions of the Beatles' 'A Hard Day's Night' and 'Help', talking his way through both numbers in character as King Richard III, Peter Sellers was resting up before filming on *Casino Royale* got under way. Questioned by the *Daily Express* regarding the forthcoming movie, he responded, 'I play the croupier, Orson Welles plays the villain and there are no fewer than five James Bonds, one of them a woman.' Signalling that negotiations with Trevor Howard were still taking place, Sellers indicated that the actor would portray Sir James Bond.[101]

---

[100] *Woody Allen: A Biography*, John Baxter, HarperCollins, November 1998.
[101] *Daily Express*, Northern & Shell Media, 25 November 1965.

The Eady Levy

From 1950 to 1985, the so-called Eady Levy was a form of taxation collected by the Government as a percentage of cinema ticket sales, which was ultimately invested into domestic and foreign-backed pictures filmed in Britain, making the country attractive to movie-makers and creating work throughout the industry. In order to secure some of this funding and offset the production costs, plans to film parts of *Casino Royale* on location in Germany and Spain were abandoned in favour of shooting mostly in the UK. Meanwhile, with yet another planned start date – 8 December 1965 – looming, Feldman had transferred his office to a suite in the Grosvenor House hotel, Park Lane, London, from where he would supervise overall production.[102]

Sellers finally signs up

Having not yet actually signed a contract to appear in *Casino Royale*, Sellers at this point received a further visit from Feldman, who set out his intention to have two male leads in the film and stated that his friend David Niven had committed himself to playing the other lead – which in fact was not entirely truthful, as negotiations with Niven were still ongoing and had yet to reach fruition. Thinking that, with Niven along, the easy-going atmosphere they had enjoyed while working together on *The Pink Panther* (1963) would be recreated, and with his fee raised to a cool $1 million, Sellers finally signed his contract three weeks before production commenced.[103, 104] Later, while taking part in a combined interview with Spike Milligan for the BBC's *Film Night* programme transmitted on 8 November 1970, Sellers would admit to interviewer Tony

---

[102] *Kiss Kiss Bang! Bang!: The Unofficial James Bond Companion*, Alan Barnes and Marcus Hearn, Overlook Press, October 1998.
[103] *Woody Allen: A Biography*, John Baxter, HarperCollins, November 1998.
[104] *Peter Sellers: The Mask Behind the Mask*, Peter Evans, Frewin, September 1969.

Bilbow, 'Everyone has their price; I proved that with *Casino Royale.*'

David Niven and Ursula Andress

Having been approached regarding the film, David Niven requested a look at the screenplay, but was informed that he could do so only at Feldman's home, and that he would not be allowed to remove it from the premises. Having finished reading a portion, in which Sir James Bond recruits Nigel Force to masquerade as Bond, Niven was very surprised when Feldman, who clearly considered the screenplay extremely valuable, quickly locked it away in a wall safe.[105] Feldman then unashamedly used Sellers' contract signing (even though the two leads would not actually share any scenes) and a salary of $500,000 entice Niven on board, and was successful in doing so.[106] Apparently others considered for the role of Sir James Bond were Laurence Harvey, Stanley Baker, Peter O'Toole and William Holden, the last two of whom ended up taking other roles in the picture, but only cameo ones.[107]

Once again shooting failed to commence on the planned date, 8 December, but then in the week before Christmas there was a major public announcement concerning two additions to the cast, both of whom had prior Bond connections. These were Ursula Andress and David Niven.[108] Unless he had managed to get Connery involved, Feldman could not have obtained the services of two more appropriate performers, as Andress had played the original Bond girl Honey Ryder in *Dr. No* and Niven had been Ian Fleming's personal choice to play the cinematic 007.[109] Andress was initially paid $250,000 to play Vesper Lynd,

---

[105] *Kiss Kiss Bang! Bang!: The Unofficial James Bond Companion*, Alan Barnes and Marcus Hearn, Overlook Press, October 1998.
[106] *Variety: Daily*, Reed Business Information, 16 May 1967.
[107] Crawley's Casting Calls website, *Casino Royale*, retrieved July 2013.
[108] *The Daily Cinema*, Cinema Press Ltd, 17 December 1965.
[109] *The Other Side of the Moon: David Niven: A Biography*, Sheridan Morley, Weidenfeld & Nicholson, October 1985.

though she accepted the role only on the understanding that she would not be redubbed in post-production to erase her strong Swiss-German accent, as had happened on *Dr. No*.[110] Andress was tagged by the press as 'the most beautiful woman in the world,' and Val Guest rated her as one of the three best actresses he had ever worked with. Apparently, she was nothing like her sophisticated media image, being very down-to-earth and extremely easy to get along with.[111] However, her agreement to become involved with *Casino Royale* was greatly influenced by Peter Sellers, who strongly advised her that she would benefit greatly from being associated with the picture.

Start of production in sight

When asked in interviews about the competition *Casino Royale* might pose to Eon Productions' own Bond films, Cubby Broccoli appeared both upbeat and apparently unworried saying, 'That's a spoof and we welcome spoofs. That's wonderful for the whole industry.'[112]

In mid-December 1965, another filming start date was issued to the popular press, indicating that production would finally commence on 10 January 1966. A couple of weeks later came reports that set construction was under way at Shepperton Studios in Surrey.[113, 114] Feldman had installed a team of scriptwriters at the Dorchester Hotel, along with various cast members, extras and Peter Sellers, who had a suite there.[115] Meanwhile, Orson Welles was entrenched in an apartment over the Mirabelle restaurant in Mayfair, where he waited for the call

---

[110] *Ursula Andress*, Patrick Meier & Philippe Durant, Favre, November 2009.
[111] Telephone conversation between Val Guest and Michael Richardson, December 2005.
[112] *Variety: Daily*, Reed Business Information, 14 December 1965.
[113] *The Daily Cinema*, Cinema Press Ltd, 17 December 1965.
[114] *Kine Weekly*, Odhams Press Ltd, 30 December 1965.
[115] *Woody Allen: A Biography*, John Baxter, HarperCollins, November 1998.

to report to Shepperton, enjoying the food and informing friends, 'I don't mind waiting, the room service is excellent.'[116]

Having now secured the services of former cast members of both *The Pink Panther* and *What's New Pussycat?*, Feldman obviously thought he had assembled the talent to create a blockbuster Bond comedy movie of huge proportions. After five years of struggle, his quest to bring *Casino Royale* to the cinema screen was finally about to succeed, and the timing could not have been better. With both Bondmania and the '60s craze for spy and secret agent movies at their peak, it seemed that *Casino Royale* was a sure-fire success just waiting to be filmed; and after so much meticulous planning, what could possibly go wrong?

---

[116] *Peter Sellers: The Mask Behind the Mask*, Peter Evans, Frewin, September 1969.

Chapter Three
The Impressionist Meets the Magician

Problems begin

Unknown to Charles K Feldman, problems were already beginning to manifest themselves when, having heard about Orson Welles' tendency to make a substantial input into the productions he worked on, Peter Sellers warned Joseph McGrath that they needed to safeguard against this happening on *Casino Royale*.

Before filming got under way, Welles and Wolf Mankowitz visited Sellers in his suite at the Dorchester Hotel for a pre-production meeting to discuss script revisions. This did not go particularly well. Sellers' attempts at humour using his impressionism abilities were not appreciated by Welles, who failed to crack a smile, let alone laugh. The slim and extremely fit Sellers then proceeded to give his visitors, who were both large men, a lecture about being overweight.

This incident appears to have been when Sellers first developed an irrational fear of being upstaged by Welles, prejudging the American as both a rival and a threat before a single scene had even been filmed.[117] Welles and Mankowitz had worked together previously, as the latter had been instrumental in arranging the BBC series *The Orson Welles Sketch Book*, a talk show screened in 1955 on which he had served as an

---

[117] *Peter Sellers: The Mask Behind the Mask*, Peter Evans, Frewin, September 1969.

uncredited executive producer.[118]

Joseph McGrath's first feature film suddenly became a nightmare when Sellers informed him that he did not consider it necessary that he appear on set with Welles for any of the baccarat game sequence. McGrath disagreed, pointing out that the casino set was a huge and lavish construction, accommodating 200 extras, and that the unit would be utilising film cameras with the latest wide-angle lens, hence he needed the two actors in shot together. Overruling McGrath, Sellers arranged with Feldman that he and Welles would be filmed on alternate days, usually in close-up, for the card game confrontation, which would be shot on Stage C at Shepperton Studios.[119]

Principal photography gets under way

Production on *Casino Royale* commenced on Monday 10 January 1966 on closed sets, which Feldman insisted upon both to create media interest and to keep secret exactly who was portraying James Bond. However, there was reportedly no coherent script ready for the cast and crew to work from, so Val Guest had to come to the rescue and cobble something together, presumably from the Mankowitz screenplay, in order to get things under way.[120] Grateful that filming was finally happening, and wanting to keep Sellers happy, Feldman bought the actor a white Rolls Royce limousine, which was delivered to his home on the first day of production.[121] Thinking that he could milk Feldman's generosity further, Sellers then ordered 45 suits from his friend, the tailor Douglas Heyward, and cheekily charged

---

[118] *Orson Welles: A Biography*, Barbara Leaming, Viking, September 1985.
[119] *Peter Sellers: The Mask Behind the Mask*, Peter Evans, Frewin, September 1969.
[120] *Woody Allen: A Biography*, John Baxter, HarperCollins, November 1998.
[121] *Peter Sellers: The Authorized Biography*, Alexander Walker, Weidenfeld & Nicolson, January 1981.

them to the movie. However, upon receiving the invoice for the garments, Feldman refused to pay, stating that the wardrobe for the film had already been provided by the costumiers Nathans, based in Drury Lane, London. This left Sellers with no other option than to settle the matter himself.[122]

Frankie Randall

The initial day of production also brought forth a press release announcing that the easy listening singer and actor Frankie Randall would be recording the theme song to *Casino Royale*, which would be released as a single by RCA Records. Further to this, Randall, who had previously appeared on *The Ed Sullivan Show* in the US, was scheduled to portray a character somewhere in the film. In the event, for some unknown reason, none of this actually happened.[123]

Peter Sellers is Evelyn Trimble

As on *What's New Pussycat?*, Sellers was quickly rewriting the screenplay, this time in conjunction with Joseph McGrath. Making amendments every night in his suite at the Dorchester, he replaced the Nigel Force character with the world's greatest baccarat exponent, Evelyn Tremble. Sellers struggled to get an angle on the Tremble character, as there was no great eccentricity for him to play with, although he did consider taking a dispirited approach, much like Tony Hancock in the sitcom *Hancock's Half Hour/Hancock*. Another idea was for him to adopt a strong Brummie accent, but again Sellers rejected this, eventually preferring a light, humorous and almost straight performance, which McGrath thought was influenced by iconic actor Cary Grant.[124, 125]

---

[122] *Woody Allen: A Biography*, John Baxter, HarperCollins, November 1998.
[123] *Variety: Daily*, Reed Business Information, 10 January 1966.
[124] *The Life and Death of Peter Sellers*, Roger Lewis, Century, April 1994.
[125] *Peter Sellers: The Authorized Biography*, Alexander Walker,

Stirling Moss and Una Stubbs

As shooting progressed during that first week at Shepperton, both ex-Formula 1 racing driver Stirling Moss and actress Una Stubbs were in attendance to make cameo appearances, as Tremble's chauffeur and a nurse respectively.[126] Moss had been brought onto the picture by Sellers, who had owned a great many different vehicles, including an Aston Martin DB5, and was an enormous car enthusiast; but the four-times runner-up in the Formula 1 world championship would ultimately go uncredited. Moss's only scene involved a single-seater racing car supplied by Lotus Cars, who had experienced the benefits of product placement on *The Avengers* television series and appeared only too pleased to become associated with the film.

'Follow that car,' Tremble instructs Moss, who instead of using the Lotus promptly sprints off camera, bringing the response, 'I'll use Fangio next time, idiot' – a reference to five-times Formula 1 world champion Juan Manuel Fangio. The scene concludes with Tremble dressed in racing overalls and white crash helmet slowly climbing into the Lotus Formula 3, uttering witty dialogue obviously written by Sellers, before driving away at speed. This sequence was essentially a variation of a gag from the second Pink Panther movie, *A Shot in the Dark* (1964), in which Sellers' bumbling police detective character Clouseau approaches a police car calling 'Back to town' and, misunderstanding the instruction, the driver simply drives off without waiting for his superior to get in the vehicle.

Although the finished film would contain a couple of dream sequences, at this point the screenplay also featured a nightmare scenario featuring Una Stubbs' nurse character. This was either removed during editing or made redundant by storyline alterations, meaning Stubbs would not actually feature on screen.

Now with the production firing on all cylinders, Mankowitz

Weidenfeld & Nicolson, January 1981.
[126] *The Daily Cinema*, Cinema Press Ltd, 14 January 1966.

thought the film would conclude the cycle of '60s espionage movies, being quoted as saying, 'I consider *Casino Royale* will be the final death knell of the spy cult.'[127]

Una Stubbs' material was filmed within the week, but Stirling Moss would spend another five days at Shepperton before his cameo role was completed.[128] Meanwhile, Sellers had given an interview to Army Archerd of *Variety*, in which he confessed, 'I'm only in one segment of the story,' and prophesied, 'This could shatter the Bond image.' The interview also mentioned that David Niven would feature throughout the entire film, which was the first indication that there would be a connecting storyline running through its different segments.[129]

Unused sequence

According to Joseph McGrath, there was a set piece filmed (possibly for a dream sequence) where Sellers was a ball on a giant roulette wheel, and the red and black divisions of the wheel were represented by women. Sellers was spun, and then stopped between the legs of a particular woman. Upon watching this footage, Sellers thoroughly disliked it, thinking that it failed to achieve the desired effect, which resulted in it being scrapped.

Linking storyline

Feldman's original concept for the film was that it would consist of four different stand-alone vignettes, each starring a different James Bond, presumably culminating in all the characters coming together at the conclusion. Sometime later, however, he reconsidered his approach, deciding that a storyline linking all the parts was needed. Val Guest was in total agreement, although he pointed out that it would probably have been far

---

[127] *The Daily Cinema*, Cinema Press Ltd, 14 January 1966.
[128] *The Daily Cinema*, Cinema Press Ltd, 14 January 1966.
[129] *Variety: Daily*, Reed Business Information, 28 January 1966.

better to have had this linking material planned out in advance, before principal filming was under way. Trusted with the task of devising the screenplay for the connecting scenes, Guest thought up a framing story featuring David Niven as Sir James Bond and Ursula Andress as Vesper Lynd, although it would be June 1966 before any filming took place from this script.[130]

Meanwhile, a sequence was shot in which Vesper visits the Buckingham Club and quickly introduces herself to Evelyn Tremble. Vesper asks the obvious question, 'Isn't Evelyn a girl's name?', to which Tremble replies, 'No, it's mine, actually.' This is followed by several lines of dialogue in which Vesper professes to having thoroughly enjoyed Tremble's book, *Tremble and Baccarat*, purring, 'I've studied it closely at night in my bed.' To which he replies, with a double meaning, 'Is that where you study it!' During this filming there were a great many uncredited extras on the Buckingham Club set, including Maxwell Craig, Jim Brady and stuntman Alan Chuntz.

Possible performers

Feldman wanted singer/actress Barbra Streisand involved in the film in some capacity, but producer Ray Stark already had her signature on a contract to make her cinematic debut in the comedy drama *Funny Girl* (1968).[131] Sellers meanwhile considered having his wife Britt Ekland appear; a scheduling conflict prevented this, however, as during January 1966 she was working in the US on the television courtroom drama *Trials of O'Brien* – although the couple communicated every day by exchanging international telegrams.[132]

Throughout January, Woody Allen had been recording new dialogue for the feature film *What's Up Tiger Lily?* (1966) at Teacher's Sound Studio in New York, assisted by some of his

---

[130] *Psychedelic Cinema* documentary, MGM Home Entertainment Inc, October 2002.
[131] *Variety: Daily*, Reed Business Information, 28 January 1966.
[132] *Milwaukee Sentinel*, Journal Communications, 29 January 1966.

friends including Mickey Rose and Frank Buxton. This film was based around a Japanese espionage thriller called *International Secret Police: Key of Keys* (1965), which was being transformed with new scenes and a rearrangement of the existing ones before being completely overdubbed. The final result, which had been financed by American International Pictures, was a comedy movie where the plotline revolved around the pursuit of the perfect egg salad.[133]

Graham Stark

Four weeks into the shooting of the film, actor Graham Stark received an approach through his agent requesting his presence the following day at Shepperton Studios. Due to the larger-than-usual fee on offer, he dropped everything and complied. Doubtless his close friend Sellers had pulled some strings to have Stark recruited, envisaging them working together and doing some good two-handed comedy. If any such material was ever filmed, however, it went unused. In the event, Sellers and Stark shared just a single scene, along with Ursula Andress, involving Tremble and Vesper Lynd arriving at the casino, and the humour was restricted to the standing dialogue joke, 'It's not for me. It's for somebody else.'[134, 135] Stark's role was as the casino cashier, and he was a replacement for the obscure actor Monti De Lyle, whose name appeared on the production call sheet dated Monday 22 February.

Duncan MaCrae

Another addition to the cast during early February 1966 was Duncan MaCrae (more usually credited as Duncan Macrae), who assumed the part of Inspector Mathis, a character adapted

---

[133] *Woody Allen: A Biography*, John Baxter, HarperCollins, November 1998.
[134] *Peter Sellers: The Authorized Biography*, Alexander Walker, Weidenfeld & Nicolson, January 1981.
[135] *Remembering Peter Sellers*, Graham Stark, Robson Books, July 1990.

from the French agent Mathis in the novel. He was rewarded with a £2,500 fee for a couple of months' work, which actually resulted in less than three minutes' screen time.[136]

Feldman wanted *Casino Royale* to begin with the image, made famous by the Eon Production Bond films, of the agent walking into view as seen through a telescopic sight, but realised that Eon and United Artists would never allow it. Thus a pre-title sequence was compiled from footage where, having arrived in France, Tremble is approached by Inspector Mathis amidst Les Beatles graffiti in a pissoir that partly obscures both men. Producing his police identification, Mathis announces, 'These are my credentials'; Tremble gives him a whimsical look and, glancing down, replies with a double meaning, 'They appear to be in order.'

Ian Hendry

As filming at Shepperton continued, the production was joined by well-known actor Ian Hendry, one of the original stars of *The Avengers*, although unfortunately, as with Una Stubbs, his performance would be omitted from the finished film.[137] Hendry's role was the unusual one of a body being disposed of, his character having apparently met his demise at Vesper's hands just prior to Tremble's arrival at her luxury Mayfair apartment – thus giving an indication of her lethal nature.[138] The apartment set was complete with all modern conveniences courtesy of production designer Michael Stringer, though the kitchen was actually provided by '60s fitted furniture manufacturer Hygena.

Sellers' silly voices

---

[136] *Wise Enough to Play the Fool: A Biography of Duncan Macrae*, Priscilla Barlow, John Donald Publishers Ltd, December 1995.
[137] *The Daily Cinema*, Cinema Press Ltd, 4 February 1966.
[138] *007 Magazine* No. 40, *Casino Royale*, Michael Richardson and Graham Rye, The James Bond 007 International Fan Club, January 2002.

As the action continues, Vesper encourages Tremble to dress up in various costumes – which is really nothing more than a sequence written in by Sellers that allowed him do impressions, including of a British army officer, Adolf Hitler, Napoleon Bonaparte and Toulouse-Lautrec. The latter of these John Huston later claimed was an in-joke at his expense, as he had directed the 1952 movie *Moulin Rouge* that featured the character.[139] Sellers obviously thought he excelled in his impersonation of Toulouse-Lautrec, as he would revive it years later as a ruse adopted by Inspector Clouseau in *Revenge of the Pink Panther* (1978).

The small, handheld 16-millimetre cine camera used by Vesper to film Tremble's various impressions was the Beaulieu 2008 S, described at the time as the most advanced home movie system in the world. This piece of hardware came courtesy of Beaulieu Cinema Ltd, Baker Street, London, who arranged publicity through *The Sunday Times Cine-Camera Colour Supplement*. Later the company would exhibit a 16-millimetre trailer for *Casino Royale* on their stand at the International Photo-Cine Fair Exhibition, held during May 1967 in the National Hall at Olympia.[140]

One version of the screenplay involved Tremble speaking German to accompany his impersonation of Hitler, and French to coincide with the appearances of Napoleon and Toulouse-Lautrec. Sellers was also expected to do an impression of Groucho Marx, but this and the foreign language aspects of the sequence were considered inessential and wound up on the cutting room floor.[141]

Canadian animator Richard Williams apparently devoted a great deal of time to producing an intricate series of line

---

[139] *John Huston: Maker of Magic*, Stuart Kaminsky, Houghton Mifflin, May 1978.
[140] *Casino Royale Press Book*, Columbia Pictures, April 1967.
[141] *007 Magazine* No: 40, *Casino Royale*, Michael Richardson and Graham Rye, The James Bond 007 International Fan Club, January 2002.

drawing identikits that would speedily assemble themselves into the faces of the various people that Tremble mimicked. These are glimpsed briefly in the film's opening titles, forming themselves into a likeness of Hitler, and would have served as lead-ins to the different personae that Tremble adopted. However, they also must have been considered surplus to requirements at some point during post-production, resulting in their non-appearance in the actual film.

Harrods

When Vesper Lynd offers to bankroll him with £100,000 to challenge Le Chiffre at baccarat, Tremble points out that his reputation as a world authority on the game means that the villain would never agree to play him. However, Vesper has already thought of this eventuality, and gives him the alias James Bond. Having accepted the assignment, Tremble presents himself to MI5's underground training facility in the basement of Harrods department store, to be equipped with assorted gadgets. However, the previous production decision not to include the same kind of gimmicks as the Eon Productions films had obviously not been rescinded, as the various gadgets devised by Q Branch are simply mentioned in the dialogue and never actually seen in action, with the exception of a two-way video wristwatch, inspired by a similar device in the American *Dick Tracy* comic strip, which replaces Tremble's Rolex.

This sequence is played mainly for slapstick laughs, with a karate expert saluting and knocking himself out and a weapons instructor collapsing from the recoil of a gun secreted within his bowler hat. An operative, played uncredited by Bob Godfrey, is seen resisting interrogation methods as two uniformed guards physically abuse him, but then all three adjourn upon the arrival of a tea lady. After taking refreshments in a civilised manner, the three men resume their training exercise, with the guards continuing to beat up Godfrey's character.

The concept of a secret establishment beneath Harrods seems to have stemmed from Sellers, as an idea along these lines had been included in another project to which his name had been attached, namely a feature film adaptation of the play *Rhinoceros*. Director/writer Alexander Mackendrick had wanted to film *Rhinoceros* as a slapstick comedy from a screenplay by John Bird, and had originally conceived it as a vehicle for Tony Hancock, who had later backed out of the project.[142] After a reassessment, Mackendrick had planned to team up Peter Sellers and Peter Ustinov to play the two central characters, working from a second screenplay by Clive Exton in which the featured rhinos now resembled Nazis having their equivalent of a Nuremberg Rally in Harrods basement. This storyline had obviously stuck in Sellers' mind and resurfaced during discussions with Feldman, who was apparently more than happy to indulge the actor with the rewriting of the *Casino Royale* screenplay to include the Harrods basement element.[143]

Rewrites continue

When later interviewed, Geoffrey Bayldon, who played gadget-master Q in the film, recalled that the screenplay called for Tremble to be transported from Harrods to the French casino on board a double-decker bus containing attractive women, musicians and various forms of foliage. However, this sequence, along with establishing footage of Harrods, was never filmed, presumably as the screenplay was rewritten. Bayldon was disappointed that his scenes were filmed on schedule, after hearing about the fantastic amounts other performers were earning because their material was running behind and they were on huge overtime payments.[144]

Feldman genuinely believed that the improvisation and constant reworking of the script was the best way forward, feeling certain that lightning would strike twice and that *Casino*

---

[142] *Kine Weekly*, Odhams Press Ltd, 19 November 1964.
[143] *The Life and Death of Peter Sellers*, Roger Lewis, Century, April 1994.
[144] *007 Magazine* No. 40, *Casino Royale*, Michael Richardson and Graham Rye, The James Bond 007 International Fan Club, January 2002.

THE IMPRESSIONIST MEETS THE MAGICIAN

Royale would be a huge hit like the similarly-made *What's New Pussycat?*. Other sources indicate that the constant rewriting necessitated the wasteful construction of additional sets, including a futuristic laboratory and the interior of a space station, that were then dismantled without ever being used.[145]

Further developments

Production was brought to a standstill for a couple of days from Monday 7 February 1966, as Ursula Andress had unfortunately sustained a slight eye injury during the previous weekend while feeding deer at Hampton Court.[146]

Having been enlisted to portray Ilya, one of the assassins employed by Le Chiffre's SMERSH – a secret organisation bent on world domination – Scottish stand-up comedian Chic Murray received his first early-morning call to Shepperton Studios on Friday 11 February. After undergoing costume fittings and lighting tests, he was introduced to director Joseph McGrath and welcomed to the production by Peter Sellers, who was familiar with his stand-up routines, though throughout the remainder of filming the two men would never have another conversation. Murray noted the tension between Sellers and Orson Welles, whom he personally found to be both charming and good-humoured. Murray's contract was for a 16-week engagement at £400 per week. His character's name was eventually changed, appearing as Chic on the closing credits, although he was never actually referred to by any name during the action, nor did he have any lines of dialogue.[147, 148]

Sellers and Welles

---

[145] *The Life and Death of Peter Sellers*, Roger Lewis, Century, April 1994.
[146] *The Miami News*, Cox Enterprises, 11 February 1966.
[147] *Just Daft: The Chic Murray Story*, Robbie Grigor, Birlinn, September 2009.
[148] *The Best Way to Walk: The Chic Murray Story*, Andrew Yule, Mainstream, October 1989.

Another embarrassing incident occurred at the Grosvenor House hotel when Sellers encountered Orson Welles and Wolf Mankowitz in the lift waiting to descend. Claiming that their combined weight would exceed the safe payload, Sellers declined to accompany them to the ground floor. Sellers considered Welles to be grossly overweight and lacking the willpower to diet – something he himself had managed to do, regarding it as a major achievement that he had been able to reach his ideal weight.[149] Welles, for his part, was unimpressed with Sellers' bad attitude, thinking he was pretentious and definitely not a great actor, frequently referring to him as 'That fucking amateur' when talking with the crew.[150]

Jacqueline Bisset

Plucking a 19-year-old photographic model called Jacky Bisset, aka Jacqueline Bisset, from the female extras on the casino set, Sellers and McGrath launched her onto bigger things. Sporting a different hairstyle, she became femme fatale Miss Goodthighs. Although her origins within the storyline are never explained, Miss Goodthighs is obviously an enemy agent whose mission involves seducing Tremble then planting a large knockout drop in his champagne, which has almost instant results. Later, Vesper Lynd revives Tremble, informing him that Miss Goodthighs has been eradicated as a threat – so it appears that further material featuring Bisset's character either went unfilmed or was possibly removed during editing. Vesper scolds Tremble for wearing glasses, saying '... James Bond doesn't wear glasses.' Gathering himself together, he replies, 'It's just I like to see who I'm shooting.' A shot where a champagne cork is popped with a round from Tremble's Walther P38 automatic would have seemed familiar to contemporary television viewers, as a similar

---

[149] *The Life and Death of Peter Sellers*, Roger Lewis, Century, April 1994.
[150] *Double Feature Creature Attack*, Tom Weaver, McFarland & Company Inc, May 2002.

one formed a component of the opening titles of the colour Diana Rigg-starring episodes of *The Avengers*, which had just begun UK transmissions in mid-January.

One extremely dangerous event occurred during filming when, after Bisset fluffed her lines, Sellers became so angry that he fired the Walther automatic toward her face. The weapon was of course loaded with blanks, but Bissett was terrified, initially thinking that she had actually been shot, and Joseph McGrath had to step in to calm the situation.[151] Sellers was obviously feeling pressurised, possibly as a result of ongoing marital problems with Britt Ekland, who after severe disagreements had retreated to her parents' home in Sweden. Sellers frequently visited Ekland over the weekends, and when he did so he was invariably late returning to Shepperton Studios, sometimes by a whole day.[152]

Sellers' bad time keeping

Having become aware of the situation with Sellers' timekeeping, Feldman telephoned McGrath with instructions to make certain the actor reported for filming on schedule. However, the Scotsman refused to take responsibility for the actor's bad attendance. McGrath stated that when Sellers was present he would supervise direction, but should he be absent then obviously production could not be suspended and the crew would improvise and film other material. The conversation concluded with McGrath stating the obvious: 'You're paying him, Charlie. You get him there on time.'

Delegating the problem, Feldman despatched associate producer John Dark to Shepperton to rectify matters, but Sellers refused to recognise his authority and simply ignored him. Undoubtedly, Feldman's reluctance to confront Sellers' bad

---

[151] *Mr Strangelove: A Biography of Peter Sellers*, Ed Sikov, Sidgwick & Jackson, September 2002.
[152] *Kiss Kiss Bang! Bang!: The Unofficial James Bond Film Companion*, Alan Barnes and Marcus Hearn, Overlook Press, October 1998.

behaviour indicated that he still believed the actor would weave his magic as per *What's New Pussycat?*, and would be the lynchpin in making *Casino Royale* a mammoth box office success.[153]

Despite having resisted working with Orson Welles, Sellers eventually conceded that their combined presence would be required for a few shots in the baccarat confrontation sequence, resulting in them sharing the casino set for at least a solitary day's filming. One source indicates that Sellers was unaware that, like himself, Welles had also been granted permission by Feldman to write his own dialogue and interpret the Le Chiffre character within the screenplay as he saw fit.[154] The dialogue between Tremble and Le Chiffre in the finished film is somewhat disjointed, suggesting that the close-up shots were indeed filmed separately on different days, then edited together without total attention to continuity. Surprisingly, Welles failed to consider this a negative aspect, feeling that it foreshadowed the surreal elements seen later in the film.[155]

With both actors allowed to improvise, Sellers fell back on his impressive impressionism abilities, while Welles used conjuring skills gained from a lifelong passion for illusion to perform several elaborate tricks. Welles was assisted in this by David Berglas, a television magician and member of the Magic Circle, who was employed by the production and credited as technical advisor. Documentation reveals that Berglas also had a casting call during February 1966, which involved him playing the chef de partie at the casino – thought to be a cameo role accorded to him due to his minor celebrity status. This performance was apparently removed during editing.[156]

---

[153] *Kiss Kiss Bang! Bang!: The Unofficial James Bond Film Companion*, Alan Barnes and Marcus Hearn, Overlook Press, October 1998.
[154] *Peter Sellers: The Authorised Biography*, Alexander Walker, Weidenfeld & Nicolson, January 1981.
[155] *007 Magazine* No. 40, *Casino Royale*, Michael Richardson and Graham Rye, The James Bond 007 International Fan Club, January 2002.
[156] *Casino Royale* call sheet, Famous Artists Productions, 22 February

THE IMPRESSIONIST MEETS THE MAGICIAN

As production continued, during the third week of February actress Tracy Reed was another addition to the cast. Peter Sellers meanwhile took another unapproved leave of absence, which lasted five days.[157] This resulted in Joseph McGrath concentrating on Orson Welles, directing his various illusions and tricks rather than allowing the schedule to be derailed and grind to a halt.[158]

Le Chiffre's uncredited ladies

Throughout the filming of the casino scenes, Welles was surrounded by an entourage of uncredited attractive female extras, whose number frequently changed from shot to shot, although he was always flanked by the long-blonde-haired Baker Twins. Jennifer and Susan Baker's previous experience included taking minor roles in the film *Every Day's a Holiday* (1965), appearing in episodes of the BBC children's television serial *Quick Before They Catch Us* (1966), doing pantomime and recording a pop single for Pye Records. Their only dialogue in *Casino Royale* comes during Le Chiffre's performance of an elaborate trick involving the flags of all nations, when they proceed to cheer and chant 'Hooray' in appreciation of his powers of illusion. Some paperwork associated with the film credits both Bakers under the same character name, Angel, although they are never referred to as such in the action.

Working roughly from left to right as they appear in shot, the actresses playing Le Chiffre's other admirers include Alexandra Bastedo, fresh from a small part in the second Morecambe and Wise film *That Riviera Touch* (1966); Maggie Wright, wearing a pink dress and sporting her distinctive hairstyle as seen the previous year when she appeared in *The Saint* episode 'The Crime of the Century'; and Heather Lowe,

---

1966.
[157] *The Daily Cinema*, Cinema Press Ltd, 18 February 1966.
[158] *Peter Sellers: The Mask Behind the Mask*, Peter Evans, Frewin, September 1969.

wearing a multicoloured dress and an elaborate necklace that complements her long hair, worn up in a detailed style. Lowe confessed to the press that what she really wanted was a role in a musical comedy, although her fee for *Casino Royale* would undoubtedly pay the rent on her apartment in London's West End until that dream job arrived.[159]

The 1965 Miss World representative from Australia, Jan Rennison, also features in the sequence, wearing a white outfit with black markings, although she is always partly obscured by Lowe, so that usually only her face is seen on screen. Sometimes positioned behind the Baker twin on Welles' right is the obscure actress Rosemary Reede, sporting a hairstyle and a dress both similar to Lowe's. Another actress restricted mainly to facial shots behind Welles as he performs some of his tricks is Anita West, who had been a short-lived presenter on the BBC children's magazine show *Blue Peter*. Usually seen behind the Baker twin on Welles' left is dark-haired Gina Warwick, who would later appear in the *Department S* television episode 'The Pied Piper of Hambledown' (1969) and in the movie *The Haunted House of Horror* aka *Horror House* (1969).

Stood between two taller women in the background for a couple of shots is blonde actress Valerie Van Ost, best known for her presence in *The Avengers* episode 'Dead Man's Treasure', which would be filmed the following year. Standing out wearing a lilac-and-peach-coloured hooded outfit is Tracy Reed, who would remain with the production until early June 1966 before going on location later in the month to Morocco for the thriller *Maroc 7* (1967). Standing aloof in a couple of shots wearing a flowing black-and-white evening gown is fashion model Suki Potier, who would later count members of the Rolling Stones rock band among her closest friends.

Beside Tracy Reed in several shots is Jacqueline Bisset, this material having been filmed prior to her elevation to the Miss Goodthighs role, and beside her as Welles performs a levitation sequence is the blonde Fiona Lewis, who would later progress

---

[159] *Daily Mirror*, Trinity Mirror Group, 3 February 1966.

from extra work to being a regular performer in both films and television shows. In other shots, Lewis is further away from the baccarat table, leaning back against a brass railing alongside fashion model Veronica Gardiner, whose black low-cut dress matches the shade of her hair. Another positioned in this area is actress Penny Brahms, wearing her long blonde hair up and sporting a dark-pink-coloured frilly dress. Brahms' acting career would include appearances in *2001: A Space Odyssey* (1968) and the *Randall and Hopkirk (Deceased)* television episode 'When the Spirit Moves You' (1970).

The *Gastonia Gazette* newspaper, published in the US state of North Carolina, later reported that no fewer than 142 actresses had been employed during the production, although it is thought that figure also took into account fashion models and extras.[160]

Uncredited male extras

Besides the unbilled female extras, there are also various uncredited male performers visible on the casino set. These include Henry Gilbert, playing the Greek tycoon sitting on Le Chiffre's immediate left. Next to him, playing another gambler, is Bob Godfrey, seen previously in the Harrods basement sequence. Josef Behrmann appears as another casino patron, coming into shot during the levitation sequence to stand beside Tracy Reed. Film extra Harold Coyne occupies the seat to Welles' immediate right, while actor Robert Lee appears fleetingly in wide-angle shots, playing a character who according to production documentation is called Mr Lee.

There are fewer uncredited performers seen behind Sellers during the card game, though walk-on exponent Pat Halpin can be spotted leaning against the brass railing smoking a cigarette. Actress Madge Brindley is also smoking as she sits beside Sellers watching proceedings.

---

[160] *Gastonia Gazette*, Freedom Communications, 7 May 1967.

Princess Margaret and Lord Snowden

Returning to Shepperton Studios on Friday 16 February 1966, Sellers quickly informed both cast and crew, including Orson Welles, that his personal friend Princess Margaret would be visiting the set along with her husband Lord Snowdon.[161] McGrath was unaware that Sellers had arranged this visit by royalty, and became very concerned when Snowdon arrived on the closed set with an expensive camera, accompanied by various assistants from *The Sunday Times* newspaper. McGrath telephoned Charles K Feldman to make him aware of the situation and ask for instructions on how to proceed. The producer decided that the damage was already done and advised the director to allow the visitors free access to all areas.[162]

Having boasted about how he would introduce Princess Margaret to everyone including Welles, Sellers was absolutely astonished when she breezed past him and went straight up to the large American, greeting him, 'Hello, Orson, I haven't seen you in days.'[163] Unknown to Sellers, the Princess had actually known Welles since his London stage performance of *Othello* in 1949. Footage from the previous week's filming was screened for the royal couple, which as Sellers had been absent consisted mainly of shots featuring Welles. Then, throughout the following meal, the Princess enthused endlessly about Welles's performance to, of all people, Sellers! The day's events would have severe consequences for the production of the film.[164]

---

[161] *Mr Strangelove: A Biography of Peter Sellers*, Ed Sikov, Sidgwick & Jackson, September 2002.
[162] *Peter Sellers: The Mask Behind the Mask*, Peter Evans, Frewin, September 1969.
[163] *Mr Strangelove: A Biography of Peter Sellers*, Ed Sikov, Sidgwick & Jackson, September 2002.
[164] *Peter Sellers: The Mask Behind the Mask*, Peter Evans, Frewin, September 1969.

Joe McGrath and John Bluthal are dismissed

Feeling upstaged, Sellers came to the irrational conclusion that Joseph McGrath – who found Welles both charming and friendly – should have known about and informed him of Princess Margaret's friendship with the American. Consequently, the working relationship between actor and director deteriorated over the next few days, ultimately leading to an argument in Sellers' caravan/dressing room about script revisions. The two men disagreed violently regarding certain aspects of the movie, and blows were exchanged until the altercation was broken up by stunt coordinator Gerry Crampton – who would himself appear in the finished film, doubling for the uncredited Andre Charisse as a French airport customs official who is punched by Evelyn Tremble in an unprovoked attack exhibiting his James Bond persona.[165] Sellers then pulled rank by having McGrath dismissed from the production.[166]

Not satisfied to stop there, Sellers then turned his attention to a fellow cast member, character actor John Bluthal, who suddenly found himself caught up in the fallout. Seeking out Bluthal at Shepperton Studios, Sellers accused him of colluding with McGrath. Bluthal protested his innocence, stating that he was a jobbing actor with no interest whatsoever in the politics of the film. Having portrayed the bowler-hatted MI5 operative seen in the Harrods basement sequence and later shadowing Tremble at the French airport, plus the casino doorman, Bluthal was originally intended to pop up throughout the film playing other different characters. However, this all came to nothing, as his contract was terminated, although Sellers never provided any proof that Bluthal was in fact conspiring against him.[167] In the future, Sellers and Bluthal would work together again, most notably on *The Return of the Pink Panther*.

---

[165] *The Life and Death of Peter Sellers*, Roger Lewis, Century, April 1994.
[166] *Mr Strangelove: A Biography of Peter Sellers*, Ed Sikov, Sidgwick & Jackson, September 2002.
[167] *The Life and Death of Peter Sellers*, Roger Lewis, Century, April 1994.

Realisation then struck Sellers that he had made a mistake of enormous proportions in having McGrath fired, and after consulting with Feldman, he telephoned the director to request that he return, saying, 'Charlie will give you a Rolls Royce if you come back. He gave me one!' Having lost all patience, McGrath refused, considering that he was better off being away from the haphazard scheduling of *Casino Royale*. He replied, 'There's no control. Nobody has any overall feeling for the film and what is happening.'

Sometime later, Sellers wrote McGrath a letter of apology for his unprofessional attitude and congratulated him on directing the dressing-up scenes in Vesper Lynd's apartment, which were his favourite part of the film. The letter concluded with the suggestion that they work together again – which, despite their differences on *Casino Royale*, they would indeed do several years later on the films *The Magic Christian* (1969) and *The Great McGonagall* (1974).[168]

Feldman needs another director

Although Feldman had always envisaged *Casino Royale* as a multi-segment production with a different director for each segment, he now suddenly found that he needed someone at short notice to assume control of the Sellers/Welles portion. The alternative was suspending production until a replacement director could be located, but this was unthinkable to Feldman, who knew that a stoppage would result in costs of tens of thousands of dollars a day. Having successfully directed the first two feature films starring the Beatles, Richard Lester was Feldman's initial choice. However, knowing both Sellers and McGrath, Lester thought that accepting would signify him taking sides in the dispute, so he refused.[169] Bryan Forbes was contacted again, but having heard that his earlier financial demands had prompted executives at Columbia Pictures to call

---

[168] *The Life and Death of Peter Sellers*, Roger Lewis, Century, April 1994.
[169] *The Life and Death of Peter Sellers*, Roger Lewis, Century, April 1994.

him 'a blackmailing whore,' he dismissed the offer without a second thought.

Feldman found a willing collaborator in Blake Edwards, who was happy to provide his services as a replacement director, but his inflated fee of $1 million was considered completely over the top, and he was ruled out.[170] Another, more surprising candidate was American actor Cliff Robertson, who was currently working in Rome as a cast member on Feldman's second production of the time, *The Honey Pot* (1967). He was approached because he had occasionally directed screen tests. Robertson declined the opportunity, feeling that he was fully occupied acting in *The Honey Pot*, although his lack of directing experience was probably also a major factor in his refusal.[171]

Having become bored with the whole situation, Orson Welles had returned to his home outside Madrid in Spain, giving Feldman the nightmare quandary of how to entice him back to Shepperton Studios. However, Feldman finally found his replacement director in multi-talented American Robert Parrish, a former child actor who had switched to working behind the camera and who also had an excellent reputation as a film editor.[172] Feldman was quietly confident that Parrish could achieve something other directors would find extremely difficult, namely persuading Welles to return to the production – which in the event proved comparatively easy, because they were old friends.[173] Meanwhile, it appeared that the majority of both cast and crew were unaware of what had actually happened. Even Sellers' close friend Graham Stark had not been informed, and he arrived early one morning at Shepperton as per his call. After spending time in make-up and putting on his

---

[170] *Mr Strangelove: A Biography of Peter Sellers*, Ed Sikov, Sidgwick & Jackson, September 2002.
[171] *Cinema Retro* Vol. 2 No. 6, *The Look of … Mayhem*, Gareth Owen, Solo Publishing, September 2006.
[172] *Mr Strangelove: A Biography of Peter Sellers*, Ed Sikov, Sidgwick & Jackson, September 2002.
[173] *This is Orson Welles*, Orson Welles and Peter Bogdanovich, HarperCollins, September 1992.

costume, he entered Stage C to be greeted by a friendly American who shook his hand and said, 'Great to be working with you, Graham. I'm Bob Parrish, and I'm directing the picture!'[174]

---

[174] *Remembering Peter Sellers*, Graham Stark, Robson Books, July 1990.

MICHAEL RICHARDSON

Chapter Four
Torture of the Mind

Robert Parrish

With principal photography on *Casino Royale* now approaching the end of its second month at Shepperton Studios, some major changes had taken place. Joseph McGrath having been removed from his position of director after six weeks' filming, a press statement was issued indicating that his segment of the film was now complete, although this was not entirely true. Having replaced McGrath, Robert Parrish had now taken control of the production, and he was continuing with the Evelyn Tremble/Le Chiffre segment.[175]

Feldman had various writers entrenched on different floors of the Dorchester Hotel, where, according to Orson Welles, they frequently lunched together and often exchanged ideas about the film. However, Feldman was unaware that this level of co-operation was occurring, as he wanted to keep the writers ignorant of each other's presence, fearing that any collaboration would cancel out their novel concepts. The writers would be summoned individually to Feldman's suite at the Grosvenor Hotel, where he would read through their material and then, ever security conscious, lock it away within a wall safe. Having written his own dialogue for Le Chiffe, Orson Welles was well aware of this procedure, knowing that Feldman considered his writers' storyline elements so groundbreaking that people would actually want to steal them. However, despite the radical

---

[175] *Variety: Daily*, Reed Business Information, 24 February 1966.

method of filming, Welles was of the opinion that *The Avengers* television series was spoofing Bond far better on a weekly basis than anything they were doing.[176]

Shortly after his arrival, Parrish had a production meeting with Feldman and Sellers, where they concluded that the screenplay was not funny enough. Hence the services of comedy writer John Law were employed.[177] Having scripted for the BBC's *Comedy Playhouse* and collaborated with Michael Bentine, Sellers' former colleague from *The Goon Show*, on his comedy sketch show *It's a Square World*, Law would some spend time at Shepperton Studios coming up with amusing dialogue for *Casino Royale*. This appears to have been concurrent with his work on the BBC's satirical sketch show *The Frost Report*, for which his contributions included the famous 'class sketch' starring John Cleese, Ronnie Barker and Ronnie Corbett. Law had a significant input to what finally appeared on screen in *Casino Royale*, which resulted in him sharing the screenplay credit with Wolf Mankowitz and Michael Sayers. Sellers always maintained throughout his time on the production that he too would receive a writing credit for his contribution to the screenplay, and this was a topic of discussion between himself and Feldman during March and the first couple of weeks of April 1966.[178] In the end, the actor received no such credit.

Media interest

During late February 1966, there was a report in the *Daily Mirror* newspaper that had Andress, playing the world's richest spy, throwing a tantrum, dressed in a skimpy costume and ending up in Peter Sellers' arms. This scene also failed to be included in the finished film.[179] In early March, a reporter from *The Sun*

---

[176] *Orson Welles: A Biography*, Barbara Leaming, Viking, September 1985.
[177] *Mr Strangelove: A Biography of Peter Sellers*, Ed Sikov, Sidgwick & Jackson, September 2002.
[178] *Mr Strangelove: A Biography of Peter Sellers*, Ed Sikov, Sidgwick & Jackson, September 2002.

newspaper talked with Andress and found her somewhat confused about the film. 'I'm in a daze. I don't know what I'm supposed to say. I don't know which script, which director, which producer, which scene. It's confusion.'

Also during March, the entertainment press was speculating about the style of the movie, though Feldman was revealing little: 'The story breaks into various sequences and we've been trying to find an ideal director for each.' Feldman went on to state that the new sequence directed by Robert Parrish highlighted the suspenseful elements of the film, adding that it would take four to five weeks' shooting to complete. Attempting to keep interest in the picture paramount, the producer also stated that a third director would be signed shortly to handle another segment, which would be a light, sophisticated comedy starring David Niven.[180]

Despite the closed set policy still being enforced, Sellers again exceeded his authority by granting permission to his friend Graham Stark to take photographs of the production. At odds with her usual easy-going attitude, Ursula Andress was extremely reluctant to pose for these. However, Sellers persuaded Urst – as he affectionately called her – to allow Gra – short for Graham – to take several snaps. Stark developed the images himself, and several days later presented Andress with a set of 10 x 12 inch glossy prints. Andress was apparently so pleased with the finished product that she explained her earlier reluctance, relating a story about a previous production on which a media photographer had hid somewhere in the scenery and used a telephoto lens to take a shot without her knowledge. The photographer had waited until Andress bent over to stamp out a cigarette butt, not realising that the flimsy fabric of her revealing evening gown had been affected by gravity. In her thick Swiss accent, Andress told Sellers and Stark exactly what had happened next: 'I open some magazine and there in ze middle pages are

---

[179] *Daily Mirror*, Trinity Mirror Group, 25 February 1966.
[180] *Variety: Weekly*, Reed Business Information, 2 March 1966.

my teets!'[181]

Haphazard production at Shepperton

Arriving on Stage C one morning, Graham Stark found everything in total confusion, with approximately 200 extras milling about unsupervised as Feldman's team of writers busied themselves rewriting dialogue in a caravan parked in the corner of the soundstage. Like a production line, the writers, including John Law, fed a steady stream of jokes and amusing dialogue to Peter Sellers, but apparently very little of this material was actually filmed. Stark recognised Tracy Reed from their having worked together on *A Shot in the Dark*, so they began chatting. They were then joined by Orson Welles. Reed was already acquainted with Welles, as her father Sir Carol Reed had directed him in the classic movie *The Third Man* (1949), 17 years previously.[182] Commenting on the massive expenditure being lavished on *Casino Royale*, Welles stated that he could produce an entire movie for the budget allocated to the casino sequence. Then a runner arrived from the writers' caravan and handed Welles a scrap of paper containing several lines of dialogue, which the actor read after the young man had departed. Screwing the paper up into a ball, Welles threw it over his shoulder and voiced his displeasure, 'God save us from amateurs!'[183]

Jerry Bresler

With the arrival of Robert Parrish, Feldman hoped to bring to the film a radical approach of pop art and psychedelic anarchy, which would result in a madcap run-around. To assist in organising and keeping track of the shooting schedule, he brought Famous Artists' head of production Jerry Bresler in as

---

[181] *Remembering Peter Sellers*, Graham Stark, Robson Books, July 1990.
[182] *Remembering Peter Sellers*, Graham Stark, Robson Books, July 1990.
[183] *Remembering Peter Sellers*, Graham Stark, Robson Books, July 1990.

co-producer.[184] Bresler had been producer on the American civil war movie *Major Dundee* (1965), and as an incentive to work on *Casino Royale*, he received the Rolls Royce that had originally been acquired to try to tempt Joe McGrath back to the picture. In true *Casino Royale* fashion, the cast and crew were not made aware of the appointment until Bresler walked onto the casino set and announced to everybody present that he was now in charge of the production at Shepperton.[185]

Within the week, continued media scrutiny of the production saw news reporter David Nathen asking a series of probing questions that Bresler attempted to answer without giving too much away, stating, 'Yes, this is a James Bond picture. No, I can't tell you who plays Bond,' and, 'No, Peter Sellers isn't James Bond.' Meanwhile, Sellers was apparently enjoying himself far more in his own interview, claiming: 'I go into this lavatory to make contact on my telephone wristwatch and a dwarf comes in and pulls the chain. I'm last seen disappearing down the lavatory.' While this might perhaps have been simply a case of Sellers resorting to Goon-style humour at the reporter's expense, it is also possible that such a scenario was actually included in one of the various drafts of the screenplay; a similar concept was referred to in another interview, although on this occasion it was stated that the dwarf would execute a covert attack on Sellers' character by climbing out of the toilet bowl. Referring to the different James Bonds required by the screenplay, the catchphrase 'Bond for a Day' was also mentioned, but this would fail to enter the nation's psyche, being replaced later by '*Casino Royale* is too much for one James Bond!'[186]

---

[184] *The Daily Cinema*, Cinema Press Ltd, 4 March 1966.
[185] *Cinema Retro* Vol. 2 No. 6, *The Look of … Mayhem*, Gareth Owen, Solo Publishing, September 2006.
[186] *The Sun*, International Publishing Corporation, 8 March 1966.

John Huston joins the production

On Tuesday 8 March, speculation ended regarding the third director destined for *Casino Royale* when there was an official announcement that John Huston would direct, write and appear in the David Niven segment.[187] There had been a verbal agreement between Feldman and Huston regarding the project for over six months, with the director wanting to cast character actor Robert Morley as Bond's superior M. However, Morley was apparently already committed to the teen musical *Finders Keepers* (1966) starring Cliff Richard. The latter film was scheduled to begin shooting in the first week of June 1966, thus any overrun of Huston's segment of *Casino Royale* would have caused Morley problems.

With Morley unavailable, Huston agreed to take the M role himself. His initial reluctance to do so was overcome when Feldman agreed to settle his outstanding gambling debts. Knowing that Huston was an art connoisseur, Feldman also offered him a valuable piece of artwork, which he rejected in favour of accepting an antique Greek bronze head sculpture that the producer owned. Years later, Huston had the bronze valued, presumably for insurance purposes, only to be advised that it was a fake and completely worthless.[188]

Having opened a second office at 36 Dover Street, London, Famous Artists Productions wrote to Huston on Thursday 10 March, associate producer John Dark informing him that production manager John Merriman had assembled a crew for his portion of the movie. Having previously worked with script supervisor Angela Allen on *Freud* (1962) and *The Night of the Iguana* (1964) Huston had requested her services for *Casino Royale* too, and Dark indicated that she had been contacted and her involvement was now a foregone conclusion – although, in

---

[187] *Kiss Kiss Bang! Bang!: The Unofficial James Bond Film Companion*, Alan Barnes and Marcus Hearn, Overlook Press, October 1998.
[188] *John Huston: Maker of Magic*, Stuart Kaminsky, Houghton Mifflin, May 1978.

the event, Allen would not actually work on the film. Dark concluded the letter by offering to meet any requirements Huston had with regard to filming, and said how much he was looking forward to working alongside the American director.

Budget increase

Feldman arranged the screening of some preliminary rushes for Columbia Pictures executives, who were so impressed with the material that they increased the film's budget to $8 million.[189] Meanwhile, production publicist John Willis relayed to the trade press the latest information regarding the Shepperton shooting on the movie, confirming that Robert Parrish was busy supervising the suspense sequence.[190]

However, work was still progressing far from smoothly. It was not unusual for the eccentric Feldman to make instant decisions with far-reaching consequences, such as deciding against the colour scheme on the set for the following day's filming and having it changed overnight. This would cause a knock-on effect for the wardrobe department, who were kept busy running up new costumes and attempting to colour-coordinate Andress's outfits and accessories. To avoid production falling behind schedule, the third assistant director would sometimes have the unenviable task of travelling to the Mirabelle to wake Orson Welles at 5.00 am and politely ask him to attend the studio, to perform in a scene that had not actually been written yet.[191]

Psychedelic sequence

A scene was scripted involving Evelyn Tremble and Vesper Lynd riding on an elephant, but later Sellers decided against

---

[189] *Kine Weekly*, Odhams Press Ltd, 10 March 1966.
[190] *The Daily Cinema*, Cinema Press Ltd, 11 March 1966.
[191] *So You Want to Be in Pictures: The Autobiography of Val Guest*, Val Guest, Reynolds & Hearn, May 2001.

this, replacing it with a psychedelic sequence featuring a Scottish marching pipe band. Costume designer Julie Harris had devised a stylish pink outfit complete with turban for Andress to wear in the elephant scene, and she became disgruntled when it was cancelled. However, Feldman then agreed that the actress could instead wear that costume in another scene, where Sir James Bond visits Vesper's stock market office.[192] Scotsman Chic Murray was approached by a senior member of the production team and asked if he knew where a traditional bagpipe band might be located, prompting him to telephone north of the border and make arrangements to fly the Edinburgh Police Pipe Band to London.[193]

In the finished film, immediately after the shot described earlier of Tremble driving away in the Formula 3 Lotus, he is seen waking up to find himself seated in a large chair, with the symbolic carpet-beater attached to it, visible over his shoulder. But what has happened to him in between? The storyline up to this point has had at least a faint semblance of coherence, despite its unevenness, but here continuity goes completely out of the window. The intended intermediate scenes of a car chase, Tremble's arrival at Le Chiffre's headquarters, his subsequent capture and possible injection with an hallucinogenic drug are all missing, apparently because Sellers never got around to filming them before his contract ran out. Feldman preferred to gloss over the absence of these scenes, deciding against using a double for Sellers to shoot the missing material, while Jerry Bresler went on record saying that he believed audiences were no longer interested in the logical plot developments of a movie.[194]

The action continues with Tremble coming under surveillance from Le Chiffre in another room surrounded by

---

[192] *Mr Strangelove: A Biography of Peter Sellers*, Ed Sikov, Sidgwick & Jackson, September 2002.
[193] *The Best Way to Walk: The Chic Murray Story*, Andrew Yule, Mainstream, October 1989.
[194] *007 Magazine* No. 40, *Casino Royale*, Michael Richardson and Graham Rye, The James Bond 007 International Fan Club, January 2002.

sophisticated equipment, and being ordered to hand over the cheque of his large casino winnings. Tremble's refusal only amuses Le Chiffre, who warns that he will undergo torture of the mind. The strange under-cranked (speeded-up) psychedelic sequence follows.

As there is no upholstery cushion in the chair, it takes Tremble several moments to extricate himself from it, after which he suffers a series of hallucinations. Featured here are shots of a beauty competition where attractive women in swimwear (called Dream Girls in publicity material), including the uncredited Greta Van Rantwyk, Carol Shaw, Heather Lowe and Jennifer White, parade through a dungeon set to an incidental music soundtrack. This footage was not originally intended for this sequence, but was utilised after Sellers' departure in an effort to conclude the Evelyn Tremble segment of the storyline. It appears to have replaced a scene, filmed on the same dungeon set, where Vesper Lynd, wearing a black mini dress and matching boots, wielded a machine gun, presumably rescuing Tremble. Further to this, photographic evidence shows two SMERSH assassins, played by Chic Murray and Jonathan Routh, a prankster on the British version of the television show *Candid Camera*, laid out on the floor, presumably having been shot by Lynd. This plotline was obviously abandoned.[195]

Getting back to what actually happens on screen, Tremble eventually finds himself dressed in traditional Scottish clothing, complete with a Dress Gordon kilt. Standing in a rolling mist, created on set by the use of dry ice, he is then suddenly confronted by the Scottish marching band, which includes Chic Murray playing a big bass drum and Jonathan Routh, alongside the hundred-plus pipers of the Edinburgh Police Pipe Band.[196]

---

[195] *Cinema Retro* Vol. 2 No. 6, *The Look of ... Mayhem*, Gareth Owen, Solo Publishing, September 2006.
[196] *The Best Way to Walk: The Chic Murray Story*, Andrew Yule, Mainstream, October 1989.

Peter O'Toole makes an uncredited cameo

On Thursday 17 March 1966, Peter O'Toole visited his friend Peter Sellers at Shepperton, where he was persuaded to make a cameo appearance in the marching band sequence. O'Toole later described his involvement as a St Patrick's Day joke. Leading a row of pipers, O'Toole breaks away and asks Sellers, 'Excuse me, are you Richard Burton?' 'No,' Sellers replies, beaming, 'I'm Peter O'Toole' – an exchange of dialogue inspired by a similar one in *What's New Pussycat?* involving O'Toole and Richard Burton. 'Then you're the finest man who ever breathed,' O'Toole adds, tugging on one of the tassels of Sellers' sporran before rejoining the pipers.

O'Toole settled for a case of champagne as payment for this endeavour, though later he regretted having become involved and wished that his appearance had not made it through into the finished film.[197]

Double agent

With a long burst of automatic gunfire, Vesper Lynd mows down all the marching band with her customised machine gun bagpipes, leaving Tremble standing alone. 'Mr Tremble,' she calls, 'never trust a rich spy,' and concluding the sequence she fires again, revealing herself as a double agent. The agents played by Chic Murray and Jonathan Routh then follow their instructions from SMERSH control and liquidate Le Chiffre inside his sanctum. The tartan outfits worn by Sellers and Andress for this sequence were both supplied by Knightsbridge-based clothing retailers The Scotch House, which in 2002 would be rebranded by the parent company GUS into a Burberry outlet.

---

[197] *Peter O'Toole: A Biography*, Michael Freedland, W H Allen, February 1983.

Dave Prowse

Watching the Scottish pipers marching through the mist from the sidelines was Dave Prowse, then billed as David Prowse, who was due to make his feature film debut in the role of Superpooh, a giant evil teddy bear who inhabits Evelyn Tremble's nightmare. Prowse, later best known for portraying Darth Vader in the first three *Star Wars* movies, was initially informed by his agent that the Superpooh role was definitely his, but upon arriving at Shepperton Studios the following morning, he found a queue of people waiting to audition for it. Storming into uncredited assistant director Dominic Fulford's office, he complained about the situation, in response to which the others waiting were then dismissed. Prowse later admitted that he had pretended to be angry, and that this had been a calculated risk that could have backfired badly. Fortunately things progressed smoothly with a couple of costume fittings, but then Prowse had to endure weeks of waiting until filming got around to his scenes.[198]

The Soviet Cultural Mission

During the third week of March 1966, Shepperton Studios was visited by the Soviet Cultural Mission, led by Vladimir Surin, the general manager of the Moscow-based Mosfilms Studios. The Soviets were given a guided tour around the Shepperton facility, which lasted an hour and a half and included a visit to the set of ITC's *Danger Man* to meet its star Patrick McGoohan. The Russian representatives also inspected various Dalek props from the recently-completed *Doctor Who* feature film *Daleks Invasion Earth: 2150 A.D.*, before stopping off to talk with Peter Sellers, who was dressed in his highland regalia for pick-up shots on *Casino Royale*. Sellers made such a good impression that he was invited to Moscow, though the proposed Anglo-Russian

---

[198] *From the Force's Mouth: The Autobiography of Dave Prowse MBE*, Dave Prowse, Filament, June 2005.

co-productions that Shepperton Studios' management hoped to generate failed to materialise.[199]

Deborah is confused

Meanwhile, having been approached and invited to play a SMERSH operative called Agent Mimi, who poses as M's wife Lady Fiona McTarry, well-known Scottish actress Deborah Kerr had apparently given her friend John Huston a verbal acceptance. However, by 25 March she still had not seen a shooting script, which made her begin to feel anxious. Writing to Huston, she confirmed her enthusiasm for the project, but pointed out that without anything on paper, she was unable to envisage her character. With the original filming date of 4 April for the David Niven segment imminent, she requested clarification and confessed to having no idea what her role would actually entail.

Budget speculation

By the fourth week of March 1966, rumours were beginning to circulate through the film industry that *Casino Royale* was seriously over budget, with less than a quarter of the screenplay having been filmed. Speculation concerning the John Huston/David Niven segment was rife, as the director was known to favour expending much time and effort to create something of quality, and this approach would surely squeeze the budget even further. American entertainment business publications reported that Columbia Pictures executive Mike Frankovich had departed from New York on Friday 18 March for a visit to take stock of the company's European-financed productions, including *Casino Royale*.[200] However, when interviewed on Thursday 24 March, Feldman insisted that there had been no production meeting with Frankovich during his

---

[199] *The Daily Cinema*, Cinema Press Ltd, 28 March 1966.
[200] *Variety: Weekly*, Reed Business Information, 23 March 1966.

visit to London, and that his presence had nothing whatsoever to do with the status of filming on *Casino Royale*.[201]

Meanwhile, Feldman was extolling the virtues of famed director John Huston, lauding him as one of the greatest talents in the movie industry. He believed that Huston's involvement would ensure that *Casino Royale* would be of major importance. At the time, Feldman was quoted as saying, 'Both Columbia and I preferred Huston and selected him from all the directors in the entire business.'[202]

Fang Girls

By now, a car-wash scene involving Sellers and Duncan MaCrae, which logically follows on from the pre-title sequence, had undergone filming. This involved four uncredited female actresses, referred to in some sources as Fang Girls, dressed in black PVC outfits complete with visors. These were Gina Warwick and Fiona Lewis, who had also appeared behind Orson Welles in the casino sequences, plus Jean Stewart and fashion model Dani Sheridan. Each of the four sported a small facial adornment: Warwick a tattoo graphic in the middle of her forehead; Lewis a dark-coloured beauty spot on her right cheek; Stewart a small metal stud in the side of her chin; and Sheridan a tattoo teardrop beneath her right eye. Besides having a successful modelling career and walk-on roles in films, Sheridan had also recorded a cover version of the Glen Campbell song 'Guess I'm Dumb', which had been released in February. The Fang Girls are apparently female operatives of SMERSH, although the film contains no dialogue confirming this. However, Tracy Reed would be credited as 'Fang Leader' for her role in the David Niven segment.

---

[201] *Variety: Daily*, Reed Business Information, 25 March 1966.
[202] *Variety: Weekly*, Reed Business Information, 30 March 1966.

Peter Sellers and Duncan MaCrae

Also in the can by now were scenes set inside the office of casino director Simmington-Jones, played by Colin Gordon, who appeared alongside Sellers, Andress and MaCrae. This footage included a close-up shot featured in the finished film, showing the tongue of a stuffed tiger moving of its own accord – the explanation for which, if it was ever filmed, did not make it through editing. One of the funniest lines in the movie appears to have been filmed concurrently with the office material, when Tremble asks Mathis, 'There's something been worrying me. You're a French police officer, but you have a Scottish accent?' To which Mathis casually replies, 'Aye, it worries me too!'

Meanwhile, Sellers was becoming temperamental again, causing the crew problems, as since mid-March 1966 he had been intermittently calling in sick. The consequence of this and his earlier absences was that by the beginning of April, fourteen-and-a-half working days had been lost on the production, leaving it with a financial deficit amounting to £705,000, according to Feldman's calculations.

Andress unhappy with slow progress

There were further signs of discontent sometime during April 1966, when Ursula Andress gave an interview to respected journalist Sheilah Graham. Dismayed that a job originally supposed to take several weeks was now not scheduled to be completed until June, Andress placed the blame for the slow progress squarely on Sellers' shoulders, claiming that whenever the actor felt tired, those in authority allowed production to slow down. Pushing himself to the point of exhaustion was something that Sellers had frequently done, even back in the '50s, when the enforced breaks resulting from this practice had played havoc with the recording schedules of BBC radio's *The Goon Show*.[203] Andress also highlighted the constant rewriting that had taken place, confirming that this practice was delaying filming on a daily basis.

Sarah Miles

Actress Sarah Miles had by this point been offered the role of Meg, one of the McTarry daughters. Despite showing great interest in accepting, she was initially denied her request to see the screenplay. However, a second request was accepted, and on 5 April 1966 she made a visit to 16 South Audley Street to go though the portion of the script that featured her character. Upon reading this, she quickly informed the Famous Artists staff that she would not participate in the film. Upon returning home, Miles wrote an apologetic letter to John Huston, outlining her reasons for turning down the role, claiming that there was no development, characterisation or proper comic scope involved. The screenplay had also revealed that Meg was to appear topless – something that Miles obviously objected to – and she concluded her correspondence by stating that any young actress with good breasts could play the part. In the event, the shooting script was later rewritten, omitting any partial nudity for Meg, a role that was then given by Huston to Alexandra Bastedo.

Potential theme singers

The American trade press had reported that Burt Bacharach and Hal David would collaborate on half a dozen compositions for *Casino Royale*, but with several songs completed, the pair discovered that the screenplay had changed so much in eight months that these no longer fitted the movie and had to be scrapped. Bacharach was in London at the time, putting the finishing touches to his score for the film *After the Fox*, after which he would apply his time and abilities to scoring *Casino*

---

[203] *Mr Strangelove: A Biography of Peter Sellers*, Ed Sikov, Sidgwick & Jackson, September 2002.

Royale.[204] Meanwhile, Feldman had interviewed Kiki Dee as a potential singer of the theme tune, and held discussions with casting director Maude Spencer regarding Lulu and Cilla Black as other options.[205] Shortly afterwards, the French actress Claudine Auger, fresh from her female lead role as Domino in Eon Productions' Bond movie *Thunderball*, had her name associated with an appearance in *Casino Royale*, but this failed to materialise.[206]

Sellers' mind games

According to Graham Stark, Robert Parrish was an 'okay guy' who quickly realised that he had walked into the middle of an undisciplined situation, although his working relationship with Sellers was generally good.[207] Parrish found that Welles was impressive during morning filming but tended to become lethargic and bored during the afternoon, and when Sellers discovered this, he formulated a scheme to turn things to his advantage. To this end, Sellers' agent Dennis Selinger telephoned Feldman, requesting that his client's scenes would benefit from being shot in the afternoon, with immediate effect, as the actor tended to suffer from memory loss during the morning. However, Feldman's patience was beginning to reach breaking point, and he demanded that the actor respond to his 9.00 am call at Shepperton the following morning, warning that he could also have memory problems and forget to post Sellers' pay cheque. Selinger obviously spoke with Sellers, as he called Feldman back almost immediately to apologise, saying that the whole thing had been an unfortunate misunderstanding and confirming that his charge would report to Shepperton at the stipulated time.[208]

---

[204] *Variety: Daily*, Reed Business Information, 5 April 1966.
[205] *The Music of James Bond*, Jon Burlingame, Oxford University Press, October 2012.
[206] *Variety: Weekly*, Reed Business Information, 13 April 1966.
[207] *Remembering Peter Sellers*, Graham Stark, Robson Books, July 1990.
[208] *Hollywood Doesn't Live Here Anymore*, Robert Parrish, Little Brown

However, Sellers continued playing mind games, and the arrival of Robert Parrish and Jerry Bresler made no difference to his unprofessional antics, which continued with more late arrivals at Shepperton. Sellers' absenteeism often resulted in an army of technicians standing idle, and hundreds of extras being called but spending their entire day confined to their dressing rooms playing cards.[209] During these stoppages, Orson Welles provided some entertainment, practising his conjuring tricks and talking about his lifetime experiences in both the movie business and restaurants around the world. Charming and polite, Welles always bid good morning to everyone and bowed when he entered the soundstage at the beginning of the working day, before turning both to the left and then to the right to repeat the greeting.[210]

On one occasion, Welles, Parrish, the crew and at least 200 extras were present on the casino set, in response to their 8.45 am call, waiting for Sellers' arrival. Sellers was meanwhile travelling around the Surrey countryside in his chauffeur-driven Rolls Royce, constantly in touch with a contact at the studio via radio-telephone, keeping updated on the reactions caused by his absence. Having kept everyone waiting, Sellers finally arrived around 11.00 am, which resulted in Welles' great baritone voice booming out across the stage, 'Welcome, Mr Sellers, how good of you to join us.' Welles had previously arranged with a stagehand for Sellers to be picked out with a spotlight upon his appearance, silhouetting him against the wall of the soundstage. Sellers was obviously unhappy about being made the centre of attention, and the additional embarrassment of Welles adding, 'Let's have a big hand for Mr Sellers,' caused the actor to storm out and not be heard from again for a couple of days.[211]

& Company Limited, March 1988.
[209] Britmovie: British Film Forum website, James Payne, retrieved December 2008.
[210] *Hollywood Doesn't Live Here Anymore*, Robert Parrish, Little Brown & Company Limited, March 1988.
[211] *Hollywood Doesn't Live Here Anymore*, Robert Parrish, Little Brown

On one occasion when absent from Shepperton Studios, Sellers was sighted in the foyer of the Dorchester Hotel by a Columbia Pictures executive who mistook him for Woody Allen. Taking Sellers to one side, the executive began reassuring him regarding the delayed production situation, saying, 'Don't worry about this guy Sellers. We'll take care of him,' before adding, 'You, Woody, are a gentleman.' Playing along, Sellers simply adopted Woody Allen's persona and allowed the executive to believe that he was the New Yorker, although the incident resulted in him not attending the studio for another week. Having taken offence at the executive's attitude toward him, Sellers disappeared once more to the home of Britt Ekland's parents in Sweden.[212]

Superpooh

Having made friends with Chic Murray and Jonathan Routh, Dave Prowse had spent weeks watching filming taking place without actually participating himself, until one Friday afternoon he finally received the call to don the Superpooh costume, in preparation for a scene with Sellers. This aspect of the film's plotline involved a simple Winnie the Pooh toy bear transforming into the monstrous Superpooh and then attempting to break through a caged area on a dungeon set in order to attack Evelyn Tremble. However, the nightmare sequence was not completed that Friday, and work had to be adjourned until the following Monday – but in the event, Sellers never filmed any further material for *Casino Royale*, so all the Superpooh footage was ultimately scrapped. This was an obvious source of disappointment to Prowse, who considered it the loss of a golden opportunity for him.[213]

& Company Limited, March 1988.
[212] *Woody Allen: A Biography*, John Baxter, HarperCollins, November 1998.
[213] *From the Force's Mouth: The Autobiography of Dave Prowse MBE*, Dave Prowse, Filament, June 2005.

Peter Sellers is dismissed

One source indicates that Sellers' contract incorporated a provision signifying that he would continue filming in the event of an overrun, but at the inflated rate of a week's salary for each additional day he worked. After his contract expired, Sellers arrived at Shepperton one Monday morning and immediately consulted the staff in the Famous Artists production office to make certain that he would receive the higher rate of pay. Feldman, however, refused. The producer would doubtless have pointed out that the actor's scenes would have been completed already had he not been absent so much in the preceding months. Not surprisingly, Feldman's decision resulted in Sellers' departure from the studio.[214]

Upon consulting a doctor, Sellers managed to get himself diagnosed with exhaustion and jetted off to Spain to recuperate, sending Feldman a message promising to return the following week.[215] Having finally had enough of the actor's poor attitude and tantrums, an angry Feldman called a meeting with Robert Parrish, Val Guest and film editor Bill Lenny, where he asked how much Evelyn Tremble material was already in the can and if there was enough to finish the segment without any further Sellers involvement. They decided that, despite some scenes having not been filmed, they possessed enough raw footage to achieve this. Feldman then responded to Sellers' message, informing him that his services on *Casino Royale* were no longer required.[216]

Despite having walked away, Sellers still found time for another short interview with the popular press, in which he confirmed that his contract had expired with material still unfilmed. He said, 'We were just about to start one week's extra

---

[214] *From the Force's Mouth: The Autobiography of Dave Prowse MBE*, Dave Prowse, Filament, June 2005.
[215] *So You Want to Be in Pictures: The Autobiography of Val Guest*, Val Guest, Reynolds & Hearn, May 2001.
[216] *Psychedelic Cinema documentary*, MGM Home Entertainment Inc, October 2002.

work when they decided not to continue. It's all very strange and I simply don't know what will happen. It's a gigantic puzzle, the whole film.' Meanwhile, Robert Parrish's response when questioned about the future of the production did not sound that confident: 'I'm sat here at a viewing machine trying to figure things out.'[217]

Later, Sellers' work on *Casino Royale* would form part of the subject matter of the biographical film *The Life and Death of Peter Sellers* (2004), with Geoffrey Rush portraying the troubled actor and Alan Williams credited as '*Casino Royale* director' but referred to in dialogue as 'Joe', identifying him as Joseph McGrath. However, both the shower scene and the car chase sequence depicted in that film are completely fictitious and never actually occurred back in 1966. The same applies to a scene where Sellers sits on the toilet reading a broadsheet newspaper with the headline 'Bond Shaken and Stirred – Fifth Director Hired as Sellers Walks off Set'. The fifth main director on *Casino Royale* would be Kenneth Hughes, but his involvement with the picture would not begin until August 1966, four months after Sellers' departure.

Feldman creates more publicity

Following Sellers' exit, Feldman's publicity machine went into overdrive, as an announcement claimed that the film would include no fewer than thirty major stars, including Sophia Loren and Barbra Streisand – both of whom had in fact already turned down invitations to take part. Others named who ultimately failed to appear were Frank Sinatra, Honor Blackman, Rex Harrison, Peter Ustinov, the up-and-coming American actress Pamela Tiffin and the Russian ballet dancer Rudolph Nureyev. In fact the only performer mentioned who *would* grace the finished film was Peter O'Toole. However, Feldman's quotes gave the clearest indication yet that the production was running out of control: 'Columbia keeps saying stop it, no more people,

---

[217] *Evening Standard*, Associated Newspapers, 15 April 1966.

but I tell them that it's a circus. I can't stop it now!'[218]

Heaven scene

Despite having been deprived of their leading man, Robert Parrish and the Shepperton unit continued filming for approximately two weeks before wrapping, though production would resume there toward the end of May 1966.[219] However, Sellers was still required to be seen in the imaginative heaven scene that was to come immediately before the film's closing credits. This would involve all the principal cast members dressed in white and standing amidst dry ice – representing clouds – as angels, complete with large wings and playing small harps. Val Guest suggested that Sellers be replaced with a life-size photographic image of Evelyn Tremble, strategically positioned as far away from the camera as possible.[220] Eventually, however, some footage of the actor wearing his highland costume and playing a small tin whistle from the hallucinogenic sequence was pressed into service. Tremble is seen pretending that the instrument is a telescope in order to see through the mist. He then attempts to clear the mist by blowing heavily, resulting in Woody Allen's character, James Bond's treacherous nephew little Jimmy Bond, descending below the clouds and becoming enveloped in a red overlay representing hell. For some unknown reason, the double agent Vesper Lynd escapes joining him there in the underworld.

---

[218] *Variety: Weekly*, Reed Business Information, 20 April 1966.
[219] *The Daily Cinema*, Cinema Press Ltd, 22 & 29 April 1966.
[220] *So You Want to Be in Pictures: The Autobiography of Val Guest*, Val Guest, Reynolds & Hearn, May 2001.

Danny La Rue

Toward the end of April 1966, Ursula Andress flew off to Tahiti. However, despite her earlier complaints regarding the slow pace of the production, she would return to Shepperton before the end of June to film linking material with David Niven.[221]

Feldman, in consultation with Wolf Mankowitz, was meanwhile wondering how to compensate for losing his major attraction, Peter Sellers. He considered replacing him with the female impersonator Danny La Rue as the character Mata Bond, a role eventually taken by Joanna Pettet, but this idea came to nothing.[222] Feldman quickly realised that, when it came to powers of mimicry, no-one could really replace Sellers. Mankowitz suggested instead having Terence Cooper play a traditional James Bond character, as originally intended. It was envisaged that this would be Sir James's nephew (although, unlike the eventual Woody Allen version, this character was not given the name Jimmy Bond), who could easily handle all the running and fighting required of an agent. The idea was that, at the end of the story, Sir James would return to his retirement and Cooper's character would be promoted to the head of Her Majesty's secret service.[223] Again, though, this idea was ultimately abandoned.

By this point, Feldman must have been ruefully recalling the earlier warning from Mankowitz about having Sellers in *Casino Royale*, which had now returned to haunt him. After the event, Mankowitz's view was no different: 'I told Charlie that Sellers would fuck everything up. He wanted different directors. He wanted to piss around with the script. He knew nothing about anything except doing silly voices.'[224]

---

[221] *Ursula Andress*, Patrick Meier & Philippe Durant, Favre, November 2009.
[222] *Woody: Movies from Manhattan*, Julian Fox, Batsford, May 1996.
[223] *The Life and Death of Peter Sellers*, Roger Lewis, Century, April 1994.
[224] *Mr Strangelove: A Biography of Peter Sellers*, Ed Sikov, Sidgwick & Jackson, September 2002.

Chapter Five
The Spy Chick Affair

The David Niven Story

With all eight soundstages at Shepperton fully occupied with the wrapping up of work on the first segment of *Casino Royale* and the making of the *Danger Man* television series, the David Niven-starring segment of the movie began filming at Pinewood Studios in Buckinghamshire on Friday 15 April 1966. With Niven, Deborah Kerr and Charles Boyer in attendance, John Huston directed the shooting of interiors set inside the home of Sir James Bond and the McTarry family castle.[225] Producer Charles K Feldman envisaged that, under Huston's control, work on this segment would run much more smoothly than that carried out at Shepperton.[226] An attempt to hide in plain sight was engineered when, to avoid press interest, shooting commenced on closed sets under the title *The David Niven Story*, but *The Daily Cinema* blew this cover story almost straightaway.[227]

Feldman had attracted Huston to the project partly by allowing him the opportunity to construct the screenplay for his segment, which is thought to have been finalised while the director/writer stayed at Claridge's Hotel in Mayfair, London, prior to filming. Hollywood scriptwriter Nunnally Johnson, who had co-written the screenplay for the concurrent

---

[225] *The Daily Cinema*, Cinema Press Ltd, 15 April 1966.
[226] *Kiss Kiss Bang! Bang!: The Unofficial James Bond Film Companion*, Alan Barnes and Marcus Hearn, Overlook Press, October 1998.
[227] *The Daily Cinema*, Cinema Press Ltd, 21 April 1966.

production *The Dirty Dozen* (1967), was also involved, sending pages of script for Huston's approval with a message indicating that, depending on his assessment, they could be either used or ripped up. Whether or not any of Johnson's material made it through into the final version is unknown.[228] Feeling that his writing endeavours would benefit from a polish, Huston submitted his shooting script to Robert Bolt, who had been responsible for the screenplays of both *Lawrence of Arabia* (1962) and *Doctor Zhivago* (1965). However, upon inspection, Bolt decided against rewriting Huston's material – and he did not hold back in his criticism of it, dismissing it as 'garbage'![229]

Casting old friends

Forever searching for star names to add to those already included in the production, Feldman invited William Holden and Charles Boyer to his suite at the Grosvenor Hotel, having previously served as theatrical agent to both of them in Hollywood. Val Guest, also present at the meeting, witnessed the producer use his personal friendship to obtain the actors' agreement to feature in the David Niven section of the film.[230] Holden would appear as a character called Ransome, and Boyer as Le Grand of the French Deuxième Bureau. Along with Huston playing M, the quartet was completed by the Austrian actor Kurt Kasznar, who was engaged to portray Russian KGB chief Smernov. Kasznar would later become better known as the cowardly Fitzhugh in the American television series *Land of the Giants* (1968-1970).

Deborah Kerr's casting as Agent Mimi/Lady Fiona McTarry had come about through consultation between Huston and Feldman. The choice appears to have been made partly with a

---

[228] *Mr Strangelove: A Biography of Peter Sellers*, Ed Sikov, Sidgwick & Jackson, September 2002.
[229] *Woody Allen: A Biography*, John Baxter, HarperCollins, November 1998.
[230] *Woody Allen: A Biography*, John Baxter, HarperCollins, November 1998.

view to avoiding the kind of behind-the-scenes friction that had arisen between Peter Sellers and Orson Welles, as Kerr was known to have a great affection for Huston, having previously been directed by him in the movies *Heaven Knows, Mr. Allison* (1957) and *The Night of the Iguana*, and David Niven was one of her closest friends.[231] Kerr was initially informed that her scenes would be completed within ten days, though Feldman included an enormous daily overtime clause into her contract to allow for the possibility of filming taking longer than scheduled. Eventually, Kerr was kept occupied for eight weeks, although she later admitted that the majority of that time was spent simply waiting around in her dressing room. Her overtime money earned from the movie was so substantial that it provided payment for a swimming pool at her home in Switzerland, which she christened the Charles K Feldman Memorial Swimming Pool. Not surprisingly, she considered the eccentric Feldman to be a kind and sweet man.[232]

Sir James Bond

The second week of May 1966 saw location filming taking place at Mereworth Castle, situated off Tonbridge Road, just outside the village of Mereworth in Kent, as Huston supervised material featuring Niven, Holden, Boyer, Kasznar and himself. Though not actually a castle, Mereworth Castle is a large 18th Century house of Palladian architectural design, complete with two matching pavilions, which stand in acres of parkland and ornate gardens. The then owner Michael Lambert Tree had placed Mereworth Castle on the market for £800,000 in February, but in the meantime he gained financial rewards by allowing Huston's film crew to undertake some shooting on site, as the exterior became the home of Sir James Bond.[233]

---

[231] *Niv: The Authorised Biography of David Niven*, Graham Lord, Orion, October 2003.
[232] *The Life and Death of Peter Sellers*, Roger Lewis, Century, April 1994.
[233] *Daily Express*, Northern and Shell Media, 7 April 1966.

When the four chiefs of the assorted spy agencies arrive at Bond's home, the retired secret agent is using an 18th Century exercise chair known as a chamber horse, while being attended by two butlers played by the unbilled Harry Hutchinson and Erik Chitty. As the plotline unfolds, we discover that this is the original James Bond 007 and that – without mentioning names – the Connery Bond is an imposter, endowed with the master's name and number in order to keep the legend alive. M explains that it was essential to maintain the high morale within Her Majesty's secret service and keep enemies of the British Empire quaking in fear, thus he created a new James Bond superspy.

Huston's screenplay includes some nice touches here, as Sir James Bond complains about his replacement, recalling his days of adventure when spies had pride in their profession and no time for romantic interludes with every female they met. Bond is also vocal in his distaste for gadgetry, describing the modern '60s operatives as joke shop spies, and he even manages a throwaway line about an Aston Martin with deadly accessories.

As the scene continues, even the four spymasters' combined presence cannot persuade Bond to relinquish his retirement and investigate the mysterious organisation that is depleting the ranks of their services. Informed that the United States, the USSR, Britain and France have all lost agents, with numerous operatives reported missing, Bond counters, 'Too much to hope my namesake's among them?' Uninterested, Bond then gives the four visitors a guided tour around his extensive ornate gardens as, someway off, an army mortar squad prepares for a signal from M, that, when received, causes dire repercussions. Bond's residence is destroyed by mortar fire – a special effect achieved by use of a highly detailed miniature – making Bond think that the nameless organisation, revealed as SMERSH in the next scene, has attacked him. M himself is accidentally killed in the bombardment.

On location in Ireland

Huston's screenplay then shifts the action to Scotland, where Sir

James Bond returns M's remains to his widow Lady Fiona McTarry and her various daughters. Presenting Lady McTarry with the only part of her late husband to survive the attack, Bond asks, 'Just how important is a toupee?', to which she replies, 'It can only be regarded as an heirloom!' Instead of executing authentic shooting north of the border, Huston moved his film unit 12 miles south of Dublin, Ireland, where a base of operations was established at the small Ardmore Studios.[234] Suggestions were made that Huston had ulterior motives for filming there, since it allowed him to spend time at St Clerans Manor House, his 18th Century home in County Galway, and to indulge his passion for fox hunting. Around this time, Huston was also involved with a consortium of investors interested in furthering Irish film production, which if successful, would have definitely involved Ardmore Studios.[235]

Bad publicity

Meanwhile, the American news magazine *Time* ran a piece regarding the movie, where they too revealed that *The David Niven Story* was in fact another element of *Casino Royale*. Preferring to concentrate on the negative aspects surrounding the production, the publication compared Feldman's spoof to the greatly troubled early '60s epic feature film *Cleopatra*, heading their article *On Location: Little Cleopatra*. Due to the closed set policy, the reporter had actually seen nothing, but voiced his opinion anyway: 'What is really shooting is Ian Fleming's first 007 book, *Casino Royale*, and from the look of what's happening, shooting may be too good for it.'[236]

Uncredited roles and missing scenes

Having already appeared uncredited in the casino sequences,

---

[234] *Variety: Weekly*, Reed Business Information, 4 May 1966.
[235] *Newsbeat* television news report, RTÉ, 27 May 1966.
[236] *Time*, Time Inc, 6 May 1966.

both Tracy Reed and Alexandra Bastedo were cast again as daughters of the McTarry clan, being credited for these roles, along with Gabriella Licudi, Tracey Crisp, Elaine Taylor and Angela Scoular. Unrecognisable beneath ginger hair and beard was Percy Herbert, credited as 'First Piper'. Amongst others featured, but unbilled, in the background during the castle interior scenes were fashion model Maureen Lynne and, as Scottish strongmen, stunt performers Joe Powell and Doug Robinson. Having previously participated in the beauty contest sequence, model Greta Van Rantwyk received a couple of lines of dialogue as an uncredited angler whose fishing rod contains a two-way radio.

In her autobiography, Anne Ibbotson recalled her time as an inexperienced actress working on *Casino Royale* for approximately two weeks at Pinewood Studios, where as a supporting artist she filmed two scenes with David Niven. After being collected by a chauffeur-driven car in London at dawn, she spent most days alone in her dressing room because filming was running behind schedule. Both of her scenes were eventually completed in a single day. Playing one of the McTarry daughters, Ibbotson was appalled when her stand-in was instantly dismissed after casually picking up her script, thus having broken a rule of the closed set, where secrecy was considered all-important. Unfortunately, like a substantial amount of other footage, Ibbotson's scenes failed to appear in the finished film.[237]

Several sources indicate that Huston had his then 15-year-old daughter Anjelica substitute her hands for Deborah Kerr's for a close-up during filming, though this footage was apparently deemed unnecessary, as no such shot appears in the picture.

During the second week of May 1966, Columbia Pictures' executive vice-president Leo Jaffe made a statement denying that *Casino Royale* was in financial difficulties caused by

---

[237] *Coming Full Circle: A Memoir*, Anne Ibbotson, Ashgrove Publishing Ltd, November 2011.

constant script changes and the addition of new cast members. It was estimated that principal photography would be concluded in another six to eight weeks, and reports indicated that at least another eight well-known names would become involved, including Harry Andrews – though, like many others mentioned before him, he would ultimately fail to contribute.[238]

Woody Allen arrives from the States

Meanwhile, sometime during the first three weeks of May 1966, Woody Allen arrived in London, originally to fulfil his scriptwriting duties on the film, having been initially contracted for six weeks. Feldman, however, appears to have had another agenda. He placed his involvement with Allen's proposed film *Take the Money and Run* on a more professional footing by taking out a legal option on the property, for which Allen was extremely grateful, feeling that he had moved a big step closer to producing his own movie; but Allen then found himself unable to refuse Feldman's suggestion that he also accept an acting role in *Casino Royale*.[239]

However, Allen was not under any misconceptions. He still remembered the unpleasant experiences he had endured while making *What's New Pussycat?*, so he expected problems from the outset. Thus, despite having commanded a large salary and expense account, Allen would later say, 'I never trusted Feldman for a second. He was an out and out proven liar to me. I worked with him knowing that.'[240] Meanwhile, keeping himself busy, Allen made a television appearance performing his stand-up routine on ATV's *Tarbuck at the Prince of Wales*, transmitted live from the London theatre on the night of Sunday 22 May 1966.

---

[238] *Variety: Weekly*, Reed Business Information, 11 May 1966.
[239] *Woody Allen: A Biography*, John Baxter, HarperCollins, November 1998.
[240] *Woody Allen: A Biography*, John Baxter, HarperCollins, November 1998.

Killeen Castle

The following day, John Huston's unit began work in Ireland with a flexible shooting schedule of approximately ten days in which to complete all their location footage. The first week's filming appears to have centred around Killeen Castle, doubling as Castle McTarry, standing in 600 acres of parkland off Killeen Road, near the hamlet of Dunsany in County Meath, about twenty miles north-west of central Dublin.[241] Although a fortified building has stood on this site since the 12th Century, the majority of what is now Killeen Castle was constructed during the 19th Century. At the time when *Casino Royale* was filmed there, the property belonged to art dealer and racehorse owner Daniel Wildenstein. In 1981, however, the building would be badly damaged by fire and abandoned. Beginning in 1997, a long-term refurbishment plan would be put into operation by a company called Snowbury Ltd, who would also landscape the surrounding area into a golf course, designed by long-time American professional golfer Jack Nicklaus and opened in 2008.

The filming attracted the attention of the Irish news programme *Newsbeat*, which devoted 14 minutes to the Killeen Castle shoot. Presenter Cathal O'Shannon interviewed both John Huston and Deborah Kerr. Huston, who came across as extremely laid back and casual, revealed that *Casino Royale* was an episodic presentation and that he was responsible for writing and rewriting the screenplay for this segment, which featured David Niven as Sir James Bond. Huston outlined how the movie featured several James Bonds and how spontaneous alterations to his script were a daily occurrence, revealing that Feldman was allowing him the same flexibility that had slowed down production on the earlier filming at Shepperton Studios.[242]

O'Shannon asked Kerr if she found it difficult adapting to the constant rewriting of the screenplay, to which she replied

---

[241] *The Daily Cinema*, Cinema Press Ltd, 20 & 23 May 1966.
[242] *Newsbeat* television news report, RTÉ, 27 May 1966.

that as an actress she enjoyed the different challenges the role was bringing her. Kerr confessed she had never done a spoof before. She appeared genuinely pleased at being reunited with John Huston, but avoided answering O'Shannon's question as to which character she was actually playing, having possibly forgotten the name. She then proceeded to give away certain elements of the plotline by announcing that her character fell in love with Sir James Bond.

Part of a sequence where Agent Mimi hangs precariously from a broken drainpipe on Killeen Castle was shown being filmed, which for safety reasons was actually done beside a ground floor window and not on the second floor as seen in the finished film.[243] The final effect involved stuntman Roy Scammell doubling for Kerr, and the use of optical printing to insert Kerr's image into a back-projection matte of filmed footage that showed both the castle and background.

An earlier treatment of Huston's screenplay had Sir James Bond discovering the real M actually being kept prisoner in the dungeons beneath Castle McTarry, before returning to London to find that his superior had renamed many of his agents as 007. This earlier version also included Vesper Lynd, Le Chiffre and little Jimmy Bond, but there was no mention of Evelyn Tremble or of Terence Cooper's eventual character, Cooper.[244]

The Wicklow Mountains

The grouse-shooting sequence featured in the finished movie was filmed somewhere in the County Wicklow mountains, with David Niven, Deborah Kerr, Tracy Reed and Gabriella Licudi, along with eight female extras employed as beaters, all on location. During this sequence, Agent Mimi arrives and, having located a homing device/button that has been planted on

---

[243] *Newsbeat* television news report, RTÉ, 27 May 1966.
[244] *007 Magazine* No. 40, *Casino Royale*, Michael Richardson and Graham Rye, The James Bond 007 International Fan Club, January 2002.

Bond's cloak, uses his braces as a catapult, firing it back in the direction of the shooting party. The radio-controlled grouse facsimile then follows, and the button finds its target. This is followed by an optically printed shot of the grouse, which plummets downwards to crash into the radio control equipment mounted on a Volkswagen pick-up truck, resulting in three large explosions.

Parts of David Niven's costume for this sequence were later sold in the Angels Star Collection of Film and TV Costumes by Bonhams auctioneers in Knightsbridge, London, on Tuesday 6 March 2007. One of the lots was Bond's green-and-brown tweed jacket, conceived by the *Casino Royale* costume designers Julie Harris and Anna Duse and made for the production by Benson, Perry and Whitley Ltd of 9 Cork Street, London. Bidding on the garment, the inside of which was stamped with Niven's name and dated 5 April 1966, surprisingly reached only £240. However, the accompanying green velvet trilby hat, complete with rope band and feather, proved of much greater interest to collectors, selling for an impressive £2,640.[245]

Additional footage was filmed near the settlement of Glencree in County Wicklow, approximately six miles west of Ardmore Studios, at a distinctive three-pronged road junction, which merges into Old Military Road. This is the location where, in the finished film, the heads of the American, British, French and Soviet secret services meet in the sequence directly after the opening titles, accompanied by Burt Bacharach's incidental music. However, none of the actors playing M, Ransome, Le Grand and Smernov was actually present; doubles stood in for them, filmed from behind. The unbilled John Le Mesurier, playing McTarry's chauffeur, was however on location. At the time, these roads were nothing more than peat tracks; only in later years have they acquired tarmac surfaces, with the exception of the left-hand fork, which appears to have fallen into disuse since the filming.

Meanwhile, a second unit had been despatched to Scotland,

---

[245] Bonhams website, retrieved September 2013.

where they filmed only a single motor vehicle shot and collected travelling matte footage for background material. A double for David Niven drove Bond's vintage 1923 Bentley, registration number K 19, in a south-westerly direction along Dochart Road in the village of Killin, near Stirling in Stirlingshire, with the Falls of Dochart waterfall seen in the background. This was augmented with static shots of Niven pretending to drive the Bentley inside a soundstage back at Pinewood Studios, at Iver Heath in Buckinghamshire; this material was then optically printed into the travelling matte.

Vintage Bentley

The Bentley was a 3-litre model, although for the production a mocked-up supercharger was fitted to the front, giving the impression that it was the more powerful 4½-litre version. A vintage 4½-litre Bentley was James Bond's mode of transport in Ian Fleming's first three novels, *Casino Royale*, *Live and Let Die* and *Moonraker*. Upon the completion of filming, the Bentley was returned to the owners, Bill and Joyce Thallon, who lived a ten minute drive away from Pinewood Studios, in Gerrards Cross, Buckinghamshire, and they elected to retain the fake supercharger. The prop addition was however removed during the '70s as the Bentley changed hands several times, being re-registered sometime after 1983 to SV 4797, eventually being acquired by the current owner, Bentley Drivers Club member Russell Browne, who frequently attends concours events with the car.[246]

The Lions of Longleat

Newly introduced to the UK was the first drive-through safari park outside of Africa, initially called The Lions of Longleat, which opened for business on Sunday 10 April 1966, boasting

---

[246] Vintage Bentleys website, *History by Chassis*, retrieved September 2013.

fifty big jungle cats in a large enclosure covering several acres. Based around Longleat House near Warminster in Wiltshire, this novel attraction had generated plenty of publicity in the months prior to opening, prompting Huston and Feldman to include what is now known as Longleat Safari and Adventure Park as a filming location. The sequence in the park begins when the Rolls Royce limousine carrying the four secret service chiefs enters the grounds of Bond's mansion and encounters numerous lions, including a lioness that was enticed onto the roof of the vehicle, which was then filmed proceeding at a slow speed.

The incidental music accompanying this footage is the theme from the movie *Born Free*, written by John Barry, who at the time was the regular composer for the Eon Productions' Bond movies. It is thought that both the Scottish and the Longleat footage was filmed under the control of second unit director Anthony Squire, whose reputation came from directing episodes of ITP/ITC television film series, such as *William Tell* and *The Adventures of Robin Hood*.

Richard Talmadge

The other second unit director working on *Casino Royale* was Richard Talmadge, who would be responsible for directing the extensive location filming for the picture's lengthy car chase sequence.[247] Born in Camburg, Germany, on 3 December 1892, and originally named Sylvester Alphonse Metz, Talmadge began his career as a circus acrobat before graduating to the film industry, where he stunt doubled for Douglas Fairbanks Snr. Progressing further, Talmadge, known as Dick to his friends, then became an actor in silent movies, though the arrival of talkies caused problems, his strong German accent proving to be a drawback, thus prompting a return to stunt work. Gaining experience and being open to new work practices, Talmadge

---

[247] *Woody Allen: A Biography*, John Baxter, HarperCollins, November 1998.

became in turn a stunt co-ordinator, a second unit director, a director and a producer. He directed the go-karting sequence that concluded the successful *What's New Pussycat?*, and Feldman obviously thought that his directing talents would also benefit *Casino Royale*.

Car chase sequence

The car chase begins with Sir James Bond leaving Scotland in his Bentley. A cream-coloured E-Type Jaguar convertible accelerates up behind the vintage car and, overtaking it, clips the offside rear mudguard, prompting the agent to drop down a gear and gun the engine, beginning his pursuit. This material was actually filmed with the vehicles heading toward the Leatherhead estate called Givans Grove on the northbound carriageway of the A24, London Road, near Mickleham in Surrey. Over the intervening decades, the landscape on this portion of the A24 has changed greatly, now looking far more congested, although the wooden bus shelter seen during an early long shot showing both cars does still exist. As with the Scottish filming, Niven and the uncredited French actress Mierille Darc, playing the Jaguar's driver, Jag, were filmed apparently driving their respective cars in close-up on a soundstage under Huston's direction, and this footage was then optically combined with Talmadge's background material.

Both vehicles were then shot a couple of miles south, still on the northbound carriageway of the A24, before executing a tyre-screeching right turn into Pixham Lane, heading toward the residential area of Dorking. This is another location that has undergone redevelopment since the '60s, as the junction is now a roundabout and the buildings seen on the north-east side of Pixham Lane have been replaced by newer structures. The props department at Pinewood Studios had adapted the interior of the E-Type, giving Jag a telescopic microphone that extended from the centre of the steering wheel, thus allowing communication with SMERSH headquarters. Actress Penny Riley portrayed Derry, the SMERSH controller, and although her character's name was used several times in dialogue, she would actually be billed in the closing credits simply as 'Control Girl'. Derry's three assistants, played by Carol Shaw, Anne De Vigier and Jennifer White, all went uncredited. Shaw and White had been involved with the production before, having both been participants in the dungeon-based beauty competition witnessed by Evelyn Tremble.

Meanwhile, both the E-Type and the Bentley drive on at speed, passing a stationary Bedford CA milk float parked outside the red-brick Dell Park Lodge, which is situated on Bishopsgate Road in Englefield Green, near Egham. The milk float is a remote-controlled vehicle directed by Anne De Vigier's unnamed character, who has a steering wheel incorporated into her workstation console and a desk monitor connected to a forward-facing camera mounted on the roof of the Bedford. The milk float carries a rooftop placard bearing the '60s advertising slogan 'Drinka Pinta Milka Day,' seen clearly when it automatically selects first gear and roars off in pursuit of Bond's Bentley. The Bentley then appears on the SMERSH monitor, as seen from the point of view of the milk float following it as it travels along the A329 Blacknest Road, also in Englefield Green.

The four SMERSH women occupy a small circular area surrounded by a much larger circular flat surface depicting a huge roadmap on which the roads are represented by lengths of Scalextric slot car track. As Scalextric did not manufacture an E-Type Jaguar model at the time, the production crew pressed into service the nearest equivalent, using a Lister Jaguar as the scaled-down version of Jag's vehicle. They were somewhat luckier with Bond's vehicle, as Scalextric had produced a vintage Bentley model for several years. As no Bedford milk float model was available, it is believed that the crew scratch-built the miniature example to match the full-size version, mounting this on a standard Scalextric car chassis.

Glancing in the Bentley's rear view mirror, Bond notices the milk float following him, then suddenly realises that it has no driver. It is in fact a rolling bomb, which is armed by the SMERSH women from their headquarters, resulting in detonators emerging from the headlights; on impact, these will trigger an explosion. However, when Bond widens the gap between the Bentley and the milk float, the SMERSH women decide to retract the detonators. All three vehicles are then seen descending Zig-Zag Road in Box Hill, near Dorking, which was already established as a location for television film series, having featured in *The Saint*, *Danger Man* and *The Baron*. Reaching a sharp bend at the bottom of the hill, the E-Type narrowly avoids a collision with a Ford Thames pick-up truck, resulting in the commercial vehicle scattering workmen as it ploughs into some roadworks. However, the editing of this sequence lacks attention to detail, as one of the crew's tripod-mounted Arriflex film cameras is visible on the extreme left of the shot.

Old Windsor

Travelling at speed, the E-Type speeds through a couple of sweeping bends, followed by both the Bentley and the milk float. This was filmed on Burfield Road in Old Windsor in Berkshire, in a typically deserted country setting. Five decades later, the suburban sprawl has swallowed up this area, with the building of housing developments on both sides of the road, the removal of trees, foliage and scrubland, and the installation of speed bumps.

As the three vehicles retrace their wheel tracks, the next section of the car chase involves them returning to Bishopsgate Road in Surrey, though this time they are seen driving in the opposite direction to the earlier footage, passing the junction with Wick Lane. A stunt sequence follows, involving the Bentley, the E-Type and two trucks. This was performed at a crossroads with traffic lights, and the footage also features some other vehicles, including a couple of lorries in the livery of Lepstone Haulage.

All three vehicles are then seen filmed from a high vantage point proceeding through Bracknell town centre in Berkshire, on Church Lane, heading in a north-easterly direction. Since the

'60s, this portion of Bracknell has undergone an almost complete redevelopment, as Church Lane is now a dual carriageway, with the only buildings still standing from that time being the Holy Trinity Church and The Old Manor pub.

Progressing further, the three vehicles return to Burfield Road in Old Windsor, though now half a mile south-east from the previous filming, encountering a truck that has shed its load of timber at the junction with Priest Hill. Taking the initiative, Bond veers left, scything his Bentley over numerous planks of wood, before turning left at the junction and placing his vehicle in front of the E-Type, which has gone around the outside of the stricken truck. When the milk float arrives, the SMERSH operative steers it straight toward the truck and, using part of the dislodged load of planks as a ramp, launches it onto the articulated flatbed trailer and literally drives over the obstacle. However, this action results in the vehicle sustaining damage to its electronic guidance system, and the desk monitor goes blank, leaving SMERSH with no option other than to place it under automatic control.

With the Bentley now leading, the three-vehicle procession continues on Straight Road in Old Windsor, alongside the River Thames, before taking a left at speed into Ouseley Road. Jag is now becoming somewhat agitated, because the milk float is directly behind her E-Type Jaguar. She asks her headquarters to reduce the speed of the mobile bomb, but control are experiencing communication problems. Unable to see what is happening, Derry orders the detonators primed again, as the procession returns once more to Burfield Road, being filmed from the gateway to the Beaumont Estate, on the junction with Ouseley Road.

The following shot, filmed from a different angle, shows the gateway's metal gates opening at the flick of a switch by Bond, as the Bentley arrives from a different direction, having obviously approached from Ouseley Road. The Bentley having entered, the gates swing to as the E-Type arrives, and the stunt driver performs a handbrake turn, spinning the sports car to sudden halt, sideways across the now closed gateway. With the milk float bearing down on her, there is not enough time for Jag to move the E-Type before the ensuing collision brings about an explosion that engulfs both vehicles. Stopping the Bentley on the Beaumont Estate driveway, Bond looks back at the mayhem, shakes his head disapprovingly and then drives off. The close-up shots of David Niven here were again filmed in the studio against a bluescreen backdrop and inserted into the action during editing. All of the location driving for the car chase was done by doubles.

Terry O'Neill

At an early stage, well known professional photographer Terry O'Neill had come to a unique agreement with Feldman that allowed him to record the production of *Casino Royale* on the closed sets. He took various stills, including some of Peter Sellers and Stirling Moss together with the Formula 3 Lotus. He also snapped Sellers with Ursula Andress, plus Orson Welles and David Niven. One photograph showed the latter in costume on set at Pinewood Studios, being visited by his friend Sammy Davis Jnr.

Filming resumes at Shepperton Studios

Meanwhile, back at Shepperton, the extensive casino set had been dismantled from Stage C and reassembled, with the addition of a staircase, on Stage H, which at the time was the largest soundstage at the studio. Richard Talmadge found himself in demand to begin shooting there during the fourth week of May 1966 on what press releases described as action sequences, though these would actually comprise the climactic massive fight scene, featuring 200 extras, that would form the picture's conclusion. Filming of this melee in the casino would go on for several weeks, and would eventually involve Val Guest as well. Supporting Talmadge in the endeavour was Nicholas Roeg, who had already worked with John Huston to capture an earlier bubble-bath sequence featuring David Niven and Angela Scoular, and who would receive a credit on the finished film for additional photography.[248] Roeg had begun his movie career during the early '50s as an assistant camera operator and focus puller, before progressing to become the cinematographer on seven episodes of the television series *Ghost Squad* during the early '60s.[249] Before *Casino Royale*, he had recently worked on the picture *Fahrenheit 451* (1966) as the director of photography, and by the '70s he would have achieved his ambition of becoming a fully-fledged movie director.

The '60s spy film craze

The novelty of Irish location filming was still generating interest, with both the *Daily Mirror* and *Variety* reporting details, though by the first week of June 1966 John Huston had returned to Pinewood Studios, where he concentrated on shooting interiors.[250] Due to the enormous popularity generated by the James Bond movies, half the pictures being produced at Pinewood Studios during that month were espionage-based thrillers. These were the first '60s Bulldog Drummond movie, *Deadlier Than the Male* (1967); the George Segal-starring *The Quiller Memorandum* (1966), based on the best-selling novel *The Berlin Memorandum* by Elleston Trevor writing as Adam Hall; and *Funeral in Berlin* (1966) from the book by Len Deighton, with Michael Caine reprising his Harry Palmer role from the earlier box office hit *The Ipcress File* (1965).[251]

John Huston departs the project

Huston admitted to having thoroughly enjoyed himself both directing and acting in *Casino Royale*, though he also stated that,

---

[248] *The Daily Cinema*, Cinema Press Ltd, 27 May 1966.
[249] *Nicholas Roeg: Film by Film*, Scott Salwolke, McFarland and Co Inc, May 1994.
[250] *Daily Mirror*, Trinity Mirror Group, 30 May 1966.
[251] *The Daily Cinema*, Cinema Press Ltd, 27 May 1966.

having begun reading the novel before beginning his segment, he had found it somewhat boring and never actually finished it.[252] Production at Pinewood Studios closed down during the first week of June 1966, with Huston making travel arrangements to fly to New York for discussions with 20th Century Fox regarding the release of his earlier religious film project *The Bible* (1966).[253]

On leaving a viewing theatre with Val Guest after they had watched some of the *Casino Royale* rushes, Huston said, thinking out loud, 'This could easily turn into a load of crap, couldn't it?' Agreeing in principle, Guest replied, 'That's why they engaged people like you, to see it doesn't.' Huston then casually mentioned that Guest would have no problems directing Deborah Kerr, because she was extremely easy to work with. This statement surprised Guest, who remarked that his schedule did not involve him directing any scenes with the Scottish actress, to which Huston responded, 'Christ, didn't Charlie [Feldman] ask you?' Huston's contract would expire shortly, but apparently some of the material for the David Niven segment remained unfilmed; the American was confident that leaving things in Guest's capable hands was the logical thing to do.[254]

---

[252] *Variety: Weekly*, Reed Business Information, 15 June 1966.
[253] *Variety: Weekly*, Reed Business Information, 8 June 1966.
[254] *So You Want to Be in Pictures: The Autobiography of Val Guest*, Val Guest, Reynolds & Hearn, May 2001.

Chapter Six
Psychedelic Cinema

Val Guest and Richard Talmadge

Despite having been on Famous Artists' payroll for seven months, Val Guest had yet to exercise his directing abilities, though that would change during the third week of June 1966, when he assumed control of the next segment of the film to go into production. Although officially based at MGM Borehamwood Studios in Hertfordshire, Guest would be the only director on *Casino Royale* who would actually supervise filming at two different studios, as he also handled material at Shepperton.

Charles K Feldman had devised the massive casino fight sequence for the film's conclusion, while Wolf Mankowitz had fleshed out the scenario in his various screenplays. Richard Talmadge's experience of directing large barroom brawls in Western movies had made him the obvious choice to direct this action.[255] However, as he was not an established mainstream director, it was decided by Feldman that the close-ups and dialogue breaks should be controlled by Guest. This resulted in Guest joining Talmadge on the ongoing shoot and the two men working together very closely to assemble the film's conclusion.

Guest also had other responsibilities included in his brief for this segment. These included directing all of Woody Allen's scenes, most of which he had co-written with the New Yorker.

---

[255] *Woody Allen: A Biography*, John Baxter, HarperCollins, November 1998.

Further to this, he would direct all of the linking scenes featuring David Niven and Ursula Andress, which he had conceived and written at Feldman's prompting.

This segment would introduce several new characters into the film, including Woody Allen as Sir James's nephew Jimmy Bond, aka Dr Noah. Since his arrival in the UK, Allen had been waiting for filming to reach his scenes. He often spent time playing high-stakes poker at the Dorchester Hotel, and used his winnings to purchase a piece of expressionist art in the form of an Emil Nolde watercolour, which he presented to his then wife Louise Lasser. Allen also acquired a sketch by Austrian artist Oska Kokoschka, which could still be seen hanging in his New York apartment many years later, plus various rare traditional jazz LP records that were unavailable in the United States, which he obtained from second-hand shops.[256]

Barbara Bouchet

Also included in this segment was Barbara Bouchet as Moneypenny. Bouchet had been chosen for the role by Feldman himself, but almost missed out on it. The producer initially received a knock-back from director Otto Preminger, with whom the actress had an ongoing contract. Bouchet herself did not learn of this until later. Then, having managed to free herself from the Preminger contract, she subsequently encountered Feldman by coincidence at an American airport. Feldman offered her the part again, but Bouchet was visiting London for a meeting with the Italian writer/director Michelangelo Antonioni, hoping for a possible role in an upcoming movie he was planning, and she felt that circumstances prevented her from accepting the producer's offer. Having crossed the Atlantic Ocean, Bouchet arrived at Antonioni's hotel only to find him disrespectful and unresponsive, claiming that he was extremely tired, causing her to leave without discussing the possible casting. Before exiting

---

[256] *Woody Allen: A Biography*, Eric Lax, Jonathan Cape, August 1991.

the hotel, Bouchet stopped off in the lobby and, telephoning Feldman, finally accepted the role of Moneypenny.[257]

Like many others who worked on *Casino Royale*, Bouchet only ever saw the pages of the screenplay that directly involved her. All of her scenes were directed by Val Guest, and most of them also featured David Niven. Although they had worked together two years previously on the movie *Bedtime Story* (1964), Bouchet admitted that she got to know Niven much better on *Casino Royale*, where she found him charming, humorous and a complete gentleman. Like Terence Cooper, Bouchet waited over a year before Feldman managed to organise the filming of *Casino Royale*, and she found the production so confusing that she now cannot remember if she appeared in any scenes that failed to be included in the finished picture.[258]

Joanna Pettet and Daliah Lavi

Though the character would be introduced in the preceding segment of the storyline (yet to be filmed), Sir James Bond's illegitimate daughter Mata Bond also featured in Guest's segment. She was portrayed by American-based British actress Joanna Pettet, who was apparently well known to Feldman, having appeared in the movie *The Group*, produced by Famous Artists' French sister company Famartists Productions, which had been released in the United States in March 1966.

Daliah Lavi was another actress who appeared in the Val Guest segment, playing a character known as the Detainer, although she was never actually referred to as such on screen, the explanation for the name having presumably become lost during more script rewrites. Sporting a large beehive hairstyle, Lavi used her strong Israeli accent to great effect, coming across as a groovy swinging '60s chick and a total femme fatale.

---

[257] *Cinema Retro* Vol. 2 No. 6, *The Look of ... Mayhem*, Gareth Owen, Solo Publishing, September 2006.
[258] *Cinema Retro* Vol. 2 No. 6, *The Look of ... Mayhem*, Gareth Owen, Solo Publishing, September 2006.

Terence Cooper as a sort of James Bond

Having waited patiently for over two years, Terence Cooper finally got the opportunity to play James Bond – though only in a manner of speaking, after a plot development that saw Sir James rename all secret service personnel '007' in order to confuse SMERSH. When interviewed in early 1966, Cooper had stated that John Huston would direct him in a romantic interlude with Ursula Andress, but in the event, Val Guest directed him getting close to both Barbara Bouchet and Daliah Lavi. Cooper later admitted that he had been attracted to Daliah Lavi, but she was recently married and her German husband accompanied her everywhere, including to every filming session, which prevented the actor making a move.[259]

Cooper claimed to have seen portions of several different *Casino Royale* screenplays prior to this, Feldman having mailed them to him at regular intervals together with telegrams that usually indicated production would commence in two months' time. One such telegram indicated that there was a film studio somewhere in Italy where all the dressing room doors had a *Casino Royale* nameplate, though this is thought to have been totally fabricated by Feldman to keep Cooper interested in the project.[260]

Wolf Mankowitz departs

Having already spent around 18 months attached to the picture, Wolf Mankowitz had become weary of the constant rewriting he was having to perform, so on 9 June 1966 he instructed his agent, John Heyman, to get him released from the project.

Heyman wrote to Feldman outlining all the reworking

---

[259] *007 Magazine* No. 40, *Casino Royale*, Michael Richardson and Graham Rye, The James Bond 007 International Fan Club, January 2002.
[260] *007 Magazine* No. 40, *Casino Royale*, Michael Richardson and Graham Rye, The James Bond 007 International Fan Club, January 2002.

Mankowitz had done, pointing out that during the last fortnight alone his client had rewritten the large-scale casino brawl finale plus the projected introduction of Terence Cooper's character. In addition, Mankowitz had scripted some linking material involving David Niven's Sir James Bond speaking on a telephone, though this could have been simply a polishing up of material originally written by Val Guest. Finally, Mankowitz had also gone through the Mata Bond storyline, trimming away what was considered unnecessary and – after discussions with Czech producer/director Karel Reisz, who was acting as a consultant on the production – writing a shooting script for that segment.[261]

Heyman went on to say that consideration ought also to be given to Mankowitz's rewrites and amendments to the Peter Sellers segment, which in the writer's opinion had been totally disorganised until he had extensively tidied it up and turned it into an ordered and effective script. Presumably Mankowitz had script-edited the Sellers/McGrath version of the screenplay, which had been developed from his earlier draft, having found it necessary to reinstate the narrative of the storyline. Having devised that storyline and then indulged both Peter Sellers and Shirley MacLaine by rewriting it to their individual requirements, Mankowitz had been easily the main driving force on Feldman's writing team. His feelings regarding the production were summed up by the opening line of Heyman's letter: 'Wolf feels that there really is very little more that he can contribute to *Casino Royale*.'[262]

Since Feldman and Mankowitz had last spoken regarding Terence Cooper's inclusion in the movie, the writer had concocted another angle for this, still envisaging him as Bond's nephew, but now with the novelty element of him being a totally inept agent. Feldman rejected this suggestion, but the general idea was subsequently developed into the character of little Jimmy Bond, played by Woody Allen, who would be

---

[261] *The Life and Death of Peter Sellers*, Roger Lewis, Century, April 1994.
[262] *The Life and Death of Peter Sellers*, Roger Lewis, Century, April 1994.

revealed as the leader of SMERSH and the conspirator behind the entire plot.[263]

Later, Mankowitz explained his storyline to reporter Barry Norman of the *Daily Mail*: 'I saw the story as a kind of trials of Hercules. Each task Bond faced needed a different talent, so someone with that talent was recruited and called James Bond to deal with it. Actually, I think it's a new concept in films, the movie version of a four-ring circus.'[264]

Action scenes at Shepperton

With Mankowitz's departure, Feldman pinned all his hopes on Val Guest and Woody Allen being able to handle any further rewriting that might be required. Meanwhile, Richard Talmadge was still supervising the shooting of the intricate action-packed finale sequence, which at its peak involved 70 stunt fights occurring simultaneously and the directing of approximately 200 extras.[265] Despite Talmadge's decades of Hollywood experience, this filming eventually extended to two months' stage time at Shepperton, which surprisingly translated into less than eight minutes' screen time in the finished film. Obviously, much more material was filmed than was used, suggesting that this sequence suffered severe editing by Columbia Pictures during post-production.

More script changes

Woody Allen provided a screenplay featuring his Jimmy Bond character that slotted into the Val Guest-directed segment of the movie; one source suggests that he also had input from his regular collaborators of the time, Mickey Rose and Frank Buxton.[266] Feldman initially disliked Allen's material and

---

[263] *The Life and Death of Peter Sellers*, Roger Lewis, Century, April 1994.
[264] *Kiss Kiss Bang! Bang!: The Unofficial James Bond Film Companion*, Alan Barnes and Marcus Hearn, Overlook Press, October 1998.
[265] *Kiss Kiss Bang! Bang!: The Unofficial James Bond Film Companion*, Alan Barnes and Marcus Hearn, Overlook Press, October 1998.

scrapped it, preferring another concept altogether. Then, however, after Allen had temporarily returned to the US, the producer changed his mind and, contacting him via transatlantic telephone call, anxiously asked him if he had retained a carbon copy. Fortunately, Allen had indeed saved a copy, so he was able to bring it with him upon arriving back in the UK during the third week of June 1966.[267] Shortly afterwards, Allen reached a primetime UK television audience, appearing alongside Spike Milligan on the Sunday night edition of ABC Television's *The Eamonn Andrews Show* transmitted on 19 June.

Filming gets underway at MGM Borehamwood Studios

The following day, Val Guest began shooting at the MGM film studios in Borehamwood, drawing his main cast together in the form of Woody Allen, David Niven, Barbara Bouchet and Terence Cooper. As with John Huston and Deborah Kerr, Feldman had again arranged a combination of director and lead actor that he knew would work well, as 18 months previously Guest and Niven had worked together on the espionage film *Where the Spies Are* (1966), which had also been based at Borehamwood. The material involving Kerr that needed finishing off, as Huston had mentioned to Guest, appears to have consisted of a scene where Agent Mimi arrives at Sir James's office dressed in a nun's habit, ostensibly seeking a charitable donation for needy girls, and leaves a receipt revealing the kidnapped Mata Bond's whereabouts.

Woody Allen participated in only five days' filming at this point, including a firing squad scene filmed on the French village standing set originally constructed the previous year for the movie *Eye of the Devil* (1966), which coincidentally had co-starred Deborah Kerr and David Niven.[268] The same set would

---

[266] *Woody Allen: A Biography*, John Baxter, HarperCollins, November 1998.
[267] *Woody: Movies from Manhattan*, Julian Fox, Batsford, May 1996.

also appear in other productions, such as the episodes 'The Schizoid Man', 'A. B. and C.' and 'Living in Harmony' in the television series *The Prisoner* (1967), and the film *Inspector Clouseau* (1968). This firing squad sequence is now the only one that Allen actually admits to having written solo, insisting that his lines were totally ad-libbed on the day, including the classic, 'I've a very low threshold of death; my doctor says I shouldn't have bullets entering my body at any time!' Seen leading little Jimmy Bond out to his apparent execution are four South American guards. Three of these were portrayed by the uncredited Pat Ryan, Walter Henry and Maxwell Craig, the last two of whom also appeared in other unbilled roles in the film.[269]

Dr Noah

Also filmed during this week was the scene where Sir James Bond and Moneypenny enter the casino, the following sequence inside SMERSH headquarters, and the confrontation with Woody Allen's Dr Noah.[270] Enticed to the casino director's office by one of his employees, Bond and Moneypenny are followed by the same two SMERSH assassins previously responsible for Le Chiffre's death – footage of Chic Murray and Jonathan Routh obviously filmed at an earlier stage – although the assassins are never featured again after this point. Upon entering the office, Bond and Moneypenny are ambushed by two bearded highlanders and a horseguard, all of whom Niven casually fends off in an amusing fight scene to the accompaniment of Burt Bacharach's jaunty incidental music first heard during the car chase sequence. However, the three antagonists all recover and, producing automatic pistols, hold Bond and Moneypenny at gunpoint. At this point, the reason for the horseguard's earlier action of pressing the stuffed tiger's

---

[268] A Guide to Avengerland website, Anthony McKay, retrieved July 2013.
[269] Britmovie: British Film Forum website, Gerald Lovell, retrieved April 2013.
[270] *Daily Mirror*, Trinity Mirror Group, 7 July 1966.

glass eye is revealed: the office doubles as a lift, which now descends beneath the casino. Once it stops, a pair of long curtains part to reveal a metallic corridor, and noted voice actor Valentine Dyall's deep bass tones are heard to announce, 'You are now entering the SMERSH headquarters of Dr Noah.'

Leading the way, Bond whispers a plan number to Moneypenny, and they both suddenly fall to the floor, causing their three assailants to trip over them. Seizing the initiative, Bond and Moneypenny escape, running along various two-tone-coloured corridors and entering moving rooms, including one where the walls and floor resemble a giant fingerprint, eventually arriving at Dr Noah's inner sanctum. Here Bond encounters his SMERSH duplicate – also portrayed by Niven – who is destroyed amidst a shower of sparks by the original using a machine gun, indicating that the SMERSH replicas are androids. Continuity takes a blow, however, when Noah's dialogue later refers to the SMERSH doubles as operatives who have undergone extensive plastic surgery. Dr Noah is then revealed as none other than Sir James's nephew Jimmy Bond, who in the presence of his famous uncle is struck dumb, having to unveil his plans for world domination via mime and a pre-recorded message. Jimmy's crazy scheme involves the release of a highly contagious bacterial solution that will make all women beautiful and eradicate all men over the height of four feet six inches.

Guard Girls

This sequence, which took two weeks to film, culminates with the arrival of a platoon of Jimmy's personal protectors, the Guard Girls, who are each armed with a Sterling L2A3 submachine gun, and who escort Bond and Moneypenny away.

The only Guard Girl actress to receive billing in the film's closing credits was actress Jeanne Roland as Captain of the Guards. Roland's career consisted mainly of supporting roles in episodes of various ITC television film series, although she was the female lead in the BBC series *Take a Pair of Private Eyes*

(1966). The striking blonde seen wearing a silver outfit with a blue sash was named as Marilyn Rickard in publicity material, but this was actually a pseudonym for German-born model and sexploitation film actress Monika Ringwald. Having already appeared as both a beauty contestant and a SMERSH control assistant, actress Jennifer White had her third and final role in the picture as another of the Guard Girls.

Also included among the uncredited Guard Girls were fashion models Vanessa Sutton, Jane Forster, Wendy Davis, Stella Grove, Yvonne Horner and, sporting a long, plaited ponytail, Louisa Rabaiotti, who several years later would appear in an episode of Gerry Anderson's *UFO* television series. Almost hidden away in the background was 17-year-old Caroline Munro, who was working for the Lucie Clayton modelling agency when the opportunity arose to become an extra in the film. Val Guest saw Munro as a future talent, and he held discussions with her parents regarding their daughter signing a contract with him. However, Munro initially favoured art as a career and decided against acting. This decision would not be reversed until after she had made an appearance in the horror movie *Dracula A.D. 1972* (1972), after which being an actress became her main priority, augmented by modelling.[271] Munro would later appear alongside Roger Moore playing the villainess Naomi in Eon Productions' Bond movie *The Spy Who Loved Me* (1977).

Paco Rabanne

Around this time, a group publicity shot of Woody Allen surrounded by 22 Guard Girls was taken outside MGM Borehamwood Studios, with Elstree Way visible in the background. This included all the aforementioned models and actresses except for Jeanne Roland. Wanting a sophisticated and unique look for the Guard Girls, Feldman had commissioned

---

[271] *Cinema Retro* Vol. 2 No. 6, *The Look of ... Mayhem*, Gareth Owen, Solo Publishing, September 2006.

costumes from Spanish fashion designer Paco Rabanne, who had come up with the idea of uniforms inspired by clothing worn by Roman centurions. The resulting costume was a metallic looking mini dress comprising chain mail made from plastic pieces held together by wire, complete with a sandal/boot and cuffs, but minus sleeves. An optional extra was a skullcap helmet that incorporated a full face visor, as seen in photographs taken behind the scenes, where Rabanne and costume designer Julie Harris prepared the outfits worn by Caroline Munro and model Julie Bevan, the latter also being seen in the group photograph.[272] Some of the Guard Girl outfits would later reappear in 'Bizarre', the last episode of *The Avengers* television series, filmed during February/March 1969, starring Patrick Macnee and Linda Thorson.

Being led away by the Guard Girls, Sir James Bond tells his nephew, 'I'm beginning to think you're a trifle neurotic.' This line was included in the script only following revisions made sometime after 31 July 1966, and replaced one where Bond attempted to charm the Guard Girls by saying, 'Haven't I seen you ladies somewhere before? No, don't tell me. Paris Lido? Latin Quarter? *Playboy*?'[273] The final query was a reference to *Playboy* magazine, whose owner Hugh Hefner had visited Shepperton during production to confer with Val Guest, probably as earlier drafts of the screenplay had included SMERSH headquarters being secreted beneath the Playboy Club in London.[274]

The impressive SMERSH sets were designed by assistant art director Norman Dorme, while Dr Noah's plain costume was based on that worn by Joseph Wiseman as the title character of the first Bond film, *Dr. No*.[275]

---

[272] *Daily Mirror*, Trinity Mirror Group, 7 July 1966.
[273] *Psychedelic Cinema* documentary, MGM Home Entertainment Inc, October 2002.
[274] *Psychedelic Cinema* documentary, MGM Home Entertainment Inc, October 2002.
[275] *Woody Allen: A Biography*, John Baxter, HarperCollins, November 1998.

The return of Ursula Andress

The following week, the last of July 1966, the popular press reported on the return of Ursula Andress to the UK to resume filming on *Casino Royale*. Her character, Vesper Lynd, would serve as the crossover between the Sellers and Niven storylines and would also appear in the film's final segment.[276]

Requiring assistance in recruiting Evelyn Tremble to play Le Chiffre at baccarat, Sir James Bond visits Vesper's business, where he points out that the world considers her deceased after being eaten by a shark. Vesper replies that the shark was actually her personal submarine. She is then informed by Bond that she owes £5 million in tax arrears, but that with his intervention an easy payment plan and considerable discount could be arranged.

Vesper's attention having been gained by the prospect of an enormous cash outlay, she agrees to adjourn with Bond to her private office to discuss his assignment for her. The outer office set featured four reel-to-reel cabinets containing the Honeywell H200, a revolutionary computer introduced in 1963, with two adjacent prop cabinet units lifting to reveal the secret entrance to Vesper's personal domain.[277] The actor playing one of Vesper's two financial assistants during this sequence had his dialogue overdubbed in post-production by Valentine Dyall. The other, who mentions the rising price of gold, was played by an uncredited Paul Ferris, who had previously appeared in eight episodes of ITC's *The Baron*.

Press launch at the Dorchester Hotel

Val Guest had meanwhile received a mysterious engraved

---

[276] *Daily Mirror*, Trinity Mirror Group, 27 July 1966.
[277] Starring the Computer website, James Carter, retrieved September 2013.

invitation from Columbia Pictures to attend a press launch at the Dorchester Hotel on Sunday 26 June 1966 to announce a new director for *Casino Royale*. Reading the invitation, Guest suddenly realised that the launch was to publicise his own appointment on the film, although his involvement had actually started back in late 1965, and this was the first indication he had had of any official event to mark the fact.[278]

Reports that appeared at this time indicating that filming would be completed by the conclusion of June were totally inaccurate, and appear to be from press releases issued back in January.[279] With Guest having only just begun working on his segment, Talmadge still shooting the large-scale fight sequence for the same segment, and filming on the Mata Bond storyline yet to get under way, Lloyd's of London suspended the film's insurance cover.[280] To keep things moving, Feldman arranged cover from a different source, but general opinion was that Columbia Pictures' $8 million budget was long gone and the producer was now throwing his own money at the project.

Woody plays the Playboy Club

On Friday 1 July 1966, Woody Allen attended the opening of the Playboy Club in Park Lane, London, where he later performed his stand-up comedy routine to an appreciative audience.[281] Three days later, Eon Productions' fifth James Bond movie *You Only Live Twice* began shooting interiors at Pinewood Studios, on a production schedule that would also involve location filming in Japan, with principal photography continuing until February 1967.[282] Meanwhile, the latest news regarding *Casino Royale* was

---

[278] *Variety: Weekly*, Reed Business Information, 29 June 1966 & *So You Want to Be in Pictures: The Autobiography of Val Guest*, Val Guest, Reynolds & Hearn, May 2001.
[279] *Kine Weekly*, Odhams Press Ltd, 21 June 1966.
[280] *007 Magazine* No. 40, *Casino Royale*, Michael Richardson and Graham Rye, The James Bond 007 International Fan Club, January 2002.
[281] *Variety: Daily*, Reed Business Information, 5 July 1966.

the imminent arrival of Joanna Pettet to join proceedings at Shepperton Studios, the actress having been contracted to the production for eight weeks.[283]

On location in London

Val Guest and his crew would now undertake location filming in central London for a long sequence beginning with an establishing shot of The Mall from Horse Guards Road and continuing with doubles for Niven and Pettet in Bond's vintage Bentley, turning off Whitehall into Downing Street. In the finished film, the vehicle appears to stop outside the Prime Minister's famous residence, 10 Downing Street, but this was actually filmed on a standing set constructed for *Casino Royale* on the MGM Borehamwood Studios extensive backlot.[284] This structure would appear later in other productions, including *Inspector Clouseau*, and it would remain intact at MGM until the studio complex was closed down and demolished in 1973 and the backlot was levelled after being sold for housing development. However, instead of sporting its previous registration number K 19, the Bentley now had number plates bearing the more appropriate JB 007. With Sir James Bond wearing a black riding hat, having an attractive female passenger at his side and driving a vintage Bentley, the sequence is highly reminiscent of *The Avengers* television series.

Unable to attend her father's meeting with the Prime Minister, Mata Bond departs Downing Street from the junction with Horse Guards Road. Joanna Pettet was on location to film this material, and the crew had easy access to Downing Street, as the large security gates present nowadays were not erected until much later, in 1991. The following shot, with the

---

[282] International Movie Database: *You Only Live Twice*, retrieved September 2013.
[283] *The Daily Cinema*, Cinema Press Ltd, 8 July 1966 & *Daily Express*, Northern and Shell Media, 18 October 1966.
[284] A Guide to Avengerland website, Anthony McKay, retrieved September 2013.

uncredited Pat Ryan and Paul Beradi appearing as a couple of passers-by, sees Mata Bond on Horse Guards Parade, where she produces a camera, intending to photograph a troupe of the Household Cavalry approaching along Horse Guards Road. However, there is diabolical villainy afoot, as the leading horseman charges forward and bodily picks up Mata, then gallops away in what onlookers think is simply a publicity stunt. Meanwhile, a large unidentified flying object spectacularly appears over London, eventually touching down in Trafalgar Square, from which Nelson's Column has been removed by Vesper Lynd earlier in the picture.

The special effects for this Trafalgar Square material were extremely impressive for a '60s production. The live action of moving traffic and milling crowds was optically printed into a matte background, including static London Transport double-decker buses. The metallic flying saucer miniature, which was also printed into this combination background, was a joint effort between effects experts Cliff Richardson and Roy Whybrow, working in conjunction with matte creator Les Bowie.

An army of uncredited extras were employed to populate areas of Trafalgar Square, and included in this number were Rita Tobin-Weske, Peter Rendall, Juba Kennerley, Dido Plumb, Ernie Rice, Alf Mangan and, doubling as a family of American tourists, Roy Beck and his family. Mike Jarvis portrayed a police constable, Guy Standeven was the driver of the stationary bus, Lewis Alexander was a passenger on the moving bus, and actor John Tatum watched events unfold from a black cab.

The London Transport double-decker used as both the moving bus and the stationary bus in the sequence was a 1950 Leyland Titan fleet number RTL 848. The vehicle had been previously sold to Passenger Vehicle Sales (London) Ltd, from whom it was hired for the film.

The Niven/Pettet footage was obviously filmed before both their contracts expired toward the end of August 1966, but records indicate that the establishing Trafalgar Square material was actually shot later, during September.[285] Additional footage showing the Household Cavalry on horseback proceeding along Horse Guards Road with The Mall in the background was also captured during this shoot.

Miniatures

Slowly a ramp extends down from the flying saucer as the horseman carrying Mata comes into the square from Admiralty Arch. They then enter the craft, which promptly takes off. From the open window of Sir James Bond's office, Moneypenny watches as the UFO rises into the sky above the River Thames – another model shot, featuring a detailed matte painting. Bond instantly appears, only to be disappointed when the RAF loses contact with the futuristic craft. Further examples of miniature effects work are seen as the flying saucer stops and hovers over some coastline and then a pair of sliding doors opens in its side, disgorging a small shuttle craft that proceeds across the water to a sliding rock-face that opens up before it. The shuttle having entered a secret dock, a life-size version is then seen in place of the model, being winched out of the water apparently under its own power, although the cable doing this is clearly visible on screen. Forcibly evicted from the shuttle, Mata finds herself in a staging area, where Valentine Dyall's uncredited Dr Noah voice welcomes her as she peers into the secret domain through a small glass section of a large steel watertight hatch.

The World Cup

Hosted in the UK, the World Cup football tournament began on Monday 11 July 1966, and David Niven bought thirty tickets for assorted games, which he presented to members of the crew in appreciation of their commitment to the film. Together with his son James, Niven himself attended the

---

[285] Buses on Screen website, Maurice Bateman, retrieved September 2013.

final between England and West Germany, held at the old Wembley Stadium on Saturday 30 July, when the home team triumphed and were awarded the Jules Rimet Trophy.

Niven apparently lived up to his easy-going image while working on *Casino Royale*, never acting like a big star and frequently playing cards with the extras at Shepperton Studios between takes.[286] He commented little regarding the production problems on the picture, though once while filming he prophesised, '*Casino Royale* is going to be a classic bit of fun or the biggest fuck-up since the flood!'[287]

The concluding melee

By the second week of July 1966, Richard Talmadge had finally completed all the large-scale filming involving the multitude of extras and stunt personnel taking part in the final melee, though Val Guest would continue shooting close-up footage for this sequence for some months.[288]

As the action continues, Sir James Bond, having escaped confinement, instructs Cooper to escort Mata and Moneypenny to safety. Then, picking up the nearest telephone, he asks the operator to connect him to Whitehall 00-07. However, he finds himself interrupted by Vesper Lynd and her chrome-plated Beretta M1934 automatic. She reveals that she has been instrumental in enticing him to the casino, to which he comments, 'The things you do for money, Vesper.' 'This time it's for love,' she counters, though this statement is never explained, and she could simply mean a love of money and power.

Rushing back into the casino foyer, Cooper announces that the American assistance are on their way – a

---

[286] *Niv: The Authorised Biography of David Niven*, Graham Lord, Orion, October 2003.
[287] *David Niven: A Biography*, Sheridan Morley, Weidenfeld & Nicolson, October 1985.
[288] *Kiss Kiss Bang! Bang!: The Unofficial James Bond Film Companion*, Alan Barnes and Marcus Hearn, Overlook Press, October 1998.

development depicted via some unidentified Wild West footage. Momentarily distracted, Vesper is suddenly overpowered by Bond, who seizes her automatic and shoots an armed casino receptionist played by the uncredited Julian Sherrier, whose dialogue was overdubbed in post-production by Italian actor Robert Rietty. This prompts one of the ginger-haired, tuxedo-attired SMERSH men, played by stuntman Joe Powell, seated at a card table, to produce a Mauser broom-handle automatic and begin firing at Bond, as the massed casino patrons scatter. However, the assistance mentioned by Cooper suddenly arrives, as various cowboys on horseback ride into the casino, with the uncredited stuntmen Larry Taylor, Billy Dean, Bill Cummings and Peter Brace among their number. Other unbilled extras seen during the build-up to this sequence include Malcolm Johns as a gambling casino patron and Cyril Kent playing a waiter pouring glasses of champagne.

'Custer's Last Stand'

Vesper Lynd's final appearance in the picture has her simply diving for cover. Val Guest's screenplay, however, presented a different scenario in which, having lost her automatic in the action with Bond, she deployed a second pistol hidden beneath her dress; obviously the original intention was that she would become involved in the final melee, entering the main casino area shooting, with Sir James Bond intent on stopping her but being waylaid by a couple of SMERSH men. Although this material does not feature in the finished film, it is possible that it was shot under Guest's direction and later discarded during editing.

The massive punch-up, dubbed 'Custer's Last Stand' by Richard Talmadge, involves the cowboys fighting the ginger-haired SMERSH men, depicted by, amongst others, unbilled stuntmen Frank Maher, Alf Joint, Nosher Powell and, as a waiter using metal spittoons as boxing gloves, Fred Haggerty.[289]

Meanwhile, having been tricked by the Detainer into swallowing his own atom bomb pill, Jimmy Bond makes his way through the casino burping coloured animated clouds as he narrowly avoids various fights. This element of the action was apparently added into the corrected script dated 29 May 1966, which indicated that Guest would direct Allen's footage, later to be slotted into sections of the Talmadge-directed sequence. Guest had written additional revisions dated 10 June 1966, including shots, not included in the finished picture, of Jimmy wandering through the casino and asking various fighting people if they know the whereabouts of his uncle, Sir James Bond. Like the missing Vesper Lynd footage, it appears likely that this additional Jimmy Bond material was filmed around the same time, but later judged surplus to requirements and omitted from the final edit.[290]

Hiding beneath a table, a female patron, played by uncredited model Jean Combie, accidentally activates a device that launches a roulette wheel, which then flies through the casino emitting laughing gas before eventually colliding with a wall and exploding spectacularly. In accordance with this aspect of the storyline, numerous uncredited extras, including brothers Pat and Gerry Judge, are seen laughing as they thoroughly enjoy themselves running around the edge of the casino set, keeping clear of the action that is taking place in the middle. Other unbilled extras playing casino patrons included little known actor Paddy Smith; Roy Beck; Walter Henry; Peter Perkins, seen fighting with a cowboy; Maltese-born performer Victor Harrington; and Joe Powell again, this time without ginger hair.

Hoisting himself onto a card table, Sir James Bond elegantly kicks several SMERSH adversaries in succession, timed perfectly to the incidental music. Part of this action was

---

[289] *Psychedelic Cinema* documentary, MGM Home Entertainment Inc, October 2002.
[290] *Psychedelic Cinema* documentary, MGM Home Entertainment Inc, October 2002.

performed not by Niven himself but by his stunt double, Jimmy Lodge. Sheer madness now reigns as, elsewhere, two sea lions attempt to bite each other, a chimpanzee wearing a ginger toupee eats bubbles and, amidst all the mayhem, a SMERSH agent attempts to control a bucking mule. Further to this, a sheepdog wearing a furry and engraved 007 collar has sunk its teeth into a SMERSH man's dinner jacket, attempting to pull him backwards while he fights with a cowboy – a story element originated by Wolf Mankowitz.[291]

Taking the mickey out of Eon Productions' James Bond

Smashing a chair over a SMERSH operative's head, Cooper is congratulated by a grinning cowboy, who shakes his hand. Another SMERSH man becomes so carried away with the situation that he also shakes Cooper's hand, but then suddenly Cooper lands a powerful punch that sends the agent, played by unbilled stuntman Terry Plummer, headlong through a large bank of mirrors to arrive inside an artists' studio. Here two artists, one of them played by an uncredited Peter Ashmore, are painting three models, including the unbilled Anne Thompson and Greta Van Rantwyk, head to toe in gold – a sideswipe at Eon Productions' *Goldfinger*, which famously featured sex symbol Shirley Eaton being similarly adorned in her role as Bond girl Jill Masterson.

Meanwhile, overhead, reinforcements are about to drop in, literally, as a party of Native Americans, complete with 007 war paint across their foreheads, skydive from a plane and parachute toward the chaos. Small plastic figures attached to wigwam-shaped parachutes are seen floating down onto the miniature building exterior, before various unbilled stuntmen, including George Leech, smash through the skylights on the casino set. Jimmy Bond continues wandering through the confusion, counting down with every burp to inevitable doom.

---

[291] *Kiss Kiss Bang! Bang!: The Unofficial James Bond Film Companion*, Alan Barnes and Marcus Hearn, Overlook Press, October 1998.

The sequence culminates in a night-time shot of the illuminated casino exterior miniature exploding violently.

Woody Allen on British television again

As filming continued at both Shepperton and Borehamwood, Woody Allen managed another UK television appearance, as guest presenter on an edition of the Associated-Rediffusion variety series *The Hippodrome Show* transmitted in some regions on Wednesday 13 July 1966 – a programme that still exists in the television archives.

Just over a week later, the American trade press reported that Burt Bacharach and Hal David were scheduled for a London meeting with Feldman regarding *Casino Royale*'s soundtrack requirements. However, this was cancelled at the last moment, as very little footage had yet undergone editing and it was thought that the songwriters would find it impossible to obtain a feel for the movie. The meeting was postponed until October.[292]

George Raft

While Val Guest was directing at Shepperton one day, Charles K Feldman suddenly appeared along with American actor George Raft, whose greatest claim to fame was having played gangster Guido Rinaldo in the 1932 movie *Scarface*. Guest was instructed to write Raft into the proceedings in such a way that they actor could perform his *Scarface* character's coin-flipping trademark while leaning against the casino bar. However, having not actually practised the coin-flipping for decades, Raft was naturally nervous, and virtually pleaded with Guest not to write him any dialogue.

Despite the actor's apprehension, everything went as planned. Raft flipped his coin without any problems, and even

---

[292] *The Music of James Bond*, Jon Burlingame, Oxford University Press, October 2012.

handled some lines of dialogue delivered to a blond-haired extra bearing a strong resemblance to David McCallum's character Illya Kuryakin from the then popular spy show *The Man from U.N.C.L.E.*.[293] 'I've been framed,' Raft informs the extra, indicating his Beretta automatic. 'This gun shoots backwards. I just killed myself.'

Raft later returned to the US, and when he attempted to re-enter the UK the following year to take up a position as a casino director, he was refused permission because of his apparent association with organised crime.[294]

Killer-Girls

Some months earlier, a memo from Mankowitz to Feldman had outlined how the film was originally intended to conclude. The huge melee in the casino was to have occurred after Tremble's defeat of Le Chiffe at baccarat. The male casino employees would have unzipped their clothing to reveal that they were really women – called Killer-Girls – who would then have advanced on Tremble, Vesper Lynd, Inspector Mathis and his men. A large scale fight, reminiscent of a mass brawl in a Wild West saloon, was to break out, orchestrated by Le Chiffre from his wheelchair. Then, after much damage had been done, assorted cowboys or the Texas cavalry would ride through on horseback and become involved. Seeing that things were not going well, Le Chiffre was to have escaped in his wheelchair, leading to a chase sequence that had not been planned in detail at the time when Mankowitz issued his memo.[295]

---

[293] *The Daily Cinema*, Cinema Press Ltd, 29 July 1966 & *So You Want to Be in Pictures: The Autobiography of Val Guest*, Val Guest, Reynolds & Hearn, May 2001 .
[294] Wikipedia website entry on George Raft, retrieved September 2013.
[295] *The Life and Death of Peter Sellers*, Roger Lewis, Century, April 1994.

Kenneth Hughes joins the production

With Val Guest entrenched at Shepperton, the first week of August 1966 saw the interiors for the Mata Bond segment finally enter production at MGM Studios in Borehamwood, where incoming director Kenneth Hughes, known to his friends as Ken, assembled cast members David Niven, Joanna Pettet, Ronnie Corbett, Anna Quayle and Joseph Furst for the initial week of filming.[296]

Three days later, the *Daily Mirror* published photographs from the Irish location shooting in May, showing John Huston in director mode, demonstrating how he required David Niven to embrace and kiss Deborah Kerr.[297]

Woddy Allen becomes bored

Despite Charles K Feldman having accepted Woody Allen's screenplay for the concluding segment of the film, it appears that the constant rewriting that had plagued the earlier stages of the production was still continuing. Allen and Val Guest collaborated on this at the latter's home, Pear Tree Cottage in St John's Wood, London, where they wrote alternate scenes and then script-edited each other's work. Although he liked Allen's humour, Feldman apparently failed to understand it at times, as when portions of the screenplay were submitted to him for inspection, he frequently crossed out the jokes. This upset Allen immensely, causing him to call Feldman 'a script murderer,' though Guest promised to reinstate the missing material when filming took place, and later proved good to his word.[298]

Unfortunately, Allen was becoming bored and very disenchanted with the project, wanting to get on with filming further material as little Jimmy Bond, although this would not

---

[296] *The Daily Cinema*, Cinema Press Ltd, 5 August 1966.
[297] *Daily Mirror*, Trinity Mirror Group, 8 August 1966.
[298] *So You Want to Be in Pictures: The Autobiography of Val Guest*, Val Guest, Reynolds & Hearn, May 2001.

occur until the arrival of actress Daliah Lavi. Writing to his New York-based publicist Richard O'Brien, Allen made his opinion of the production very apparent: 'Saw the sets for my scenes. They are the height of bad pop art expensive vulgarity. Saw rushes and am dubious to put it mildly.'[299] Throughout his time working on the movie, Allen disliked the production and his creation of Dr Noah, and he was convinced that *Casino Royale* would be a massive box office failure. Decades later he would freely admit that he had never actually watched the film, claiming that some of his close relatives had done so and advised him, 'It's a uniquely ghastly experience.'[300]

Daliah Lavi and Woody Allen

Daliah Lavi joined the production at MGM during the second week of August 1966, performing two-handed scenes with Allen that involved her being held captive reclined naked on an upholstered bench, with thick metal straps protecting her modesty.[301] Although she appeared to be naked during this scene, Lavi actually wore underwear; filming was always done from an angle that avoided revealing this.

This scene begins with Jimmy dismissing the five Guard Girls, two of whom were portrayed by Vanessa Sutton and Louisa Rabaiotti. Lavi's first dialogue in this scene as the Detainer is, 'Why was I abducted from the roulette table and subjected to this?', but as no such abduction scene exists in the finished picture, evidently it was either unfilmed or, more likely, became another casualty of editing.

Confessing that he finds her the most attractive of his uncle's 007s, Jimmy attempts to impress the Detainer with his abilities as a concert pianist and bronco rider, though he fails miserably. 'They called Einstein crazy,' he cracks. 'No-one ever called Einstein crazy,' she replies. 'Well, they would have, had he

---

[299] *Woody Allen: A Biography*, Eric Lax, Jonathan Cape, August 1991.
[300] Crawley's Casting Calls website, *Casino Royale*, retrieved July 2013.
[301] *Variety: Daily*, Reed Business Information, 9 August 1966.

carried on like this!' he claims.

Changing tactics, the Detainer begins to flatter Jimmy, securing her release, though not until he has thoroughly explained his greatest invention, the atom bomb pill. It looks like an aspirin, it tastes like an aspirin, but really it contains 400 tiny tablets that slowly explode, starting a chain reaction, eventually turning the person involved into a walking time bomb. After the Detainer agrees to become his mate, Jimmy releases her somewhat excitedly, saying, 'I'll unlock you immediately and we'll run amok. If you're too tired we'll walk amok.'

Jimmy then gives the Detainer a guided tour of his space plane populated with duplicates, including her own double, dressed as an air hostess, and his personal barman, played by Peter Ashmore, who went uncredited again. Standing on a circular section of flooring that lifts him several metres high, Jimmy proceeds to deliver a speech regarding the plight of the little man, which Allen appears to have read from the palm of his hand.

These Allen/Lavi scenes work well, accepting the fact that both their characters have contributed little to the overall storyline until now, having logged up less than twenty minutes' screen time between them. Jimmy Bond is endowed with Allen's early comedy persona, which is extremely close to the characters he later portrayed in movies such as *Bananas* (1971) and *Sleeper* (1973): incompetent underdogs with feelings of sexual inadequacy. Jimmy is simply a progression of Allen's monologue stand-up routine of the time, taken one step further to include some acting and the physical comedy elements of slapstick and mime.

Val Guest – coordinating director?

Relying on Val Guest's abilities to assemble and create whatever was necessary to finish the movie, Feldman wanted him to accept the additional credit of 'coordinating director'. Guest rejected this, pointing out that the picture was more haphazard than coordinated, although later he mellowed somewhat and accepted an 'additional sequences' credit, besides his billing as one of the main directors.[302]

To connect the John Huston/David Niven storyline to his final segment, Guest wrote several linking scenes, including one where Sir James Bond deduces that the enemy is utilising the abilities of female agents. Instigating the AFSD (Anti-Female Spy Defence), Bond has Moneypenny research all reserves to locate the male agent whom all women want, and then train him to resist all women. Working her way through eight agents, including one played by uncredited actor Peter Burton, who had portrayed the armourer Major Boothroyd in *Dr. No*, Moneypenny comes across Terence Cooper, who possesses that extra something. Later, as Moneypenny continues gathering evidence in pursuit of her quest, Cooper advises her that she could address him as 'Coop' for short, to which she replies, 'Sounds like something for keeping birds.' Coop was actually a nickname that Cooper, the actor, encouraged his friends to call him by, indicating that he probably contributed a little to the screenplay.[303]

Fast-tracked into rigorous training in a gym, Cooper proves immune to the kisses of a number of extremely attractive and scantily-clad women, three of whom were portrayed by the uncredited models Stella Grove, Yvonne Marsh and Susan Sampson. Sporting a white bikini complete with a sheathed knife, almost identical to the one worn by Ursula Andress as Honey Ryder in *Dr. No*, a woman called Lorelei drops down from some wall bars and advances toward the agent. Lorelei was played by the unbilled Susanna Hunt, who at the time was married to Ronnie Lane, bass player in the Small Faces group, and who recorded a couple of single records for the CBS label under the name Geneveve. Having been unaffected by Lorelei's

---

[302] *So You Want to Be in Pictures: The Autobiography of Val Guest*, Val Guest, Reynolds & Hearn, May 2001.
[303] *It Seemed Like a Good Idea at the Time*, Sue Lloyd and Linda Dearsley, Quartet, October 1998.

kiss and caress, Cooper uses a judo throw to dispose of her. He then repeats the process with his next challenger, Ting Ling, played by Jeanne Roland, who also went uncredited for her role. Shirley, played by Stella Grove, moves forward next, but is stopped by a mysterious figure portrayed by Daliah Lavi, who announces that she is the new secret weapon and has just been perfected. However, she fares no better, also receiving a judo toss from Cooper.

Brigitte Bardot and William Holden

Meanwhile, determined to include more big names into the casino finale, Feldman telephoned Val Guest one evening with instructions to write Brigitte Bardot into the sequence, as she was currently in London. Having worked late into the night constructing a role for the French actress, Guest received another call from Feldman the following evening, announcing that Bardot had imposed too many requirements on her appearance and so he should forget her.[304] Guest's opinion of the producer was mixed to say the least: 'Charlie Feldman was a madman. There were days when you could hug him and then other days when you could throttle him!'

Around this time, Guest visited Feldman's suite/office at the Dorchester Hotel, where the door was opened by William Holden, who casually mentioned that he would be playing the latest James Bond. Believing that this would mean another hasty rewrite, Guest was far from happy. However, realising that his joke had backfired somewhat, Holden then quickly assured the director that he would simply be doing a cameo reprising his CIA character, Ransome.[305]

---

[304] *Woody Allen: A Biography*, John Baxter, HarperCollins, November 1998.
[305] *So You Want to Be in Pictures: The Autobiography of Val Guest*, Val Guest, Reynolds & Hearn, May 2001.

Jean-Paul Belmondo

During the final week of August 1966, Jean-Paul Belmondo also filmed a cameo, appearing with David Niven on the casino set in character as a French Legionnaire, who translates his greeting into English so that Sir James Bond can understand it.[306] Shaking hands, Bond quickly warns the Legionnaire that someone is about to attack him from behind, resulting in the Frenchman turning around and punching an assailant, hurting his hand in the process and exclaiming a single word in his native language, 'Merde!' Consulting his translation book again, he informs the inquisitive Bond that he has just said 'Ouch!' – although actually 'merde' translates as 'shit'. A popular actor on the continent at the time, Belmondo was brought onto *Casino Royale* after Feldman discovered that he was romantically involved with Ursula Andress and then constantly badgered the actress to use her influence to get him involved.[307]

Dave Prowse as the Frankenstein Monster

Having escaped from their confinement cell, Sir James, Mata, Moneypenny and Cooper narrowly avoid being machine-gunned by the massed Guard Girls, whose bullets penetrate the lining of SMERSH headquarters, allowing seawater into the base. Amidst loud alarms, armed men in black and more Guard Girls, the four secret service operatives try to appear inconspicuous as they approach an intersection in the metallic corridor, where they encounter the Detainer, who has escaped from Dr Noah's space plane. Various people scurry around in the background, including a creature in the likeness of the Lon Chaney Jnr example of the Wolf Man, first seen in the 1941 movie of the same name. Then the Frankenstein Monster – another of the doubles controlled by

---

[306] *Kine Weekly*, Odhams Press Ltd, 26 August 1966.
[307] *Woody Allen: A Biography*, John Baxter, HarperCollins, November 1998.

Jimmy Bond – lumbers into view.[308]

Four months after his aborted Superpooh role, Dave Prowse had received a strange telephone call from a production assistant at Famous Artists Productions' office at MGM Borehamwood Studios, asking him if he could report to the studio as soon as possible for a fitting of the Frankenstein Monster costume. The caller was embarrassed, as he was not certain which actor – it was not Prowse – had been measured up for the costume originally. Luckily for Prowse, the outfit – based on the classic Boris Karloff/Universal Pictures version, featuring electrodes in the neck and a flat headpiece – fitted to perfection. Prowse was happy finally to be able to get his movie career under way, even if the part was restricted to a solitary scene with David Niven, predating by four years his second appearance as the Monster, in Hammer Film Productions' *The Horror of Frankenstein* (1970).[309]

Although disjointed and lacking complete explanations, the film has managed some semblance of order up to this point in the action, but now that disappears and absolute lunacy takes over. Assuming command, Sir James announces to his colleagues that he will handle the situation. Addressing the Monster, he asks it for directions, but it totally ignores him and relentlessly walks away down a corridor, colliding with some sliding doors. 'That's very civil of you, sir,' Sir James announces, as his party come under fire from more Guard Girls, played by Jeanne Roland and Marilyn Rickard. Having located the office/lift thanks to the Monster's inadvertent pointer, Sir James quickly instructs Mata to place her finger in the stuffed tiger's ear, which will activate the mechanism and return them to the casino. Arguably, this action constitutes another a lapse in continuity, as previously the horseguard made the office descend by pressing the animal's glass eye.

---

[308] *Psychedelic Cinema* documentary, MGM Home Entertainment Inc, October 2002.
[309] *Straight From the Force's Mouth: The Autobiography of Dave Prowse MBE*, Dave Prowse, Filament, June 2005.

The Detainer exits

More danger awaits Sir James's group as they realise that they now have to pass through the casino. This results in Daliah Lavi's character, the Detainer, opting to exit by sliding down a drainpipe, via a diversion through the ladies' room. Lavi was very noticeably written out at this point, as she was committed to her next movie project, *Jules Verne's Rocket to the Moon* (1967), which had entered production on location in Ireland on Monday 12 September 1966.[310] Lavi was still contracted to *Casino Royale* until the final week of September, but somewhere along the line a decision was taken to avoid her having to participate in any Shepperton footage, and Val Guest wrote the short scene concluding her involvement.[311]

Despite *Casino Royale* having been in production for nine months, principal photography still went on, on what had become a mammoth undertaking.

---

[310] *Variety: Daily*, Reed Business Information, 7 October 1966.
[311] *Kine Weekly*, Odhams Press Ltd, 22 September 1966.

Chapter Seven
The Cold War in Borehamwood

Hughes and Guest liaise

Kenneth Hughes' filming of the Mata Bond segment of the picture at MGM Borehamwood Studios continued concurrently with Val Guest's work at Shepperton Studios on his segment. Richard Talmadge having now completed filming of the action sequences for the finale, his director of photography, Nicholas Roeg, transferred from Shepperton to Borehamwood to fulfil the same function with Hughes. Like almost everyone else involved with the production, Hughes never saw a complete screenplay, only a version with blank spaces where other directors' material should have been, supporting the theory that during production only Feldman ever had a complete script. Concerned over this lack of information and wanting to know the bigger picture, Hughes telephoned Guest at Shepperton, and they discussed exactly how they could get their two segments to dovetail together.[312]

Le Chiffre's art collection

Besides the main players – David Niven, Joanna Pettet, Ronnie Corbett and Anna Quayle – Hughes' segment would also feature prominent performances by Derek Nimmo, Bernard Cribbins

---

[312] The Sabotage Times website, *A Cocktail Recipe for Disaster*, Richard Luck, retrieved June 2013.

and Vladek Sheybal. Noted comedy actor Nimmo spent a great proportion of his time socialising in Niven's caravan/dressing room, where he was constantly entertained by the elder actor's endless stories about working in the film industry and life in general.[313] The initial week of filming involved Hughes mounting a sequence of the auction of Le Chiffre's art collection – which actually consists of nothing more than slides showing military officers in compromising positions with half-naked women, including *Playboy* model Dolly Read. This story element evolved from the idea of Le Chiffre's blackmail photographs in the Ben Hecht screenplay a couple of years earlier, before the film was reformatted as a madcap run-around comedy.

In this sequence, the '60s superpowers, Russia, China, the United States and Britain, have all sent military delegations hoping to acquire the potentially embarrassing material. The Chinese decide to bid only while standing; the Americans, wanting to be different, elect to bid only while seated; and the British, under an indecisive leader played by Richard Wattis, settle on doing both. Of the actors cast as the delegates, only Wattis would receive on-screen billing. The Russian leader was played by veteran Austrian actor Joseph Furst, while his fellow Soviets were portrayed by actress Bee Duffell and stuntmen Bill Sawyer, Larry Martin, Bill Cummings and Doug Robinson. Burt Kwouk was cast as the Chinese leader, backed by stunt performers Alan Chuntz and Max Faulkner amongst others. The head of the Americans was portrayed by Hal Galili. Amongst the British delegation are a Brigadier General played by 65-year-old Ian Wilson, and another army officer played by stuntman Joe Powell, taking his fourth uncredited role in the picture.[314]

---

[313] *007 Magazine* No. 40, *Casino Royale*, Michael Richardson and Graham Rye, The James Bond 007 International Fan Club, January 2002.
[314] *The Daily Cinema*, Cinema Press Ltd, 5 August 1966.

Temple dance routine

Apparently money was no object on the production, as Charles K Feldman gave Hughes an unlimited budget, and also authorised the building of a Javanese temple set costing $30,000.[315]

Having been informed by Agent Mimi that her instructions originated from International Mothers' Help in East Berlin, Sir James suddenly decides that the perfect agent to infiltrate the establishment would be his illegitimate daughter Mata. Apparently conceived from a liaison between Sir James and the Dutch World War One spy Mata Hari, Mata Bond now resided in an Indonesian temple after being entered into an orphanage aged three and having used her father's monthly retainer on psychiatrists' fees. Joanna Pettet's look was changed considerably for the filming of this part of the picture; she now sports a long blonde hairpiece and a large ornate tiara, as opposed to a short mod hairstyle seen in the Val Guest-directed segment.

Bond's introduction to his daughter comes as she performs an atmospheric dance routine along with 12 uncredited exotic dancers, including actress Antonia Ellis. Pettet's experience in the performing arts had obviously assisted her in getting cast as Mata.[316] The next scene, where Bond persuades Mata to follow the family tradition and take up spying, features several other unbilled actors, including John Hollis as the high priest, Fred, and Maurice Browning as a servant, Charlie. One-time professional wrestler, the Indian-born Milton Reid, also failed to receive a credit for his role as a temple guard; for Eon Productions' Bond films he had previously appeared uncredited in *Dr. No* and would later be seen opposite Roger Moore in *The Spy Who Loved Me*.

---

[315] *Bondage* No. 15, *The Forgotten Bond*, Leonard Thomason, The James Bond 007 International Fan Club, May 1987.
[316] *FAB* No. 48, *Antonia Ellis Interview*, Martin Gainsford, Fanderson, February 2004.

More location filming in London

Central London location filming for this segment was restricted to an establishing shot of Horse Guards Avenue, viewed from Whitehall, where a police constable is seen directing traffic. Both Joanna Pettet and Derek Nimmo, playing secret service operative Hadley, were filmed leaving 10 Whitehall Place (East Block) SW1, with Pettet departing, supposedly for Berlin, in an Austin black cab driven by Bernard Cribbins. Plans to film on location in Berlin as well had been abandoned sometime earlier, though the German capital would be represented by standing sets in a night-time shoot on the backlot at MGM Borehamwood Studios.

MGM Borehamwood Studios backlot

Shots of the German border checkpoint and the fictional Feldmanstrasse – named after the producer – were filmed on the largest exterior standing set at MGM, which had been assembled for *Casino Royale* from three different sources. One part had originally been constructed early in 1964 as a Parisian suburb for the second Pink Panther film, *A Shot in the Dark*. This had then been dismantled, moved from its original position and reassembled together with a larger Paris set, built the following year for the movie *Return from the Ashes*. In addition to this, some smaller building frontages, assembled back in 1961 as portions of a Sicilian settlement for the drama movie *Village of Daughters*, had undergone reconstruction, and they were also now amalgamated into the larger set.[317]

Now minus headlights and with smoke coming from beneath its bonnet, the Austin cab – its dilapidated condition suggesting another missing sequence – arrives in Berlin and is parked beside a breezeblock wall that divides the standing set square into the city's allied and Soviet sectors. Having amassed an outstanding fare of £482, 15 shillings and 9 pence, Mata declines to pay,

---

[317] E-mail from Anthony McKay of A Guide to Avengerland to Michael Richardson, September 2013.

claiming not to have any change, as an American border guard, played by extra Maxwell Craig in his third unbilled role, watches from a distance. Cribbins' taxi driver alights from his vehicle, directing complaints about missing his lunch toward a passing American GI smoking a cigar. 'Any fish and chip shops around here, mush?' he asks.

Anna Quayle and Ronnie Corbett

International Mothers' Help has been identified as a SMERSH undercover spy school situated in what was once Mata Hari's dance academy during World War One. Gaining access to the espionage school, Mata Bond finds that it possesses a strange haunted house-like quality of German expressionism, evoked to great effect by production designer Michael Stringer, who created the sets. Mata then encounters the school proprietors, the double act of Frau Hoffner and Polo, played by Anna Quayle and Ronnie Corbett respectively. Polo's life-functions are powered by a battery strapped across his chest.

Seeing Mata's resemblance to her mother, Hoffner is convinced that her request to enrol in their facility is genuine, while Polo has an enormous crush on the newcomer, thinking that Mata Hari has returned from the dead. Hoffner brags about the great spies that have graduated from the school, prompting Polo to mention several names, including that of Peter Lorre, the actor who portrayed Le Chiffe in the 1954 televised version of *Casino Royale*. Leading Mata up the staircase to her late mother's room, Polo struggles as his battery begins running down: 'My, my, my battery needs recharging.' 'Might be your head needs examining?' Mata counters. 'No', he replies matter-of-factly, 'I had that examined last week.'

Putting himself through a rigorous personal schedule, Ronnie Corbett worked on *Casino Royale* for six weeks, while also appearing nightly at the nightclub of female impersonator Danny La Rue, where he performed cabaret. However, it was Corbett's wife Anne Hart who became responsible for making certain that he met his commitments, ensuring that he had sufficient time to travel to Borehamwood by waking him at 6.00 am every day. Corbett would return home at 6.00 pm and go straight to bed, before being woken again by Hart at 10.00 pm, thus allowing him travelling time to the nightclub. Returning home at 2.00 am, he would then start going through the routine once more.[318]

Crossed wires

As the auction continues, the cabbie arrives and, having retired with Mata to the adjacent corridor for privacy, introduces himself as Carlton-Towers of the Foreign Office, with instructions that under no circumstances is she to allow the art collection to be sold. Stealing the incriminating slides, Mata activates a war programme simulation within the viewing theatre to keep the various delegates occupied, then disposes of the slides down a toilet before retracing her steps back to her room. Finding herself confronted by Polo, she pretends to be friendly toward him and casually disconnects the wires from his battery.

Reconnecting the wires, Polo mumbles about being unable to differentiate between positive and negative, and inevitably touches the wrong terminals. This results in him running around the room backwards at high speed, before entering the bathroom in reverse and landing on the toilet, activating a hidden revolving section that then rotates uncontrollably. This amusing sequence was achieved by under-cranking, a process that involves reducing the frame rate of the camera while filming so that the action appears in fast-motion when shown at normal speed. The footage was simply played in reverse to achieve the desired effect of Polo running around backwards and out of control.

Mata Bond escapes

Mata has a brief altercation with Frau Hoffner, which sees the latter meet her demise after falling backwards onto the seated

---

[318] *Ronnie Corbett My Autobiography: High Hopes*, Ronnie Corbett, Ebury Press, October 2000.

body of Otto, a long-dead German officer, whose automatic pistol is still loaded and fires a single shot upon impact. Finding her path blocked by the combined delegates, Mata fends them off singlehandedly in a slapstick, action-packed staircase fight scene, in the course of which she knocks Doug Robinson's character over the landing balcony. Mata then sprays fire-extinguisher foam into the faces of various assailants, including the one played by Joe Powell, while Carlton-Towers reappears and somewhat evens the odds, throwing aside the Doug Robinson and Larry Taylor characters. Mata and Carlton-Towers are then able to escape.

Bacharach's accompanying incidental music for this sequence, called 'Home James, Don't Spare the Horses', would be heard again decades later in the DVD release *Family Guy Presents Stewie Griffin: The Untold Story* (2005).

Emerging back into the city – again represented by the standing set on the MGM backlot – Mata leads Carlton-Towers toward a manhole cover as a foolproof method of losing their pursuers. When it is opened, however, there is heard the sound of a female voice singing the theme song to *What's New Pussycat?*. Carlton-Towers disagrees with Mata's suggested escape route and they return to the cab, leaving under a hail of gunfire from Le Chiffre's representative, played by Vladek Sheybal, who had previously appeared in the Eon Bond movie *From Russia with Love*.

David Niven departs the film

Despite American trade press reports that principal filming on *Casino Royale* had been completed, shooting would continue unabated at both Shepperton and Borehamwood for some time yet.[319]

Additional filming for the art auction sequence was required during the last week of August 1966. One industry publication advised that, due to ill health, this would be Ian Wilson's final

---

[319] *Variety: Weekly*, Reed Business Information, 10 August 1966.

movie, but in fact he would continue working in the industry until the early '70s.[320]

Upon the completion of all his scenes, and having devoted four and a half months to the project, David Niven departed the picture around this time.[321]

The Keystone Kops

Having already contributed greatly to the production, Richard Talmadge suggested the addition of something different: a silent film-style sequence filmed in black and white and featuring the Keystone Kops. This celebrated comedy ensemble had been created in 1912 by Canadian-born Keystone Studios head Mack Sennett, the acknowledged innovator of silent slapstick, and had featured in more than a dozen films over the following few years. Portraying incompetent American police officers, the troupe had an ever-changing line-up, including Roscoe 'Fatty' Arbuckle and on at least one occasion Charlie Chaplin. Feldman agreed that a slapstick silent film sequence, accompanied by a tinkling piano background, would make an ideal element of Evelyn Tremble's psychedelic experience while being held prisoner by Le Chiffre.[322]

Talmadge, who was 70 years old when *Casino Royale* was made, had actually taken part in some Keystone Kops movies in Hollywood early in his career, and had also worked with Chaplin on the New York stage. Not only did he direct the silent film sequence for *Casino Royale* but, with the addition of a long, droopy fake moustache, he also portrayed a Kop, as did Chaplin's daughter Geraldine. The filming was executed at Shepperton on the exterior standing street set originally constructed in 1964 for the romantic period comedy *The Amorous Adventures of Moll Flanders* (1965).[323]

---

[320] *The Daily Cinema*, Cinema Press Ltd, 26 August 1966.
[321] *Niv: The Authorised Biography of David Niven*, Graham Lord, Orion, October 2003.
[322] *Daily Express*, Northern & Shell Media, 21 September 1966.
[323] A Guide to Avengerland website, Anthony McKay, retrieved

Geraldine Chaplin thoroughly enjoyed becoming involved in the action, saying, 'It is great to be taught by a man who was actually there at the time. I had a lot of fun.'[324] Unfortunately, however, neither she nor Talmadge are recognisable in the finished film, as during editing a decision was taken to reduce the sequence to only a couple of long-shots, showing the Kops leaving their police station and climbing on board a Model T Ford. Then, in a complete change of plan, the sequence was repositioned in the picture, being added to the overall mayhem of the mass brawl finale, after the casino director Simmington-Jones calls the police for assistance.

Editing begins

Filming at Borehamwood was completed by the final week of September 1966, although pick-up shots and special effects footage would continue to be worked on at Shepperton until mid-October.[325] After playing a part in the comedy movie *30 is a Dangerous Age, Cynthia*, (1968), Duncan MaCrae performed some post-synching work for *Casino Royale* before returning to his home in Glasgow during early October.[326]

The end of September also saw film editor Bill Lenny sitting down at Shepperton Studios and beginning to piece together the movie from twenty reels of raw footage, for a proposed Christmas 1966 release. Lenny was among a select few who ever saw a complete *Casino Royale* screenplay, and was quoted as saying, 'I'm convinced it's going to be a really top-notch picture in spite of all this crazy way of making it.'[327] However, Lenny apparently struck problems, and although he received assistance from Feldman, Guest and Jerry Bresler, another editor, Russell

---

September 2013.
[324] *Daily Express*, Northern & Shell Media, 21 September 1966.
[325] *Kine Weekly*, Odhams Press Ltd, 22 September, 6 and 13 October 1966.
[326] *Wise Enough to Play the Fool: A Biography of Duncan Macrae*, Priscilla Barlow, John Donald Publishers Ltd, December 1995.
[327] *Kine Weekly*, Odhams Press Ltd, 29 September 1966.

Lloyd, was engaged as an uncredited post-production supervisor. Lloyd had a great reputation for his skill in cutting movies together, having previously worked extensively with director John Huston on various films including *Moby Dick* (1956) and *The Roots of Heaven* (1958).

On location in France

Sometime during October 1966, Val Guest headed a small unit, including doubles for David Niven and Ursula Andress, undertaking filming along the French Riviera, around the Cap Ferrat district of Nice. Upon hearing that Guest was on location with her double, Andress telephoned him person to person and complained bitterly about not being allowed to do the filming herself. In the event, however, the excursion proved to be another wasted effort, as none of this material was included in the finished picture, save for brief footage of a Boeing 707 airliner of the defunct American airline Pan Am landing at Nice airport.[328] This was used to indicate Evelyn Tremble arriving in France ready for his high-stakes baccarat game with Le Chiffre.

Footage shot in Malta?

It appears that some filming for the movie may also have taken place in Kalkara, Malta, at what is now Mediterranean Film Studios but was originally Malta Film Facilities. Established by special effects technician Benjamin Hole in 1964, this was at the time nothing more than a shallow horizon water tank created for simulated ocean shooting. It was first utilised for the war movie *The Bedford Incident* (1965), but records show that *Casino Royale* was the second production to have footage filmed there. However, Mediterranean Film Studios now have no details regarding this, and *Casino Royale* contains no footage that would have

---

[328] *So You Want to Be in Pictures: The Autobiography of Val Guest*, Val Guest, Reynolds & Hearn, May 2001.

required the use of such specialised facilities.[329]

Burt Bacharach and Hal David arrive

According to Feldman's paperwork, the composer Henry Mancini approached the producer on Thursday 13 October 1966, enthusiastically putting himself forward to provide the soundtrack for *Casino Royale*. Despite Mancini's impressive reputation for writing film themes and soundtracks, Feldman elected to remain faithful to Burt Bacharach, who had now been associated with the project for 14 months.[330] On Monday 17 October, Bacharach and Hal David arrived in London, where they spent a week viewing a rough cut of the movie and meeting regularly with Feldman and Columbia Pictures' music executive Jonie Taps. Bacharach informed Feldman that because the screenplay had been ever-changing, he now required approximately ten weeks to compose all the incidental music. This scuppered the proposed Christmas release date, so Easter 1967 was pencilled in instead.[331, 332]

Press interest

Meanwhile, on 16 October 1966, the Sunday magazine *Parade*, distributed across the US in more than 600 different newspapers, contained a feature on Jacqueline Bisset and her involvement with *Casino Royale*.

The movie gained a further mention in the press toward the end of October, when *The Australian Woman's Weekly* magazine ran an interview with fashion model Jean Shrimpton and she revealed that she had turned down an invitation to appear in

---

[329] Mediterranean Film Studios website, retrieved June 2010.
[330] *The Music of James Bond*, Jon Burlingame, Oxford University Press, October 2012.
[331] *Variety: Weekly*, Reed Business Information, 7 December 1966.
[332] *The Music of James Bond*, Jon Burlingame, Oxford University Press, October 2012.

the picture: 'I was offered a part in *Casino Royale*, but James Bond films bore me silly and I dislike all spy films.'[333]

As October became November, the tabloid press continued coverage of the film, as the *Daily Mirror* printed a photograph of Barbara Bouchet, dressed only in a bikini, feeding deer in Richmond Park.[334]

A couple of days later, Eon Productions held a press conference at Pinewood Studios regarding their current Bond picture, *You Only Live Twice*, but naturally several reporters also asked burning questions about the rival 007 movie *Casino Royale*. Albert R Broccoli dismissed Feldman's extravaganza as not posing any real competition, describing it as 'a sort of enlarged *What's New Pussycat?* and just a harmless spoof.' Meanwhile, Jerry Bresler would as usual reveal absolutely nothing about *Casino Royale*, preferring to keep details of both the plot and the format secret: 'Wait till you see the picture, it's impossible to describe in advance.'[335] However, those expecting a battle of the Bonds at the box office would be disappointed, as *Casino Royale* would arrive in cinemas a couple of months before *You Only Live Twice* premiered.

Columbia Pictures grow restless

Having provided a multimillion dollar budget and then waited patiently while production and editing took place at a snail's pace, Columbia Pictures were by November 1966 becoming impatient for the blockbuster Feldman had promised them. Defending the situation, Feldman admitted that problems existed but claimed that these revolved mainly around the soundtrack – which was somewhat unfair on Burt Bacharach, as he had been involved with the project for over a year now, but had only just been able to start composing.[336] Bacharach had also taken on the

---

[333] *The Australian Woman's Weekly*, Bauer Media Group, 26 October 1966.
[334] *Daily Mirror*, Trinity Mirror Group, 2 November 1966.
[335] *Kiss Kiss Bang! Bang!: The Unofficial James Bond Film Companion*, Alan Barnes and Marcus Hearn, Overlook Press, October 1998.

scoring duties on the comedy film *Luv* (1967), but managed to get released from that contract in late November, allowing him then to focus his full attention on *Casino Royale*.[337]

Val Guest departs

Meanwhile, having devoted approximately a year to the production, Val Guest concluded his association with it at around this time, needing a break before entering pre-production on his next film project, which would become the spy thriller *Assignment K* (1968).[338]

'Have No Fear Bond Is Here'

In what appears to have been an extremely late decision, Feldman telephoned Bacharach long distance on Monday 12 December 1966 and informed the composer that he required a comedy song to accompany the movie's opening titles. Bacharach and David returned to London on Tuesday 3 January 1967, where they presented various compositions to Feldman, including the proposed title song, referred to as 'Little French Girl, Little French Boy'. Feldman was unimpressed with this and rejected it as the title song, although it would be included in the finished film in instrumental form, minus lyrics, accompanying both the car chase sequence and the fight scene where Sir James takes on the two pipers and the horseguard. Having anticipated the situation, the songwriters already had to hand another comedy song, which Feldman called 'the baroque number', but its lyrics were also judged unacceptable for use over the opening titles, hence Hal David devised new lyrics and changed the title to 'Have No Fear Bond Is Here'.[339] Feldman

---

[336] *The Music of James Bond*, Jon Burlingame, Oxford University Press, October 2012.
[337] *Variety: Daily*, Reed Business Information, 23 November 1966.
[338] *So You Want to Be in Pictures: The Autobiography of Val Guest*, Val Guest, Reynolds & Hearn, May 2001.
[339] *The Music of James Bond*, Jon Burlingame, Oxford University Press,

thought that this revised version fitted the bill perfectly, and Bacharach found the ideal vocalist in Mike Redway, who had previously sung with the Mike Sammes Singers.

Redway excelled during the recording session for 'Have No Fear Bond Is Here', nailing the number on only the second take, although later he would make a second recording for a vinyl single release on Deram Records. Feldman, however, then had a change of mind, and decided against using Redway's rendition for the opening titles; instead, it would play over the closing credits. Despite failing to receive an on-screen credit, Redway appeared genuinely grateful to have been invited on board such a big-budget project. He was later quoted as saying, 'I didn't know that it was for the closing titles, but I didn't mind.'[340]

Redway also performed another song to accompany part of the Tremble dream sequence after he is drugged by Miss Goodthighs, where he pretends to play keyboards on the torso of the reclining Vesper Lynd. This short ditty, which on the later soundtrack album was entitled 'Dream on James, You're Winning', is reprised at the movie's conclusion, with Redway singing a different verse regarding seven James Bonds at *Casino Royale*. Bacharach wanted this track sung novelty fashion in an over-the-top upper class Noel Coward accent, which Redway achieved with ease.

Romantic interlude

Charles K Feldman had definite views regarding the romantic interlude between Evelyn Tremble and Vesper Lynd, which Joe McGrath had directed: 'Take that arty farty shit out. I want Sellers being funny.' However, persuasion from a combination of McGrath and Bacharach convinced him that the sequence should be retained, as the right background music, in the form of a romantic ballad, would transform it by creating the correct

---

October 2012.
[340] *The Music of James Bond*, Jon Burlingame, Oxford University Press, October 2012.

atmosphere. Bacharach composed the tune for this sequence, drawing inspiration from Ursula Andress's beauty and the bossa nova number 'The Girl from Ipanema', and Hal David provided lyrics that resulted in the song being called 'The Look of Love'.[341]

Johnny Rivers

It seems that Feldman and Bacharach wanted someone with more of an international appeal to perform the movie's opening theme song, which they apparently intended to be another version of 'Have No Fear Bond Is Here', this time under the title 'Casino Royale'. Having met American vocalist Johnny Rivers the previous month at a party hosted by actor Steve McQueen, Bacharach put his name forward. On being approached, the singer was enthusiastic about making a recording for the film. He had recently scored an American chart-topping hit record called 'Poor Side of Town', and back in March 1966 had reached number three with his song 'Secret Agent Man', which had been used as the theme for US network transmissions of *Danger Man*, retitled *Secret Agent* in that territory. Rivers arrived in London on Wednesday 18 January 1967, but returned to the US virtually straightaway, having heard the song Feldman and Bacharach wanted him to record and instantly decided that it was not his style.[342] This left the issue of the opening theme song unresolved.

Recording the soundtrack

The recording of the soundtrack began on Saturday 21 January 1967 at CTS Studios in Wembley, Greater London, where Bacharach conducted between 50 and 60 musicians on more than 100 different cues over the course of eight days. Bacharach arranged for his friend, the New York based recording producer

---

[341] *The Music of James Bond*, Jon Burlingame, Oxford University Press, October 2012.
[342] *The Music of James Bond*, Jon Burlingame, Oxford University Press, October 2012.

and engineer Phil Ramone, to be present and supervise the sessions, although UK union rules prevented him from actually engineering them. CTS employee Jack Clegg oversaw the schedule from the control room, with American orchestrators Jack Hayes and Leo Shuken also on hand to arrange the passages and cues. On the night of Wednesday 25 January, the Animals pop group either auditioned or recorded a song for the film at CTS, but total mystery surrounds this event, which was never publicised. Presumably the Animals failed to capture the desired atmosphere with the number they worked on that night, and their opportunity to become involved with the picture came and went.[343]

'The Look of Love'

There was no debate about who should record 'The Look of Love', as everyone agreed that Dusty Springfield was the correct choice. The singer had previously impressed Bacharach and David with renditions of a couple of their other songs, and she was also Feldman's favourite singer. With director Joe McGrath in attendance, Springfield recorded two versions of 'The Look of Love', one for the soundtrack and the other for a single release, at Philips London sound studio in Stanhope Place, London on Sunday 29 January 1967. However, at some point, versions sung in French, German and Italian were also recorded by French songstress Mireille Mathieu, and these would replace Springfield's on prints of the film destined for those three European countries.[344]

---

[343] *The Music of James Bond*, Jon Burlingame, Oxford University Press, October 2012.
[344] *The Music of James Bond*, Jon Burlingame, Oxford University Press, October 2012.

Herb Alpert

With the soundtrack recording now complete, Feldman and Bacharach returned to considering their options for the opening theme song that Johnny Rivers had rejected. They identified two possibilities. The first option was to offer the opportunity to sing 'Casino Royale' to Tom Jones, following his powerful performance of 'What's New Pussycat?' for Feldman's earlier box office hit. The second option was to abandon the lyrics altogether and settle for an instrumental version performed by easy listening exponent Herb Alpert who, together with his backing band the Tijuana Brass, had popularised a Mexican brass sound in the mid-'60s.[345] Eventually the producer and composer decided to go for option number two.

Bacharach had already recorded a backing track with the assembled musicians at CTS, which he played over the telephone to Alpert, who was in New York, suggesting that it could be augmented by his distinctive brass sound. A master tape was forwarded to Alpert, who simply double tracked his trumpet and added some light percussion sounds before returning it to London. It is believed that the musicians who comprised the Tijuana Brass did not perform on the track, despite being credited along with Alpert under what appears to have been a contractual agreement of the time. Records indicate that members of the Tijuana Brass did spend two days in February 1967 making a recording of 'Casino Royale' in a studio in Los Angeles, but this seems to have been shelved, presumably because the version Bacharach already had was considered superior.[346]

Opening titles and closing credits

Feldman was overjoyed with Bacharach's contribution to the picture, feeling that the composer had completely captured the

---

[345] *The Music of James Bond*, Jon Burlingame, Oxford University Press, October 2012.
[346] *The Music of James Bond*, Jon Burlingame, Oxford University Press, October 2012.

atmosphere of the production and that his incidental cues enhanced its comedy aspect. With the music now complete, animator Richard Williams had the task of creating a set of intricate opening titles to go with the opening theme, and also a set of closing credits.

The opening titles consisted of a series of animated psychedelic montages incorporating portions of filmed footage. Williams had begun his career by animating short films in the late '50s, although by the mid-'60s he had provided the titles for several features, including *The Liquidator* (1965), *A Funny Thing Happened on the Way to the Forum* (1966) and Feldman's *What's New Pussycat?*. To reduce Williams' workload and enable him to complete his task as quickly as possible, a decision was made to credit only forty cast members and approximately half the production crew.

The screenplay credit on screen went to Wolf Mankowitz, John Law and Michael Sayers, omitting all other contributors including Peter Sellers, Joseph McGrath, Terry Southern, Orson Welles, Ben Hecht, John Huston, Terence Cooper and Val Guest. Woody Allen had insisted that his contribution toward the script also go uncredited – which meant that, if they did have any input into his material, his frequent collaborators Mickey Rose and Frank Buxton were treated likewise. Over the years, there have been suggestions that material was also contributed to the project by scriptwriter and one-time MGM president Dore Schary[347] and by American writer Donald S Sanford[348], but there is no substantial evidence to support this.

British Board of Film Censors

Meanwhile, on 2 February 1967, the British Board of Film

---

[347] *Woody Allen: A Biography*, John Baxter, HarperCollins, November 1998.
[348] *This is a Thriller: An Episode Guide, History and Analysis of the Classic 1960s Television Series*, Alan Warren, McFarland & Company Inc, April 2004.

Censors evaluated a version of *Casino Royale* that ran for 142 minutes and 29 seconds. They decided that it warranted no cuts on censorship grounds and awarded it a Universal rating, meaning that it was suitable for cinemagoers of all ages. However, as the soundtrack recordings had been completed only three days earlier, this version is thought to have been a rough cut minus any incidental music, submitted on the understanding that the shorter release print would be assembled from what had already been seen.

Playboy magazine

Playboy magazine assisted in promoting the movie by running in its February 1967 edition a 13-page pictorial entitled *The Girls of Casino Royale*, for which Joanna Pettet, Barbara Bouchet and Fiona Lewis all posed. Also included were a mixture of stills and publicity photographs featuring Ursula Andress and Guard Girls played by Marilyn Rickard, Jane Forster and Vanessa Sutton, plus various shots taken during production, including some of action not featured in the finished film. Woody Allen provided the amusing copy that accompanied the large number of images, which also featured *Playboy* models Samantha Jewell, Toni Burnett and Dolly Read.

Columbia Pictures take control

Editors Bill Lenny and Russell Lloyd, with assistance from Feldman and Jerry Bresler, eventually managed to transform the twenty reels of raw footage into a finished film, which had a running time of about three hours. Columbia Pictures, however, were totally aghast at the picture they were presented with. Having put enormous faith in Feldman's abilities to assemble an assured box office hit, they felt badly let down. With the London premiere looming, Columbia promptly took the picture completely out of Feldman's hands and undertook a major re-editing. In the process they trimmed out a huge amount of material, making the actual release print only 131 minutes long.[349]

Premiere announced

During the second week of March 1967, there was an announcement in the trade press that *Casino Royale* would receive a royal premiere in the presence of Princess Alexandra on 13 April at the Odeon Cinema in Leicester Square, London. This would also be a charitable event, benefitting both the 'Hurt Minds Can Be Healed' campaign of the Mental Health Trust and the Italian Art and Archives Rescue Fund.[350]

'The Look of Love' cover versions

The first record release associated with the film was a 45 rpm single that became available on Friday 31 March 1967 on the Decca label. This was a vocal version of 'The Look of Love', backed by an interpretation of 'Have No Fear Bond Is Here', both credited to Roland Shaw and his Orchestra. Seven days later came the release of another cover version of 'The Look of Love', this one performed by singer/actress Shani Wallis, the single's B-side in this instance being another Bacharach and David composition written for the movie, called 'Let the Love Come Through'. The latter song had been rejected for inclusion in the picture by Feldman, although an instrumental version was used to accompany the action of Mata Bond and Carlton-Towers arriving in Berlin.[351]

With only four days to go until the long-awaited official premiere, BBC1's late night series *The Look of the Week* devoted an entire programme to *Casino Royale* in its edition transmitted on Sunday 9 April.

Royal premiere

---

[349] *007 Magazine* No. 40, *Casino Royale*, Michael Richardson and Graham Rye, The James Bond 007 International Fan Club, January 2002.
[350] *The Daily Cinema*, Cinema Press Ltd, 8 March 1967.
[351] 45Cat website, retrieved September 2013.

On Thursday 13 April 1967 the *Daily Express* contained a half page advertisement for the royal premiere of *Casino Royale*, which would take place that evening at the Odeon in Leicester Square, where the doors opened at 7.30 pm for the 8.15 pm screening. Princess Alexandra was joined by Charles K Feldman, Jerry Bresler, Val Guest, John Huston, Kenneth Hughes, Joanna Pettit, Barbara Bouchet and Daliah Lavi. Others in attendance included Tracy Reed, Tracey Crisp, Elaine Taylor, Angela Scoular, Jeanne Roland, Chic Murray, Caroline Munro, Vicky Hodge and John Huston's daughter Anjelica, plus famous actors James Mason, Jack Hawkins, Laurence Harvey, Mia Farrow and Catherine Deneuve together with her then husband, professional photographer David Bailey.[352, 353] Conspicuous by their absence were the film's A-list cast members, David Niven, Ursula Andress, Woody Allen, Orson Welles and, perhaps not surprisingly, Peter Sellers. Apprehensive regarding the audience's reaction to the movie, John Huston whispered to Val Guest, 'Do you think we're wise to be here?'[354]

---

[352] *Kine Weekly*, Odhams Press Ltd, 22 April 1967.
[353] *Just Daft: The Chic Murray Story*, Robbie Grigor, Birlinn, September 2009.
[354] *So You Want to Be in Pictures: The Autobiography of Val Guest*, Val Guest, Reynolds & Hearn, May 2001.

MICHAEL RICHARDSON

Chapter Eight
The Fun Movement

Promotional items

The day after the *Casino Royale* premiere, a special screening was arranged at the nearby Columbia Cinema (now the Curzon Soho) in Shaftesbury Avenue for Rank cinema managers, each of whom brought along a reporter from their local newspaper. After this screening, everyone moved to the Odeon in Leicester Square, where there was a trade show in progress, unveiling a large number of promotional items created as part of a massive marketing campaign under the slogan 'Join the *Casino Royale* fun movement'. The items included three life-size posters by Italian artist Giorgio Olivetti, each depicting two characters from the film, and a special James Bond 007 newspaper.[355] The characters as depicted by Olivetti in his paintings also came on individual door panels, and five different examples were even made available as bookmarks – which are now extremely rare. Other items produced included three colourful round badges, complete with the slogans 'David Niven Bathes with Girls', 'Barbara Bouchet Is a Bond-Aid' and 'Tijuana – What Brass!' Each of these badges had a different coloured edging around the main lettering and incorporated the smaller wording 'Casino Royale Fun Movement' and 'James Bond 007'.

The assembled group were addressed by Jerry Bressler,

---

[355] *Kine Weekly*, Odhams Press Ltd, 22 April 1967.

with additional promotion being provided by various models wearing body stockings matching the naked, colourfully tattooed woman illustrated on both the movie poster and the twenty-third, twenty-fourth and twenty-fifth printings of the Pan paperback edition of Ian Fleming's *Casino Royale* novel. The poster was the work of American artist Robert McGinnis, a prolific illustrator of both paperback book covers and movie advertising material, who had also painted the posters for *Thunderball* and the second Matt Helm spy picture, *Murderers' Row* (1966). Over the weekend of 15 and 16 April, a number of the body-stocking-clad models were driven around London in a Ford Mustang convertible, taking part in a promotional drive and giving away posters to various businesses, including fashion boutiques and nightclubs. Further publicity was created by huge banners carried along the sides of London Transport double-decker buses.[356] Meanwhile, Moët and Chandon had already anticipated the benefit of an association with the movie, as bottles of their champagne were featured in the on-screen action, and the company provided five-feet-tall dummy magnums for cinema lobby displays.

Tie-in record releases

Meanwhile, the Deram release of 'Have No Fear Bond is Here' by Mike Redway had taken place on 14 April 1967. 'Casino Royale', credited to Herb Alpert and the Tijuana Brass, also became available sometime during the month on Alpert's own A&M Records, with some examples being sold in picture sleeves, after the original plan to release the record on Pye International fell through.[357] This recording peaked at number 27 on both the US Billboard chart and the UK chart, spending a total of 14 weeks on the latter, and later went on to be included on various Herb Alpert compilation albums.[358]

---

[356] *Kine Weekly*, Odhams Press Ltd, 22 April 1967.
[357] 45Cat website, retrieved September 2013.

Newspaper reviews

The morning after the film's premiere, the daily newspaper reviews began appearing. They included one by Donald Zec of the *Daily Mirror*, who said, 'I can honestly say with my hand on my stomach that *Casino Royale* is the worst film I ever enjoyed.' Others were less charitable. Tom Milne of *The Financial Times* called the film 'Sheer unadulterated hell,' and the *Daily Mail*'s critic also pulled no punches, stating that is was 'The biggest, loudest and most inconsequential of all the Bond pictures.' Meanwhile, the tabloid journalism of *The Sun* summed up Feldman's extravaganza as 'A triumph of clumsiness.'

A couple of days later, the Sunday newspapers were unfortunately just as scathing. Ernest Betts of *The Sunday People* opined that the film was: 'A two hour burlesque of all the James Bonds you've ever seen; not a single scene makes sense.' Penelope Gilliatt of *The Observer* was left feeling frustrated: 'Every scene was ambushed by some preening gag or egomaniacal bit of business. It was just a rash of a picture.' Dilys Powell of the *Sunday Times* was just as savage, turning the film's publicity slogan back on itself: '*Casino Royale*, as the adverts say, is too much for one James Bond. I find it too much for one critic.' Understandably, Feldman was very disappointed by the reviews, but he received encouragement from an unexpected source when Peter Sellers telephoned him and said, 'The notices are rough, but *Casino Royale* could still surprise everybody.' It seemed the actor might be right: despite the mainly bad reviews, *Casino Royale* did more box office business at the Odeon, Leicester Square, during its first week than any other Columbia movie had managed there, coming close to breaking the house record for attendance.[359]

---

[358] *The Guinness Book of British Hit Singles*, Paul Gambaccini, Mike Read, Tim Rice & Jo Rice, Guinness, November 1977 & *The Billboard Book of US Top 40 Hits*, Joel Whitburn, Billboard, July 1983.
[359] *Daily Mirror*, Trinity Mirror Group, 18 April 1967.

The Friday 21 April 1967 edition of the American magazine *Life* included a three-page colour feature that paved the way for the movie's general US opening the following Friday. Stateside reviews were mainly along the lines of those seen in Britain, such as Bosley Crowther's piece in *The New York Times*, describing the movie as: '… disconnected nonsense.'[360]

Success at the box office

Despite all the adverse publicity, box office receipts for *Casino Royale* told a different story, as it was the top grossing film across the US for the next six weeks, eventually becoming the thirteenth most popular film for the year.[361] Opening in 18 different cinemas in New York and the surrounding area, *Casino Royale* made more money during the first three days of business than any previous Columbia film had over this initial period. Feldman was so pleased when this occurred that he telephoned Val Guest sometime later from the US to inform him, forgetting the time difference, and the director was woken in London by his telephone ringing at 4.00 am.[362]

More record releases

Coinciding with the film's general release, the American soundtrack LP record went on sale during the third week of April 1967 on Colgems Records, reaching number 22 on the Billboard album chart, on which it remained for nine weeks. The following month, in the UK, Philips released 'The Look of Love' by Dusty Springfield, but failing to recognise its potential, they placed it on the B-side of her then current single 'Give Me Time', which later reached number 24 in the chart.[363, 364] The

---

[360] *The New York Times*, The New York Times Company, 29 April 1967.
[361] *Variety: Weekly*, Reed Business Information, 3, 10. 17, 24 and 31 May and 7 June 1967.
[362] *So You Want to Be in Pictures: The Autobiography of Val Guest*, Val Guest, Reynolds & Hearn, May 2001.

sides were later reversed for the American release, which for some unknown reason did not happen until October. May 1967 also witnessed the release of a Burt Bacharach instrumental based on the incidental cue that accompanies the Berlin auction brawl sequence. Called 'Home James, Don't Spare the Horses' on the soundtrack album, it was renamed 'Bond Street' for the A&M single.[365] The British soundtrack LP on RCA Records would not become available until June, with the movie still receiving media attention and the film magazine *Photoplay* devoting both its cover and three and a half pages to promoting the picture.

Award and nominations

At the annual Laurel Awards presented by the American *Motion Picture Exhibitor* magazine, *Casino Royale* was awarded a Golden Laurel after being considered the third best comedy film of the year. Later in 1968, 'The Look of Love' was nominated for an Oscar as the Best Original Song, losing out to 'Talk to the Animals', from the family film *Doctor Dolittle* (1967), written by Leslie Bricusse, who later confided to Hal David that he thought the track from *Casino Royale* was far superior.[366] There were also nominations at the Grammys for Burt Bacharach, for the Best Original Score Written for a Motion Picture, and at the BAFTA awards for Julie Harris, for Best British Costume, which unfortunately neither won.

---

[363] *The Guinness Book of British Hit Singles*, Paul Gambaccini, Mike Read, Time Rice & Jo Rice, Guinness, November 1977 & 45Cat website, retrieved September 2013.
[364] 45Cat website, retrieved September 2013.
[365] 45Cat website, retrieved September 2013.
[366] *The Music of James Bond*, Jon Burlingame, Oxford University Press, October 2012.

Rolls Royce

Some time after *Casino Royale*'s release, Charles K Feldman saw Joseph McGrath, and admitted that he had become totally confused by the film's production schedule: 'I think that film drove me crazy. I didn't know what had been shot and what hadn't been shot ... I lost control.'[367]

Two years after working on the film, McGrath was in Los Angeles when he was approached by a man driving a Rolls Royce. He was surprised when the man introduced himself as Jerry Bresler and invited him to inspect the limousine. Bresler then went on to explain that this was the vehicle Feldman had been prepared to give to McGrath if he had consented to return to the production. McGrath's refusal had allowed Feldman to use it instead to entice Bresler to become involved.[368]

Final cost

Despite Columbia Pictures' official figure of $8 million, *Variety* estimated the final cost of *Casino Royale*'s production to have been around the $9 million mark, while Joe McGrath reckoned that over double that amount was more accurate.[369] Wolf Mankowitz felt certain that the excesses he had witnessed during filming had pushed costs even further than anyone had ever imagined; he thought that the final expenditure could easily have approached $28 million. Whatever the truth, Feldman was not saying.[370] However, the personal cost to the producer was much greater; during the film's production, he had both suffered a heart attack and been diagnosed with cancer. Charles K Feldman passed away on 25 May 1968,

---

[367] *Kiss Kiss Bang! Bang!: The Unofficial James Bond Film Companion*, Alan Barnes and Marcus Hearn, Overlook Press, October 1998.
[368] *Dr. Shatterhand's Botanical Garden website, It's a Mad, Mad, Mad, Mad Royale*, Stuart Basinger, retrieved July 2013.
[369] *Variety: Weekly*, Reed Business Information, 12 October 1966.
[370] *Woody Allen: A Biography*, John Baxter, HarperCollins, November 1998.

following unforeseen complications after undergoing surgery for cancer of the pancreas, later being interred at the Hollywood Forever Cemetery in Los Angeles, California.[371]

Television transmissions, CD soundtrack and VHS video releases

Having established itself at the cinema, *Casino Royale* arrived on American television on 18 September 1970, though a further three years passed before it was transmitted in the UK, on BBC1 on Boxing Day 1973, as part of the Christmas ratings war. Three and a half years passed before the movie was again scheduled by the BBC. Then it reappeared on ITV in May 1981 and began doing the rounds of the various independent regional companies until 1985, whereupon the UK screening rights returned to the BBC.

The soundtrack recording was reissued on vinyl and also made its initial appearance on CD in the UK, when the American label Varese Sarabande offered it in both formats during November 1990.

Having been available on sell-through VHS video cassette in the US for several years, the film was finally issued in the UK during 1990 under the RCA Columbia International branding, as part of their Hollywood Spy Collection. It was reissued the following year, now sporting a different artwork cover design, again by RCA Columbia International, but this time retailing for the budget price of £7.99.

Meanwhile, the BBC gave their third and final television screening to the movie on 9 November 1991. The rights then passed across to Sky, who would show it eight times over the next four years on their Sky Movies Gold channel.

In 1994, Columbia Tristar issued the film in the short-lived laserdisc format for American consumption; this appeared in retail outlets on 23 November.

---

[371] Wikipedia: Charles K Feldman, retrieved September 2013.

A rival James Bond franchise?

Having already remade *Thunderball* once in 1982/1983 as *Never Say Never Again* (1983), Kevin McClory announced his intention to rework it again in 1996 under the title *Warhead 2000 AD*. By October 1997, the concept had been expanded by Columbia Pictures, who revealed plans to develop a whole new James Bond franchise. This was based around McClory's contention that as his original *Thunderball* screenplay predated *Dr. No*, he was partly responsible for establishing the cinematic James Bond character. Eon Productions and their financial backer of the time, MGM, were unwilling to see this happen, and they vigorously defended their rights by starting legal proceedings, which continued for over a year.[372, 373]

Apparently, McClory had waited too long to produce another remake. The court judgement he had obtained during the '60s was now deemed out of date, and his only recourse was to obtain some financial recompense by selling all his interests in *Thunderball* to Eon Productions. Meanwhile, in February 1999, legal representatives of both MGM and Columbia's parent company Sony Pictures Entertainment settled their differences out of court, resulting in the latter dropping their plans for any future James Bond product. Part of the agreement involved Columbia selling all their rights to Ian Fleming's original *Casino Royale* novel plus Charles K Feldman's movie version to MGM for £10 million.[374, 375]

Austin Powers

Two years earlier, in 1997, inspiration from *Casino Royale* was clearly seen in the spy spoof *Austin Powers: International Man of*

---

[372] Universal Exports: The Home of James Bond 007 website, Kevin McClory, Sony.
[373] *Bond: A History Lesson*, Greg Goodman, retrieved October 2013.
[374] Universal Exports: The Home of James Bond 007 website, Kevin McClory, Sony.
[375] *Bond: A History Lesson*, Greg Goodman, retrieved October 2013.

Mystery, and its producer, writer and star Mike Myers stated that he had been especially influenced by Burt Bacharach's soundtrack.[376] This initial Austin Powers movie also featured 'The Look of Love' by Dusty Springfield. Its success was such that it spawned two sequels, *Austin Powers: The Spy Who Shagged Me* (1999) and *Austin Powers in Goldmember* (2002).

More television screenings and soundtrack releases

More regional television screenings of *Casino Royale* took place on ITV throughout the late '90s. The film was then issued on DVD in the UK by MGM on Tuesday 24 April 2001, complete with the theatrical trailer and a making-of featurette called *Psychedelic Cinema*, involving Val Guest.

On Friday 29 June 2001, the Mods and Rockers Psychedelic Festival was a celebration of '60s films and pop culture that took place at the Egyptian Theatre at 6712 Hollywood Boulevard in Los Angeles. The event got under way by showing *Casino Royale*, followed by a discussion session with Guest, who was amazed when the movie was greatly appreciated by the audience, admitting, 'It's quite good.'

UK television screening rights had now been acquired by Channel 5, who transmitted the film once in 2001 and again in April 2002. Now-defunct satellite channel Carlton Cinema then showed it five times before the end of 2002.

Varese Sarabande reissued the soundtrack album on CD, complete with new cover artwork depicting a version of the tattooed lady, though this time in silhouette, and this became available in the United States on 15 October 2002.

SFX magazine dated March 2003 featured an interview with Guest, in which he talked extensively about his career, including *Casino Royale*, and commented, 'There's a whole film to be made about the filming of *Casino Royale*.'

---

[376] *Casino Royale* soundtrack booklet, Gergely Hubai, Quartet Records, February 2012.

There were no UK television transmissions of the film during 2003, but ITV acquired the rights again in 2004, screening it on eight occasions over the next three years, sometimes fully networked, on their channels ITV1, ITV3 and ITV4.

The soundtrack underwent another American reissue on 3 March 2005, although this time Varese Sarabande reverted to the original tattooed lady image for the cover.

Daniel Craig

Eon Productions finally used the *Casino Royale* novel as the basis for a reboot of their own Bond movies. This version, released in November 2006, introduced a grittier James Bond character, played by Daniel Craig.

Further television screenings

During February and March 2009, Feldman's original *Casino Royale* received half a dozen satellite screenings courtesy of Sky Movies Premiere 4, before being given a further nine transmissions on ITV channels, beginning in August 2010 and going through to September 2012.

Remastered CD with additional tracks

American soundtrack specialist Kritzerland reissued the soundtrack once again on CD on 18 January 2011, although this limited edition of 1,000 copies featured three additional tracks, including Mike Redway's 'Have No Fear Bond is Here'. However, this Kritzerland issue was only a taster, as on 28 February 2012, the Spanish company Quartet Records unveiled their totally remastered double CD set, restricted to 1,500 copies, which incorporated an additional 25 minutes of previously unreleased music. The first disc contained all the cues placed in their running order from the film, while the second was the original 13-track soundtrack, remastered from a half-inch stereo master tape discovered in the Spanish vaults of Sony Music Entertainment.

Further television rights moves

When the UK television rights lapsed again, Sky quickly snapped them up, and between October 2012 and February 2013 they showed the film a dozen times, using their channels Sky Movies Showcase HD and Sky Movies Modern Greats. In 2014 the rights returned once again to ITV, allowing them to schedule two screenings within the space of a week during August that year. The following year, ITV4 gave the movie another couple of screenings within a week during June, in what had become almost a regular summer ritual.

In conclusion

Charles K Feldman had gambled heavily on showcasing Peter Sellers' comedy genius as the main element of what was always envisaged as a multifaceted extravaganza assembled by different contributors. Even if Sellers had filmed all of his scheduled material, it appears likely that principal photography would still have taken considerably longer to complete than originally planned. The constant improvisation and rewriting of the various screenplays could have been supervised much more closely by Feldman, with more attention focused on making the various episodic storylines fit seamlessly together. Apparently Feldman visited Shepperton Studios only three times during production, preferring to control everything from his suite at the Dorchester Hotel, which perhaps was not the best approach to film-making, lacking a producer's usual hands-on involvement.

In 1992 Orson Welles was quoted as saying, 'How this picture was a success I can't imagine,'[377] though on another

---

[377] *This is Orson Welles*, Orson Welles and Peter Bogdanovich, HarperCollins, September 1992.

occasion he jokingly commented that the naked tattooed lady on the film poster was the reason the movie had been a box office winner.[378] Around the time of the premiere, David Niven described *Casino Royale* thus: 'The picture is a hodgepodge of nonsense, hardly a critic's film. But I bet Charlie Feldman makes money.'[379] Wolf Mankowitz was far less charitable, calling it, 'A frightful mess!'[380]

But the atmosphere of disappointment that initially surrounded *Casino Royale* appears now to have been largely reversed, as the film's disjointed storyline has apparently helped to make it a swinging '60s cult classic, which is still screened regularly on television. The impressive cast, the humour, Burt Bacharach's excellent score, the various plotlines and James Bond elements have all combined to create an entertaining experience of huge proportions.

---

[378] *Orson Welles: A Biography*, Barbara Leaming, Viking, September 1985.
[379] *The Blade*, Block Communications, 30 April 1967.
[380] *Orson Welles: A Biography*, Barbara Leaming, Viking, September 1985.

PART TWO
BIOGRAPHIES

Biographies

WOODY ALLEN (JIMMY BOND/DR NOAH)

Allan Stewart Konigsberg, aka Woody Allen, entered the world on 1 December 1935 in Brooklyn, New York. He found his way into showbusiness during the '50s, penning gags and writing humorous books. Moving into television, he began scriptwriting for comedy series including *The Sid Caesar Show* and television movies such as *At the Movies*. He then managed his big break into feature films by providing the screenplay for and acting in *What's New Pussycat?*. This led to a contract with producer Charles K Feldman and eventually his involvement with *Casino Royale*. Along the way, Allen also managed numerous television appearances, appearing as a panellist on game shows, doing his stand-up routines and taking part in sketches on *The Andy Williams Show*.

However, Allen wanted a career in movies, and he quickly became an all-rounder as he progressed into devising his own big screen projects, which he would not only write but also star in and direct. The first of these was *Take the Money and Run*, released in 1969. This was followed in the early '70s by *Bananas*, *Play It Again Sam*, *Everything You Always Wanted to Know about Sex* (*But Were Afraid to Ask)* and *Sleeper*. Toward the end of the '70s Allen abandoned this comedic approach, preferring to create comedy-dramas based around love stories, and he made the successful *Annie Hall*, *Manhattan* and *Stardust Memories*.

Manhattan was Allen's last film for 14 years with actress Diane Keaton, with whom he had shared a personal relationship during the '70s. He then had a 12-year relationship with another actress, Mia Farrow, with whom he had one child and adopted two others, and she also appeared in 13 of his movies. Now revered as a serious auteur, Allen continued making critically-acclaimed pictures throughout the '80s, including *Broadway Danny Rose*, *Hannah and Her Sisters* – for which he received an Oscar for Best Original Screenplay – and *Radio Days*.

Averaging one film per year, Allen bid the '80s farewell with *Crimes and Misdemeanors*, released in 1989. He continued working into the next decade, the highlights of his '90s output being *Manhattan Murder Mystery*, co-starring Diane Keaton, *Bullets Over Broadway*, for which Dianne Wiest was awarded an Oscar as Best Supporting Actress, and *Everybody Says I Love You*.

Entering a new sphere of entertainment, Allen became a voice-over artist for the 1998 animated feature film *Antz*, before returning to his own productions, where he decided upon a change of scenery as, for the first time, he began regularly setting his pictures in places other than New York. London provided the backdrop for the 2007 film *Cassandra's Dream*, while the following year's *Vicky Cristina Barcelona* was filmed partly on location in Spain, and in 2011 the title *Midnight in Paris* gave away that film's locale.

URSULA ANDRESS (VESPER LYND)

Ursula Andress was born in the Ostermundigen district of Bern, Switzerland on 19 March 1936. She began her acting career by appearing in Italian film comedies during the mid-'50s, before gaining a role in an episode of the American television anthology series *Thriller*. Plucked from obscurity, she was chosen to play the first Bond girl after being cast as Honey Ryder in *Dr. No*, making a unforgettable entrance as she emerged from the surf wearing a white bikini. Appearances in smaller films followed, until in 1964 she was cast as the female lead in Hammer Films' *She*, as part of an agreement between the house of horror, her then husband John Derek and backers Seven Arts.

Andress joined the cast of Charles K Feldman's *What's New Pussycat?*, billed as a guest star, before taking part in the French films *Les Tribulations d'un Chinois en Chine* (aka *Up to His Ears*) and *The Tenth Victim*. From there Andress performed alongside George Peppard and James Mason in the World War One movie *The Blue Max*, then followed up with John Derek's World War Two film *Once Before I Die*. Turning full circle, she returned to both James Bond and Charles K Feldman for *Casino Royale*. She then decided to reduce her workload, and averaged only one film per year until 1976, when she acted in four.

Resuming her usual busy routine, Andress then worked through to the turn of the decade, gracing the big screen in feature films including *The Fifth Musketeer* and the original version of *Clash of the Titans*. In the early '80s she moved into television, guest-starring in episodes of the American series *Manimal* and *The Love Boat*, then three instalments of the soap *Falcon Crest*. The late '80s and '90s brought her work in television movies and a variety of obscure European films. Her career came to a close with the movie *Die Vogelpredigt* in 2005.

JACQUELINE BISSET (MISS GOODTHIGHS)

Winnifred Jacqueline Fraser-Bisset was born in Weybridge, Surrey on 13 September 1944. She entered the acting profession by playing an uncredited extra in the 1965 film *The Knack ... and How to Get It*. The following year, she was credited as Jackie Bisset for her appearance in another film, *Cul-de-sac*, and then as Jacqueline Bisset for her supporting role in the comedy movie *Drop Dead Darling*. After *Casino Royale*, she was cast in several more films where she simply made up the numbers, before winning female lead roles in *The Sweet Ride* and then *Bullitt*, both released in 1968.

Further movies followed, and during the first half of the '70s Bisset briefly became a significant player in the industry, collecting credits in a stream of major productions including *The Life and Times of Judge Roy Bean*, *The Thief Who Came to Dinner* and *Murder on the Orient Express*. Toward the end of the decade, however, her volume of work began decreasing, although she was the female lead in the underwater adventure *The Deep*, based on the best-selling novel by Peter Benchley, and in *The Greek Tycoon*.

Bissett started the '80s by averaging about a film every year, then drifted into small screen productions after being cast as the title character in a television movie adaptation of *Anna Karenina* and as Josephine in the mini-series *Napoleon and Josephine: A Love Story*.

For the remainder of the '80s Bisset continued acting in a mixture of feature film and television roles, but then over the following two decades she came to focus mainly on the latter. She played parts in the series *Ally McBeal* and *Law and Order: Special Victims Unit*, had a recurring role in seven episodes of *Nip/Tuck*, and appeared in three episodes of *Rizzoli & Isles* and four of *Dancing on the Edge*.

BARBARA BOUCHET (MONEYPENNY)

Barbara Goutscher, aka Barbara Bouchet, was born on 15 August 1943 in the town of Reichenburg, which at that time was in Germany, though due to border alterations after World War Two it was renamed Liberec and is now part of the Czech Republic. When she was a child, her family immigrated to the US and settled in San Francisco, where during her teens she began entering beauty contests (under the name Bouchet), which led on to fashion modelling and then appearances in television commercials. Bouchet's good looks and impressive figure were then responsible for getting her cast in a minor role in the Bob Hope comedy *A Global Affair*, released in January 1964. Having come to the attention of Hollywood casting directors, Bouchet then found herself working on several features over the next three years, though these appearances usually went uncredited.

However, Bouchet's attributes had also been discovered by television, for which she guest-starred and was credited in episodes of *The Rogues*, *The Man from U.N.C.L.E.* and *Voyage to the Bottom of the Sea*. She then co-starred in *Agent for H.A.R.M.*, originally conceived as a television pilot for a potential series but ultimately given a theatrical release.

After playing Moneypenny in *Casino Royale*, Bouchet returned to the spy genre again in *Danger Route*, then back on television had supporting roles in the Western series *The Virginian* plus *Star Trek* and *Tarzan*.

More film work followed, in *Sweet Charity* and the action movie *Surabaya Conspiracy*. However, feeling typecast, and also being unable to gain lead roles, Bouchet then decided to relocate to Italy, where a whole new world of cinema awaited her. Throughout the '70s she appeared in a large number of productions, realising her ambition of playing leads and in the process becoming a major actress in Italy. She was tempted back to the States on only one occasion, to take a role in the *Cool Million* pilot film.

During the first half of the '80s, Bouchet branched out into other European movies and then the multinational television movie *The Scarlet and the Black*, appearing alongside Gregory Peck and Christopher Plummer. Then, with the acting work drying up, she diversified into other areas by becoming a television celebrity, establishing a production company in 1985 and then producing a range of fitness videos and books, which eventually led to the opening of an exercise studio in Rome.

Resuming her acting career with the film *Our Tropical Island*, released in 2001, Bouchet continued with *Gangs of New York* the following year and then various Italian television series and movies up to the present day.

TERENCE COOPER (COOPER)

Carnmoney, Belfast, Northern Ireland, was the birthplace of Terence Cooper, who arrived in the world on 5 July 1933, going on to make his initial film appearance in the 1955 movie *Oh ... Rosalinda!!*. He then found his feet in various television series of the time, appearing in 14 episodes of the swashbuckling adventure show *The Buccaneers*, as well as episodes of *The Vise*, *William Tell* and *H.G. Wells' Invisible Man*. During the early '60s he also trod the boards, making an impression in various plays, including the musical *Lock up Your Daughters*, besides continuing to appear in television film series like *The Four Just Men* and *Danger Man*.

As the swinging '60s progressed, Cooper left television behind and concentrated on appearing in feature films. Then, after *Casino Royale*, there was a break of three years, when he worked neither in movies nor in television.

Resurfacing in Australia in 1971, Cooper began winning roles in television series such as *Barrier Reef* and *Boney*, and this provided him with work through until the early '80s. After that he became involved with a number of feature films made in New Zealand, and then spent time in the States, working on more movies and in 1986 an episode of the television series *Hotel*.

Returning down under, Cooper once again found supporting roles in movies and television productions made in Australia and New Zealand. His final credit, though, came on the 1995 American film *Hell's Belles*.

CHARLES K FELDMAN (PRODUCER)

Charles Gould, aka Charles K Feldman, was born on 26 April 1904 in New York. During his early twenties he gained work in the camera departments of various film studios, which included serving as a second assistant cameraman for director John Ford, in order to pay his university tuition fees. After attending the universities of both Michigan and Southern California, Feldman became a lawyer. He quickly formed his own law practice in 1928, but then dissolved it again four years later to join the staff of the Famous Artists talent agency, eventually rising to become its president. He personally managed the careers of stars John Wayne, Lauren Bacall, Stan Laurel, Richard Burton, Kirk Douglas, William Holden and Charles Boyer, proving most adept at negotiating on their behalf.

However, the draw of making movies proved irresistible for Feldman, and throughout the '40s he also became involved in various productions as either producer or executive producer (sometimes uncredited), beginning in 1942 with *The Lady is Willing*. This situation continued, though to a lesser degree, through the '50s and into the early '60s, when eventually Feldman turned Famous Artists from a management agency into a production company, starting with the television series *The Tab Hunter Show*. This was followed in 1962 by Famous Artists Productions' initial feature film, *Walk on the Wild Side*, a co-production with the Columbia Pictures Corporation, with Feldman once again occupying the position of producer.

As Feldman's productions always seemed to be successful, he quickly acquired the nickname 'the King Midas of Celluloid'. The next film he was involved with was *The 7th Dawn*, although this was not a Famous Artists production. It would be late 1964 before filming commenced in Paris on *What's New Pussycat?*, when Feldman and Famous Artists, financed by Columbia Pictures, assembled a talented cast to make what proved to be a big box office hit. There were two more Famous Artists film projects, *The Group* and *The Honey Pot*, before Feldman managed to get his mammoth production of *Casino Royale* under way in January 1966.

VAL GUEST (DIRECTOR & ADDITIONAL SEQUENCES)

Born in London on 11 December 1911, Valmond Guest was a multi-talented filmmaker who turned his hand to acting, writing, composing, directing and producing throughout a long and fruitful career in both movies and television.

Acting gave him his initial taste of the business when he appeared uncredited in the 1932 film *Old Spanish Customers*, and three years later he completed his first writing assignment by providing dialogue for the film *No Monkey Business*. The following year he provided lyrics for a song heard in the film *Public Nuisance No. 1*. Working continually throughout the late '30s and the early years of World War Two, he came to the 1943 musical *Miss London Ltd*, on which, besides writing the screenplay and the songs, he added another string to his bow by directing.

From then on Guest mostly left song-writing behind and focused on writing screenplays and directing his own material, eventually making the logical progression to producer with the 1952 film *Penny Princess*, made by his own production company Conquest.

Guest next formed an association with Hammer Films. This started in 1955 with *The Quatermass Xperiment*, which he both co-scripted and directed. Two years later, he returned for a repeat performance with *Quatermass 2*, followed by *The Abominable Snowman* and *The Camp on Blood Island*. Then, away from Hammer, he turned his attentions to the comedy film *Up the Creek* and its sequel *Further up the Creek*.

Trying something different, in 1959 Guest directed the British beat classic *Expresso Bongo*, starring a young Cliff Richard. He then took on both scripting and directing duties on *Life is a Circus* and *Hell is a City*. In the early '60s he was busy writing most of the screenplay for the comedy film *Dentist in the Chair* and both scripting and directing the science fiction drama *The Day the Earth Caught Fire* and the crime movie *Jigsaw*. He completed the drama *80,000 Suspects* in 1963, before making *The Beauty Jungle* the following year and then joining the spy movie craze with *Where the Spies Are* in 1965.

Upon completing *Casino Royale*, Guest quickly embarked upon another espionage film, *Assignment K*, once again assuming the dual roles of director and co-writer. In 1970 he fulfilled the same functions on the science fiction musical *Toomorrow*. That year also saw him make a brief return to Hammer Films for their prehistoric epic *When Dinosaurs Ruled the Earth*, before he became involved with ITC's television film series *The Persuaders!* and *The Adventurer*. Later, he resumed his usual practice of directing his own screenplay for the heist movie *The Diamond Mercenaries*, with an international cast that included Telly Savalas and Christopher Lee. Returning to television, he then directed three episodes of Gerry Anderson's *Space: 1999*.

After an absence of several years, Guest assumed the director's chair again in 1979 for nine episodes of the television series *Sherlock Holmes and Doctor Watson*, filmed on location in Poland. Over the following year he also directed the television movie *The Shillingbury Blowers* and all six episodes of its short-lived spin-off series *Shillingbury Tales*.

Resuming his usual double role of director and co-writer, Guest worked on the comedy movie *Dangerous Davies: The Last Detective* with Bernard Cribbins, before teaming up with Cannon and Ball for *The Boys in Blue*, based on the 1939 comedy *Ask a Policeman*. His career concluded in the early '80s, when he directed three feature-length segments of the television anthology series *Hammer House of Mystery and Suspense*.

KENNETH HUGHES (DIRECTOR)

Born on 19 January 1922, Liverpudlian Kenneth Hughes decided during his teens that he wanted a future in film production, which he managed to achieve by being proficient in both scriptwriting and directing. He got his break into the business by directing the comedy drama film *Wide Boy*, released in 1952, which paved the way for him to become involved with the *Scotland Yard* shorts being filmed at Merton Park Studios. Directing seven of these B-movies, which were originally used as supporting features to the main attraction in UK cinemas, Hughes also provided the screenplays for five of them. He returned to Merton Park in the mid-'50s to direct a couple more. A temporary transfer to television brought Hughes to the American anthology series *Alcoa Theatre*, for which he wrote a solitary segment in 1958, and then to the six-part BBC serial *Solo for Canary*, on which he was sole scriptwriter.

Hughes' favourite project was the 1960 film *The Trials of Oscar Wilde*, which he both directed and wrote. After this he worked on a mixture of movies and television productions, including ITC's *Espionage*. By 1966 he had both written and directed the comedy film *Drop Dead Darling*. The came his involvement with *Casino Royale*.

Subsequently Hughes again doubled up on writing and directing on both *Chitty Chitty Bang Bang* and, at the start of the

'70s, the historical movie *Cromwell*. After this however his scriptwriting duties were usually confined to television productions. Between 1973 and 1974 he wrote material for three BBC series: *Menace*, *Colditz* and *Dial M for Murder*. Meanwhile he also directed the 1974 film *The Internecine Project*.

Hughes' last combination of writing and directing came in 1976 with the picture *Alfie Darling*. This was followed by directing duties on the film adaptation of the comedy play *Sextette* and, his final work, the 1981 slasher movie *Night School*.

JOHN HUSTON (DIRECTOR)

John Marcellus Huston was born in the town of Nevada in Vernon County, Missouri, USA, on 5 August 1906. Like his friend Orson Welles, he became a respected director and all-round exponent of film production.

Huston began his involvement with the industry in 1929 by performing small and usually uncredited roles in various films, before turning his attention to scriptwriting to supply the screenplay for the 1931 movie *A House Divided*. Having diversified, he gained other writing assignments, though some of these were in an uncredited or dialogue-only capacity, until he established himself toward the end of the '30s.

Huston's introduction to directing came with the 1941 film noir classic *The Maltese Falcon*, for which he also provided the script, and this began an association with its star Humphrey Bogart. He then concentrated on directing, and reached his peak in this field toward the end of the '40s and during the '50s, commanding the action on several popular feature films. During 1947 and 1948 there were directing duties on *The Treasure of the Sierra Madre* and *Key Largo*, both starring Bogart, followed in 1950 by the heist movie *The Asphalt Jungle*. The success continued through to the late '50s, with high profile films such as *The Red Badge of Courage*, *The African Queen*, *Moulin Rogue*, *Beat the Devil*, *Moby Dick* and *Heaven Knows, Mr. Allison*. Along the way, he proved his great versatility by also occupying the position of producer and writing the screenplay for some of these movies.

As demand for his directing talents waned in the '60s, Houston returned to acting. However, there were still some major directing assignments in the early part of the decade, on *The Unforgiven*, *The List of Adrian Messenger* and *The Night of the Iguana*. This led to his involvement with *Casino Royale*, as both an actor and a director.

Dividing his time between acting and directing, Huston then continued working in films through into the early '70s, where he controlled events on *The Life and Times of Judge Roy Bean* and *The MacKintosh Man*, both starring Paul Newman.

Bringing Sean Connery and Michael Caine together for the 1975 film *The Man Who Would be King*, Huston both directed and co-wrote the screenplay, while around the same time he also appeared before the cameras in *Chinatown* and *The Wind and the Lion*. The following year, he played Professor Moriarty in the television movie *Sherlock Holmes in New York*, which was just one of many diverse roles he took on the big screen up to the end of the decade.

Huston's abilities as a director surfaced again in the first half of the '80s, with the World War Two football movie *Escape to Victory*, the feature film adaptation of the Broadway musical *Annie* and the black comedy *Prizzi's Honor*. A rare television appearance came in 1985 in a segment of the revived anthology series *Alfred Hitchcock Presents*, and there was another acting job the following year in the feature film *Momo*.

Huston's final contributions to the visual medium were his directing of the film *The Dead* and his portrayal of the Soul Collector in the television movie *Mister Corbett's Ghost* in 1987.

DEBORAH KERR (LADY FIONA/AGENT MIMI)

Deborah Jane Kerr-Trimmer was born in Helensburgh, Scotland, on 30 September 1921. Her initial screen appearance in the picture *Contraband*, released in 1940, was edited out before release. However, her following roles in the movies *Major Barbara* and *Love on the Dole* remained intact, and later she portrayed three different characters in the film *The Life and Death of Colonel Blimp*. By the beginning of the '50s she had progressed to leading roles, including in *King Solomon's Mines*, *Quo Vadis*, *The Prisoner of Zenda* and the 1953 adaptation of Shakespeare's *Julius Caesar*. A steady stream of further movie work followed, including in *From Here to Eternity*, *The King and I* opposite Yul Brynner and *Heaven Knows, Mr. Allison* alongside Robert Mitcham.

Kerr's career continued into the '60s with parts in mainstream films such as *The Sundowners*, *The Chalk Garden* and *The Night of the Iguana*, plus a solitary UK television appearance in Granada's *Play of the Week*. After completing her involvement with *Casino Royale*, she made another film with her close friend David Niven, when they both appeared in *Prudence and the Pill*.

Kerr effectively retired from acting after the 1969 picture *The Arrangement*, but was enticed back 13 years later, when she appeared in an instalment of the BBC's *Playhouse*. She then continued acting until the mid-'80s, concentrating on television movies with the exception of the feature film *The Assam Garden*, released in 1985. Her final credit came the following year with a major role in the television movie *Hold the Dream*.

DALIAH LAVI (THE DETAINER)

Daliah Levenbuch, aka Daliah Lavi, was born in the village of Shavei Tzion, in what was then the British mandate of Palestine – now Israel – on 12 October 1940. After studying dance she managed to obtain a supporting role in the 1955 Swedish film *The People of Hemso*. However, failing to capitalise on this breakthrough, she returned to Israel for active duty in the armed forces, and it was 1960 before she began appearing in a mixture of European-produced feature films. In 1965 she was cast in her first British film, *Lord Jim*, then after working in mainland Europe again, she became part of the multinational cast of Agatha Christie's *Ten Little Indians*.

With her strong accent and sultry femme fatale looks, Lavi found herself in the right place at exactly the right time, and she was suddenly in demand for the swinging '60s cycle of spy movies generated by the James Bond films. Major roles followed in the first Matt Helm film *The Silencers*, the spoof *The Spy with a Cold Nose*, *Casino Royale* and the light-hearted adaptation of Jules Verne's novel *From the Earth to the Moon*, filmed as *Jules Verne's Rocket to the Moon*. The espionage theme continued with *Nobody Runs Forever* and the second '60s Bulldog Drummond film, *Some Girls Do*, though with the spy fad burning itself out during the early '70s, Lavi found her acting opportunities becoming very scarce.

After co-starring alongside Yul Brynner and Leonard Nimoy in the spaghetti Western *Catlow*, released in 1971, Lavi found herself relegated to minor celebrity status on television programmes such as *Sez Les* and *Whodunnit?*. Seeing no future as a film actress, she relocated to Germany, where she began a new career as a recording artist, producing several highly successful hit records and also becoming a concert performer. Eventually, during the '90s, Lavi was tempted back to the visual medium, initially to take part in a television movie and later to appear in an episode of a German television series.

JOSEPH McGRATH (DIRECTOR)

Glaswegian Joseph McGrath, sometimes credited as Joe McGrath, was born in 1930 and entered the television industry by producing Michael Bentine's BBC comedy sketch series *It's a Square World*. He later directed and co-wrote an instalment of the BBC's drama anthology *Festival* and produced the short-lived BBC1 sitcom *The Big Noise*. He really established his name by directing and producing the first season of the BBC2 Peter Cook and Dudley Moore comedy sketch show *Not Only ... But Also*, and he also produced the BBC2 Frankie Howerd special *East of Howerd*.

After directing on *Casino Royale*, McGrath gravitated to the world of feature films, commanding the action on *30 is a Dangerous Age, Cynthia* and *The Bliss of Mrs Blossom*. He also directed a one-off Thames television version of BBC radio's *The*

Goon Show, transmitted on 8 August 1968. Having both written and directed the movie *The Magic Christian*, filmed at the beginning of 1969, McGrath then briefly returned to television as a director on the BBC2 Spike Milligan vehicle *Oh in Colour*.

After spending time away from the visual medium for a couple of years, McGrath resumed his involvement, penning the screenplay for the movie *Secrets of a Door-to-Door Salesman* and directing the family film *Digby, the Biggest Dog in the World*. In 1974 he directed both an episode of the Thames drama series *Zodiac* and the comedy movie *The Great McGonagall*. Then came the short presentation *Girls Come First*, on which he was credited under the name Croisette Meubles.

The Sherlock Holmes spoof *The Strange Case of the End of Civilization as We Know It* followed in 1977, with McGrath doubling up as writer and director. He then formed an association with Leonard Rossiter for an episode of *The Losers* and the *Rising Damp* feature film.

Mixing disciplines during 1983, McGrath co-wrote the comedy series *Goodnight and God Bless* and directed the final Morecambe and Wise film *Night Train to Murder*. His career concluded in 1984 with the television movie *The Mating Call*.

CAROLINE MUNRO (GUARD GIRL)

Originally from Windsor in Berkshire, Caroline Munro was born on 16 January 1949. She became involved with the media after being entered in the Face of the Year competition by her mother and photographer David Bailey. Chosen as the winner of the competition, held by *The Evening News*, Munro found this led to several modelling assignments and then a small role in the 1965 film *Smoke over London*, where she was credited as Beautiful Brunette. Her next roles were uncredited glamour parts in the short film *G.G. Passion* and the feature length movies *Casino Royale* and *Joanna*, though she maintained her modelling links, and in 1969 she became the face of Lamb's Navy Rum on billboard advertising for the next ten years.

Munro's career as an actress took an upturn when she

found herself cast and credited in the Spanish-filmed comedy Western *A Talent for Loving* and in the British movie *Where's Jack?*. However, her following minor roles in the early '70s films *The Abominable Dr. Phibes* and its sequel *Dr. Phibes Rises Again* were again uncredited.

Meanwhile, Muno's acting abilities had been recognised by director Alan Gibson, who cast her in a major credited role in Hammer Films' *Dracula A.D. 1972*. She then took the female lead part in the fantasy film *The Golden Voyage of Sinbad*.

Returning to Hammer, Munro appeared in *Captain Kronos: Vampire Hunter*. Then, taking advantage of her fantasy and horror movie experience, she took further film roles in *I Don't Want to be Born* and the Amicus adaptation of *At the Earth's Core*. Diversifying, she made her first television appearance alongside comedy actor Frankie Howerd in a segment of *The Howerd Confessions*, before returning to feature films to play the villainess Naomi in the Roger Moore Bond picture *The Spy Who Loved Me*. She then surfaced playing another bad girl in *The New Avengers* episode 'Angels of Death', and followed this up by assuming the female lead in the 1978 Italian science fiction film *Starcrash*. Munro then gained something of a reputation as the queen of slasher films, after starring in *Maniac*, *The Last Horror Film* and *Slaughter High*, which took her through to 1986 and the television movie *Cinderella: The Shoe Must Go On*.

The remainder of the '80s saw Munro doing a couple of European horror pictures, a television movie based on the French detective Maigret and an episode of the obscure television series *Cue Gary*. In the '90s, however, the acting work fizzled out, resulting in just two appearances, in the Canadian television series *Sweating Bullets* and the comedy drama film *To Die For*.

After the millennium, Munro experienced an upturn in her fortunes, and by 2003 she was back in demand, working on the horror fantasy *Flesh of the Beast*. As the decade progressed, she also appeared in the films *Domestic Strangers* and *The Absence of Light*. In 2013 she played up to her Hammer horror image by portraying a character credited as Evil Priestess in the *Midsomer Murders* story 'Death and the Divas'.

DAVID NIVEN (SIR JAMES BOND)

Born in London on 1 March 1910, David Niven arrived in showbusiness by performing an uncredited walk-on role in the 1932 film *There Goes the Bride*, before following up with similar roles over the next couple of years. Having gained a measure of experience, he began winning a steady stream of credited roles, beginning with the movie *Without Regret* in 1935. Having previously served for a time with the Highland Light Infantry, Niven re-enlisted during the Second World War, though during this period he was also allowed to appear in a couple of films, *The First of the Few* and *The Way Ahead*, as they were considered to have high propaganda value for the war effort.

After hostilities ceased, Niven took up residence in Hollywood, where he averaged a couple of film appearances a year, including in the 1950 release *The Elusive Pimpernel*. In the early '50s he began getting cast in American television productions, and in 1952 he co-founded the production company Four Star Television. For the next five years he became a recurring participant in the company's anthology series *Four Star Theatre*, playing a range of different characters.

In 1955 Niven began filming his defining role as Phileas Fogg for *Around the World in Eighty Days*, based on the Jules Verne novel, after which he appeared in multiple episodes of *Alcoa Theatre*, *Goodyear Theatre* and *Zane Grey Theatre* for American television.

Starting in April 1959, the American NBC network screened the anthology series *The David Niven Show*, with the actor introducing all 13 segments, although he starred in only one of them. As the '50s became the '60s, the actor refocused his attention on feature films, starring with Doris Day in *Please Don't Eat the Daisies* and then in *The Guns of Navarone*, adapted from the novel by Alistair MacLean.

The historical drama *55 Days at Peking* and *The Pink Panther* were Niven's cinematic outings for 1963. After this came Four Star's television co-production of *The Rogues*, which began transmission the following year, and in which he portrayed a goodhearted conman.

Unable to avoid the current trend of '60s espionage movies, Niven next assumed the role of amateur spy Dr Jason Love in *Where the Spies Are*, then returned to the subject after a couple more films for *Casino Royale*. In the late '60s he remained in demand as a leading man, appearing in the romantic comedy *Prudence and the Pill*, *The Impossible Years*, *The Extraordinary Seaman* and the light-hearted Franco-Italian heist movie *The Brain*.

During the early '70s Niven completed only a couple of films, but in 1974 normal service was resumed with *Vampira*, *Paper Tiger* and *Murder by Death*, in the latter of which he played Dick Charleston, a spoof of Dashiell Hammett's private detective character Nick Charles, aka the Thin Man.

Niven was cast in the Disney movie *Candleshoe*, released in 1977, then assumed the role of Colonel Race in the feature film adaptation of Agatha Christie's *Death on the Nile*. 1979 brought a major role amongst ITC's all-star cast for *Escape to Athena*, plus the mini-series *A Man Called Intrepid*. The following year saw him take parts in *Rough Cut* and alongside his good friend Roger Moore in *The Sea Wolves*.

Director Blake Edwards persuaded Niven to reprise his role of Sir Charles Lytton, originally seen in *The Pink Panther*, for both *Trail of the Pink Panther* and *Curse of the Pink Panther*, with his filming for both movies being completed within a week. The actor's final screen performance came under the direction of Bryan Forbes in the 1983 comedy film *Better Late than Never*.

ROBERT PARRISH (DIRECTOR)

Born on 4 January 1916 in Columbus, Georgia, USA, Robert Parrish was appearing uncredited in small film roles before his teens, though he later transferred behind the scenes, becoming an editor in 1939. He initially edited documentaries, but later progressed to cutting feature films, and received an Academy Award for working on the boxing drama *Body and Soul* released in 1947. Having advanced through the ranks, he then became a director in 1951 on *Cry Danger*, the first of a dozen feature films he was associated with during the decade.

Trying something different in 1959, Parrish moved across to television, where he directed an episode of the detective show *Johnny Staccato* and three segments of *The Twilight Zone*, before returning to films in 1963 with *In the French Style*. After completing the World War Two movie *Up from the Beach*, released in 1965, Parrish became involved with *Casino Royale*, where he obviously made an impression on Peter Sellers, going on to direct his next film, *The Bobo*. From there he went on location to Spain to direct the crime film *Duffy*. This was followed by Gerry Anderson's science fiction movie *Doppelgänger* and then the Western *A Town Called Hell*, released in 1971.

The French-based thriller *The Marseille Contract*, starring Michael Caine, Anthony Quinn and James Mason, provided Parrish with his penultimate directing assignment in 1974, after which he effectively retired from the visual medium. Nine years later, he returned briefly and collaborated with French director Bertrand Tavernier on a documentary called *Mississippi Blues*, about the history of blues and gospel music.

JOANNA PETTET (MATA BOND)

Joanna Jane Salmon, aka Joanna Pettet, was born on 16 November 1942 in London. She studied performing arts at the Neighborhood Playhouse: School of the Theatre in New York, and this led to roles in various Broadway plays, a 1964 episode of the series *Route 66* and then as a regular in the soap *The Doctors*. Moving to Hollywood, she made further television appearances, including in *The Fugitive*. Progressing further, she landed a recurring role in the medical series *Dr. Kildare* and became involved with the feature films *The Group* and *The Night of the Generals*, before being cast in *Casino Royale*.

Continuing her career, Pettet assumed the female lead in the British crime movie *Robbery*, but although she continued to make regular feature film appearances throughout the late '60s, by the early '70s she was employed far more on television work. She graced episodes of *Mannix*, *Banacek*, *McCloud* and *Police Story*, before making a rare return to the UK for a couple of segments of ATV's anthology series *Thriller*.

The concluding half of the '70s brought Pettet roles in a mixture of television movies and mini-series such as *Captains and the Kings*, and then the motion picture *The Evil*, released in 1978. She began the '80s by appearing in an episode of *Charlie's Angels*. She also played a supporting role in the television movie *The Return of Frank Cannon*, before taking on the lead in an instalment of Anglia Television's *Tales of the Unexpected*.

Although she still won occasional movie parts, the '80s brought Pettet a steady stream of American television work, including on three episodes of both *The Love Boat* and *Fantasy Island*, plus nine of the soap opera *Knots Landing*. More of the same followed, including a guest-starring role in *Knight Rider* and parts in *Hotel* and *Murder She Wrote*. She then disappeared from the screen for a while, but returned for her final acting work in the 1995 movie *Terror in Paradise*.

PETER SELLERS (EVELYN TREMBLE)

Richard Henry Sellers, aka Peter Sellers, was born into a theatrical family on 8 September 1925 in Southsea, Hampshire. He enlisted in the Royal Air Force during World War Two, and there met future collaborators Spike Milligan, Harry Secombe and Michael Bentine. Returning to civilian life after the war, Sellers followed in the family tradition by entering showbusiness, becoming involved in a travelling revue, for which he both played drums and did impressions. Wanting to progress further, he then teamed up with Milligan, Secombe and Bentine for the BBC radio comedy series *Crazy People*, which from its second season in 1951 was renamed *The Goon Show*. This zany, ground-breaking and extremely popular radio series provided the perfect vehicle for Sellers' impressive powers of mimicry, as he brought to life many strange and eccentric characters, including the famous Bluebottle.

During the early '50s there were attempts to transfer Goon humour to feature films with *Penny Points to Paradise* and *Down among the Z Men*, but Sellers' real breakthrough in motion pictures came in 1955 with *The Ladykillers*.

Having already sampled television work with the BBC sketch show *And So to Bentley*, Sellers then became involved with several short-lived ITV comedy series, namely *The Idiot Weekly, Price 2d*, *A Show Called Fred*, *Son of Fred* and *Yes, It's the Cathode-Ray Tube Show!*. As both the '50s and *The Goon Show* on radio reached their end, the actor returned to movies, where his talents were winning him increasingly significant parts in productions such as *Up the Creek*, *I'm All Right Jack*, *Carlton-Browne of the FO* and *The Mouse That Roared*, in the latter of which he played three different roles.

In 1960 *The Millionairess* saw Sellers co-starring alongside Sophia Loren, with whom he later performed the novelty song 'Goodness Gracious Me', which reached number four on the British record charts. Sellers' reputation as a first division comedy actor was cemented during the early part of this decade, when he worked on feature films such as *Two Way Stretch*, *The Wrong Arm of the Law* and *Heavens Above!*.

1963 saw a return to the Goons, when Sellers provided voices for the BBC1 puppet adaptation *The Telegoons*, and also the actor's first collaboration with director Blake Edwards on *The Pink Panther*, playing the bumbling Inspector Clouseau. Having taken a small part in Stanley Kubrick's *Lolita*, Sellers assumed three different roles for the same director's next film, *Dr. Strangelove or: How I Learned to Stop Worrying and Love the Bomb*, for which he received an Oscar nomination. The next few years brought further memorable film appearances in the second Inspector Clouseau movie *A Shot in the Dark*, the Anglo-Italian production *After the Fox* and Charles K Feldman's hit extravaganza *What's New Pussycat?*.

The success of *What's New Pussycat?* led to *Casino Royale*, after which Sellers starred in movies such as *The Bobo* with his then wife Britt Ekland, *The Party* for Blake Edwards and, alongside Ringo Starr, *The Magic Christian*. High-profile film roles continued during the early '70s, with top billing in both *Hoffman* and *There's a Girl in my Soup*, followed by a much smaller part in *A Day at the Beach*, for which Sellers was credited as 'A Queen'. There was a brief return to television when he joined his old friends Eric Sykes and Hattie Jacques on their BBC1 comedy series *Sykes* for an episode entitled 'Stranger', transmitted on 19 October 1972.

Sellers' career then entered a downturn, which began with negative reviews for the medical comedy *Where Does it Hurt?*, filmed during 1972. His next project, *Ghost in the Noonday Sun*, was made for Columbia Pictures, who considered it too limited in its appeal and refused to release it, eventually selling it for television screenings more than ten years later in 1984. Sellers' almost straight acting role in *The Blockhouse*, filmed in 1973, also went unseen in the UK at the time, as the film failed to find a distributor, hence had no cinematic release. However, the slide was halted by another straight role in the more successful 1973 film *The Optimists of Nine Elms*, and then a further multi-character performance the following year in *Soft Beds, Hard Battles*.

Teaming up with Spike Milligan again, Sellers appeared in *The Great McGonagall* in 1974, before being enticed back by Blake Edwards for *The Return of the Pink Panther* and *The Pink Panther Strikes Again* the following year, which resulted in him regaining mainstream popularity. 1976 saw the release of *Murder by Death*, in which Sellers took the role of Sidney Wang (originally offered to Orson Welles), a spoof of the famous Chinese detective character Charlie Chan. However, the actor was convinced the film would be a major flop, and before its general release he persuaded the producers to buy back his percentage of the profits, thus inadvertently causing himself to lose out when it became a success.

Two years later Sellers made his final appearance as Inspector Clouseau in *Revenge of the Pink Panther*, then went on to co-star alongside his fourth wife, Lynne Frederick, in the historical send-up *The Prisoner of Zenda*. Having read Jerzy Kosinski's novel *Being There* in 1972, Sellers thought that it would make a great motion picture, and this eventually occurred in 1979, with him assuming the role of Chance the gardener, which brought him another Oscar nomination.

Sellers' final film was *The Fiendish Plot of Dr. Fu Manchu*, in which he performed the dual roles of Nayland Smith and Fu Manchu, and this opened for business in the United States in August 1980. The actor died just before that, on 24 July 1980.

ORSON WELLES (LE CHIFFRE)

Hailing from the city of Kenosha in Wisconsin in the USA, Orson Welles was born on 6 May 1915, and would become a well-respected film-maker who could turn his hand to virtually any area of production.

After the death of his father, Welles travelled to Europe, and while in Ireland he managed to bluff his way into the acting profession in 1931 by performing in several plays staged at the Gate Theatre in Dublin. Having gained experience, Welles returned in 1935 to the USA, when he acted in a New York stage production. By the following year he had expanded his talents to include dramatist and director. Branching out into radio drama brought him some notoriety when his adaptation of H G Wells' novel *War of the Worlds*, broadcast on 30 October 1938, apparently caused some listeners to experience a mixture of fear and confusion, as they thought they were listening to news reports of an actual alien invasion.

Although he had already been involved in a couple of short films for the cinema, Welles' real entry into the industry came when RKO Radio Pictures offered him a two picture deal, which would result in him directing, producing and scripting *Citizen Kane* and *The Magnificent Ambersons*. Although now generally acknowledged as two of the greatest American films ever, both pictures were commercial failures at the time, and RKO then downgraded Welles' status, giving him the task of filming a South American documentary called *It's All True*. However, this failed to proceed as planned, as Welles took it upon himself to add a subplot involving the real-life plight of four poor fishermen who travelled 1,500 miles on a raft to petition the Brazilian president regarding their working conditions. RKO withdrew their support from the project and, arriving back in the USA, Welles found that neither they nor any other major film studio required his services, forcing a temporary return to radio.

Then, however, Welles managed to attract the company International Pictures to co-finance *The Stranger*, a thriller that he directed and cast himself in, the success of which partly restored his reputation with the major Hollywood studios.

Welles' early experiences in film-making had left him with an attitude of disliking and distrusting the powerful American film companies and the way they worked. Preferring more control over his celluloid endeavours, in 1947 he moved to Europe, and two years later was rewarded by playing the lead in and assisting (uncredited) in scripting another classic movie, *The Third Man*. Returning briefly to the US in 1953, he made his first television appearance performing the title role in a production of *King Lear* for the multi-format CBS series *Omnibus*. However, it was then back to Europe again, where he worked on two short British television series called *The Orson Welles' Sketch Book* and *Around the World with Orson Welles*.

Having by this point contributed to a large number of different productions, including in such varied areas as set and costume design, editing, music and cinematography, not to mention directing, producing, writing and acting, Welles was now in a position to work only on his own projects or those that interested him. One such venture was the 1958 crime drama *Touch of Evil* , one of the last classic film noirs, which he wrote, directed and co-starred in. However, the studio, Universal, re-edited the finished picture against his wishes. Preferring to avoid further involvement with large studio-backed movies, Welles then scaled down his producing and directing and concentrated more on his acting roles during the '60s, when he appeared in such diverse pictures as *Casino Royale* and *Oedipus the King*.

During the '70s Welles also relegated his writing and directing work to occasional outings as he amassed many more acting credits, including on the World War Two film *Catch-22* and the historical epic *Waterloo*. 1974 saw the start of transmissions of Anglia Television's anthology series *Orson Welles' Great Mysteries*, each episode of which opened with an introduction recorded by the actor.

The remainder of the '70s brought mainstream movie parts in *Voyage of the Dammed* and *The Muppet Movie*. Due to his distinctive deep voice, Welles was also in demand for narration and voice-over duties, including on a couple of episodes of *Magnum P.I.*, for which he voiced the character Robin Masters.

Welles' final television work was an introduction for the *Moonlighting* episode 'The Dream Sequence Always Rings Twice' in 1985, while his last feature film performance was a voice-over for a character in *Transformers: The Movie* in 1986. He was seen by cinemagoers one final time in the drama *Someone to Love*, released in 1987, although this had actually been shot a year earlier, before *Transformers: The Movie*.

APPENDICES

Appendix One
Production Details

A Famous Artists Productions Ltd production for Columbia Pictures

Screenplay: Wolf Mankowitz, John Law, Michael Sayers
Uncredited Screenplay: Woody Allen, Terence Cooper, Val Guest, Ben Hecht, John Huston, Joseph McGrath, Peter Sellers, Terry Southern, Orson Welles
Suggested by the novel *Casino Royale* by Ian Fleming
Directors: John Huston, Kenneth Hughes, Val Guest, Robert Parrish, Joseph McGrath
Additional Sequences: Val Guest
Certificate: U

Cast: Peter Sellers (Evelyn Tremble [James Bond – 007]), Ursula Andress (Vesper Lynd [007]), David Niven (Sir James Bond), Orson Welles (Le Chiffre), Joanna Pettet (Mata Bond), Daliah Lavi (The Detainer [007]), Woody Allen (Jimmy Bond [Dr Noah]), Deborah Kerr (Agent Mimi [alias Lady Fiona]), William Holden (Ransome), Charles Boyer (Le Grand), John Huston (McTarry [M]), Kurt Kasznar (Smernov), George Raft (Himself), Jean Paul Belmondo (French Legionnaire), Terence Cooper (Cooper [James Bond – 007]), Barbara Bouchet (Moneypenny), Angela Scoular (Buttercup), Gabriella Licudi (Eliza), Tracey Crisp (Heather), Elaine Taylor (Peg), Jacky Bisset (Miss Goodthighs), Alexandra Bastedo (Meg), Anna Quayle (Frau Hoffner), Derek Nimmo (Hadley), Ronnie Corbett (Polo), Colin Gordon (Casino Director), Bernard Cribbins (Taxi Driver), Tracy Reed (Fang Leader), John Bluthal (Casino Doorman and MI5

APPENDIX ONE: PRODUCTION DETAILS

Man), Geoffrey Bayldon (Q), John Wells (Q's Assistant), Duncan Macrae (Inspector Mathis), Graham Stark (Cashier), Chic Murray (Chic), Jonathan Routh (John), Richard Wattis (British Army Officer), Vladek Sheybal (Le Chiffre's Representative), Percy Herbert (1st Piper), Penny Riley (Control Girl), Jeanne Roland (Captain of the Guards).

Uncredited Cast (identified on screen): Lewis Alexander (Bus Passenger), Peter Ashmore (Barman and Artist Painting Woman Gold), Jack Arrow (Casino Patron), Jennifer Baker (Le Chiffre's Companion [Angel]), Susan Baker (Le Chiffre's Companion [Angel]), Alexandra Bastedo (Casino Patron), Roy Beck (American Tourist [Father] and Casino Patron), The Beck Family (American Tourists), Joseph Behrmann (Casino Patron [Business Man]), Paul Beradi (Passer-by in Horse Guards Parade), Jacky Bisset (Casino Patron [Giovanna]), Peter Brace (Cowboy), Jim Brady (Buckingham Club Patron), Penny Brahms (Casino Patron), Madge Brindley (Casino Patron [Miss Brindley]), RSM Ronald Brittain (Sergeant Major), Maurice Browning (Charlie), Diana Burford (Casino Patron [Daffy]), Peter Burton (British Agent), Andre Charisse (Customs Official), Eric Chitty (Sir James Bond's 2nd Butler), Alan Chuntz (Buckingham Club Patron and Chinese Army Officer), George Claydon (Gnome Spy), Jean Combie (Casino Patron), Harold Coyne (Casino Patron), Maxwell Craig (Buckingham Club Patron, Firing Squad Guard and Berlin Border Guard), Bill Cummings (Russian Army Officer and Cowboy), Mireille Darc (Jag), Wendy Davis (Guard Girl), Billy Dean (Cowboy), Anne De Vigier (Control Assistant), Alexander Doré (Casino Patron), Bee Duffell (Russian Army Officer), Valentine Dyall (Voice of Dr. Noah and Voice of Vesper Lynd's 2nd Assistant), Max Faulkner (Chinese Army Officer), Paul Ferris (Vesper Lynd's 1st Assistant), Jane Forster (Guard Girl), Joseph Furst (Russian Army Officer), Hal Galili (American Army Officer), Henry Gilbert (Casino Patron [Greek]), Bob Godfrey (Casino Patron [Peters] and Interrogation Prisoner), Stella Grove (Shirley and Guard Girl), Fred Haggerty (Waiter with Spittoons), Pat Halpin

MICHAEL RICHARDSON

(Casino Patron), Victor Harrington (Casino Patron), Delilah/Dee Hart (Levitated Casino Patron), Walter Henry (Firing Squad Guard and Casino Patron), John Hollis (Fred), Yvonne Horner (Guard Girl), Susanna Hunt/Geneveve (Lorelei), Ken Hutchins (Berlin Border Guard), Harry Hutchinson (Sir James Bond's 1st Butler), Mike Jarvis (Police Constable), Malcolm Johns (Casino Patron), Alf Joint (Casino Patron), Gerry Judge (Casino Patron), Pat Judge (Casino Patron), Juba Kennerley (Bystander in Trafalgar Square), Cyril Kent (Waiter), Burt Kwouk (Chinese Army Officer), Catherine Lancaster (Casino Patron [Tulip]), John Le Mesurier (M's Driver), Robert Lee (Casino Patron [Mr Lee]), George Leech (1st Native American), Fiona Lewis (Casino Patron [Penny], Car Wash Girl and Girl in Gym), Heather Lowe (Casino Patron [Charlie], Beauty Contestant and Guard Girl), Frank Maher (Casino Patron), Alf Mangan (Bystander in Trafalgar Square), Yvonne Marsh (Girl in Gym), Stirling Moss (Chauffeur), Caroline Munro (Guard Girl), Peter O'Toole (Piper), Peter Perkins (Casino Patron), Dido Plumb (Bystander in Trafalgar Square), Terry Plummer (Casino Patron), Suki Potier (Casino Patron), Joe Powell (Scottish Strongman, British Army Officer, Casino Patron with Black Hair and Casino Patron with Ginger Hair), Nosher Powell (Casino Patron), David Prowse (Frankenstein Monster), Louisa Rabaiotti (Guard Girl), Tracy Reed (Casino Patron), Rosemary Reede (Casino Patron [Reggie]), Milton Reid (Temple Guard), Peter Rendall (Bystander in Trafalgar Square), Jan Rennison (Casino Patron [Split]), Ernie Rice (Bystander in Trafalgar Square and Casino Patron), Marilyn Rickard (Guard Girl), Robert Rietty (Voice of Casino Receptionist), Doug Robinson (Scottish Strongman and Russian Army Officer), Jeanne Roland (Ting Ling), Robert Rowland (British Agent), Pat Ryan (Firing Squad Guard and Passer-by in Horse Guards Parade), Susan Sampson (Girl in Gym), Bill Sawyer (Russian Army Officer), Arnold Schulkes (Casino Patron), Carol Shaw (Control Assistant and Beauty Contestant), Dani Sheridan (Car Wash Girl), Julian Sherrier (Casino Receptionist), Paddy Smith (Casino Patron), Gary

APPENDIX ONE: PRODUCTION DETAILS

Standeven (Bus Driver [Stationary Bus]), Jean Stewart (Car Wash Girl), Philip Stewart (Casino Patron), Vanessa Sutton (Guard Girl), John Tatum (Man in Cab and Casino Patron), Larry Taylor (Russian Army Officer and Cowboy), Leon Thau (Johnson), Anne Thompson (Gold Painted Girl), Rita Tobin-Weske (Bystander in Trafalgar Square), Robin Tolehurst (Casino Patron [Robin]), Jim Tyson (Casino Patron), Valerie Van Ost (Casino Patron), Greta Van Rantwyk (Girl Fishing, Beauty Contestant and Gold Painted Girl), Gina Warwick (Casino Patron [Chocolate] and Car Wash Girl), Mona Washbourne (Tea Lady), Anita West (Casino Patron), Jenny White (Control Assistant, Beauty Contestant and Guard Girl), Ian Wilson (British Army Officer), Maggie Wright (Casino Patron [Blossom]).

Uncredited Cast (identified only in documentation, publicity material and photographic evidence): June Abbey (Casino Patron [Jake]), Hermione Baddeley (Headmistress), Sue Bardolph (Casino Patron [Rose]), David Berglas (Chef de Partie), Julie Bevan (Guard Girl), Lacey Bishop (Extra), Jasmin Broughton (Extra), Geraldine Chaplin (Keystone Kop), June Cooper (Extra), Frances Cosslett (Michele), Monti De Lyle (Cashier), Alexis Drury (Casino Patron [Pansy]), Antonia Ellis (Temple Dancer), Barbara French (Casino Patron [Violet]), Veronica Gardiner (Casino Patron [Jackey]), Helen Goss (Casino Patron [Mrs Goss]), Suzanne Heimer (Extra), Ian Hendry (Vesper's Victim), Vicky Hodge (Extra), Katherina Holden (Extra), Anjelica Huston (Agent Mimi's Hands), Anne Ibbotson (Daughter of the McTarry Clan), Mary Johnson (Extra), Yootha Joyce (Extra), Virginia Lane (Extra), Lisa Leigh (Extra), Dian Lloyd (Casino Patron [Alex]), David Lodge (Buckingham Club Patron), Maureen Lynne (Daughter of the McTarry Clan), Angela McDonald (Extra), Barry Melrose (Unknown Role), Arthur Mullard (Maintenance Man), Barry Noble (Extra), Peter Newman (Bus Driver), James Payne (Casino Patron), Ian Quarrier (Casino Patron [Jones]), Christine Rogers (Casino Patron [Farthing]), Dani Sheridan (Casino Patron [Melba]),

MICHAEL RICHARDSON

Christine Spooner (Casino Patron [Miss Russell]), Valerie Stanton (Extra), Laura Stephen (Extra), Karina Sterry (Casino Patron [Lily]), Jean Stewart (Casino Patron [Glory]), Una Stubbs (Nurse), Richard Talmadge (Keystone Kop) Virginia Tyler (Casino Patron [Heather]), Paul Weston (Native American).

Crew: Charles K Feldman, Jerry Bresler (Produced by), Jack Hildyard BSC (Director of Photography), John Wilcox BSC, Nicholas Roeg BSC (Additional Photography), Michael Stringer (Production Designer), Julie Harris (Costume Designer), Bill Lenny (Film Editor), Richard Williams (Titles and Montage Effects), John Dark (Associate Producer), Douglas Pierce, John Merriman, Barrie Melrose (Production Managers), John Howell, Ivor Beddoes, Lionel Couch (Art Directors), Roy Baird, John Stoneman, Carl Mannin (Assistant Directors), Chris Greenham (Sound Editor), James Shields (Dialogue Editor), Alan Strachan (Assistant Film Editor), John W Mitchell, Sash Fisher, Bob Jones, Dick Langford (Sound), Norman Dorme, Tony Rimmington (Assistant Art Directors), Bill MacLaren (Construction Manager), Richard Talmadge, Anthony Squire (Second Unit Directors), Tutte Lemkow (Choreographer), Terence Morgan (Set Dresser), Maude Spencer (Casting), Neville Smallwood (Chief Make-Up Artist), John O'Gorman (Make-Up for Ursula Andress), Joan Smallwood (Chief Hairdresser), Betty Adamson (Wardrobe Supervisor), Cliff Richardson, Roy Whybrow (Special Effects), Les Bowie (Special Matte Work), David Berglas (Technical Advisor).

Uncredited Crew: John C Shepridge (Pre-Production Supervisor), Russell Lloyd (Post-Production Supervisor), Anna Duse (Costume Designer), Dominic Fulford (Assistant Director), Renée Glynne (Continuity), Graham Fowler (Production Assistant), Assheton Gorton, Vincent Korda (Art Directors), Tristam Cary (Electronic Sound Effects), Richard Best Jr (Assistant Sound Editor), Leslie Dear (Visual Effects), Wally Armitage, Garth Inns, John Richardson (Special Effects), Gerald Larn, John Grant, Bob Cuff (Matte Painters), Errol Le Cain,

APPENDIX ONE: PRODUCTION DETAILS

Richard Williams (Titles and Montage Designers), Errol Le Cain, Helga Galler, Roy Jackson, Sergio Simonetti, Stephen Zavrel (Titles and Montage Animation), Rex Neville, Bill Rhodes (Titles Camera Effects), Gerry Fisher, Alex Thompson, Ken Worringham, Jack Lowin (Camera Operators), Ted Deason, Wally Fairweather, Anthony B Richmond (Focus Pullers), Trevor Coop (Camera Trainee), Pamela Green, Douglas Webb (Stills Photographers), Maurice Gillett (Supervising Electrician), Paul King (Set Dresser), Stuart Craig (Draughtsman), Michael Murray (Runner), John Collingwood (Production Accountant), John Wills (Publicist), Gerry Crampton (Stunt Co-ordinator).

Uncredited Stunt Performers: Gillian Aldam, Bob Anderson, Peter Brace, Ken Buckle, Jack Cooper, Gerry Crampton, Bill Cummings, Billy Dean, Tex Fuller, Rusty Hood, Arthur Howell, George Leech, Jimmy Lodge, Peter Munt, Keith Peacock, Terry Plummer, Dinny Powell, Joe Powell, Nosher Powell, Terry Richards, Roy Scammell, Tony Smart, Terry Yorke, Mike Reid (Stunt Driver), Richard O'Brien (Stunt Rider).

Additional Credits:
Costumes for Ursula Andress and Joanna Pettet by Bermans of London
Music Composed and Conducted by Burt Bacharach
Main Title Theme played by Herb Albert and the Tijuana Brass
'The Look of Love' sung by Dusty Springfield
Music by Burt Bacharach
Lyrics by Hal David
From Paris: Chombert (Furs for Ursula Andress), Paco Rabanne (Guard Girl Dresses), Guy Laroche (Casino Dresses)
Made at Shepperton Studios – England and Pinewood and MGM Studios – England

Uncredited Additional Credits
Lord Bolton: Grouse shooting stand-in for David Niven
Jewellery for Ursula Andress designed by Andrew Grima
Soundtrack Orchestrators: Jack Hayes, Leo Shuken

'Theme from Born Free' composed and performed by John Barry
'What's New Pussycat?' composed and written by Hal David and Burt Bacharach
'Have No Fear Bond is Here' composed and written by Burt Bacharach and Hal David, sung by Mike Redway

Appendix Two
Missing Scenes and Footage

Producer Charles K Feldman was naturally extremely displeased with Columbia Pictures' severe cutting back of his spectacular from around three hours to 131 minutes. This obviously begs the question: what exactly were the contents of the missing fifty minutes or so? Without having access to Feldman's original master print or screenplay, the only way to answer that question is to look at production stills showing action not present in the finished film, along with information from publications of the time, and to speculate and draw logical conclusions. The following missing scenes and footage have been identified:

A. There was a scene where Sir James Bond discovers John Huston's M being held prisoner along with his family in the dungeons of McTarry Castle, partly witnessed in the opening tiles and shown in a production still from the movie. **Source:** *007 Magazine* No. 40, *Casino Royale*, Michael Richardson and Graham Rye, The James Bond 007 International Fan Club, January 2002.

B. More footage was filmed on the Buckingham Club set than actually appears on screen, as there is photographic evidence showing Evelyn Tremble carrying out his duties as a croupier, with Sellers' close friend, actor David Lodge, sat beside him. Lodge does not appear in the finished picture. **Source:** *Cinema Retro* Vol. 2 No. 6, *The Look of … Mayhem*, Gareth Owen, Solo Publishing, September 2006.

APPENDIX TWO: MISSING SCENES AND FOOTAGE

C. Photographic evidence exists showing a scene of Sir James Bond inside 10 Downing Street talking with the tea lady played by Mona Washbourne (a character also seen on screen in the Harrods basement sequence) and a maintenance man portrayed by Arthur Mullard. **Source:** *007 Magazine* No. 40, *Casino Royale*, Michael Richardson and Graham Rye, The James Bond 007 International Fan Club, January 2002.

D. There was a scene of Vesper Lynd assassinating in her apartment a secret service agent played by Ian Hendry. **Source:** *007 Magazine* No. 40, *Casino Royale*, Michael Richardson and Graham Rye, The James Bond 007 International Fan Club, January 2002.

E. After leaving London in pristine condition, the black cab driven by Carton-Towers of the FO arrives in Berlin in a rundown state, suggesting a missing scene that would explain the damage.

F. The bathroom scene where Sir James Bond contacts Vesper Lynd was originally longer, as it included the large animated eye of King Kong, created by Richard Williams, seen through a window. This footage was actually included in prints of the movie screened on television until 1990, before being inexplicably purged for both televised transmissions and the VHS video release that year. The missing material was not reinstated when the film was later mastered onto DVD. Source: *The Life and Death of Peter Sellers*, Roger Lewis, Century, April 1994.

G. Another photograph shows Evelyn Tremble on the bedroom set brandishing his automatic pistol, with three throwing knives embedded in the units behind him, indicating that footage was edited from the Miss Goodthighs sequence. **Source:** *Cinema Retro* Vol. 2 No. 6, *The Look of ... Mayhem*, Gareth Owen, Solo Publishing, September 2006.

H. Photographs surfaced in the popular press showing Vesper Lynd in her underwear throwing a tantrum with Evelyn Tremble, filmed on the same bedroom set as the first dream sequence. **Source:** *Daily Mirror*, Trinity Mirror Group, 25 February 1966.

I. Another still shows that the beauty competition seen during Evelyn Trimble's psychedelic experience was originally longer, though it is unknown if this was connected to the footage filmed on the same set involving Vesper Lynd wearing a black mini dress. More production images show Vesper in this outfit, having apparently saved Tremble after machine-gunning two SMERSH assassins played by Chic Murray and Jonathan Routh, who are lying on the floor. **Source:** *Cinema Retro* Vol 2 No 6, *The Look of … Mayhem*, Gareth Owen, Solo Publishing, September 2006.

J. The Scottish marching band sequence that replaced the elephant riding scene involved some strange additional footage that was cut from the movie, featuring Sellers in full highland regalia but also wearing diving flippers. **Source:** *Cinema Retro* Vol 2 No 6, *The Look of … Mayhem*, Gareth Owen, Solo Publishing, September 2006.

K. There is an image of Orson Welles as Le Chiffre sat behind a console unit totally different from the one where, in the finished film, he meets his demise after being shot by one of the SMERSH assassins. **Source:** *007 Magazine* No. 40, *Casino Royale*, Michael Richardson and Graham Rye, The James Bond 007 International Fan Club, January 2002.

L. Logically there should be a scene where Sir James Bond is informed of Mata Bond's abduction, possibly while in conference with the Prime Minister.

M. There was originally footage of Mata Bond running though Dr Noah's underground pop art graphic-decorated headquarters, as glimpsed in both the opening titles and the closing credits.

APPENDIX TWO: MISSING SCENES AND FOOTAGE

Stills of this also exist. **Source:** *Cinema Retro* Vol 2 No 6, *The Look of… Mayhem*, Gareth Owen, Solo Publishing, September 2006.

N. There is no explanation in the finished film as to exactly how the Detainer becomes Jimmy Bond's prisoner, although her dialogue does give some indication: 'Why was I abducted from the roulette table and subjected to this?' This suggests the deletion of a casino scene, which could have featured Cooper as well, as it is never revealed how he suddenly turns up in the SMERSH confinement area with Sir James, Mata and Miss Moneypenny, who are all captured by the enemy on screen. **Source:** *007 Magazine* No. 40, *Casino Royale*, Michael Richardson and Graham Rye, The James Bond 007 International Fan Club, January 2002.

O. There are a couple of photographs showing a scene where Sir James Bond and Miss Moneypenny in scuba gear arrive near the rock-face entrance to the SMERSH headquarters, prior to their appearance in the casino. The headpiece of Moneypenny's wetsuit incorporates a fake seagull as camouflage, which would be visible on the surface when she is underwater – an idea copied from Eon Productions' *Goldfinger*. **Source:** *Playboy, The Girls of Casino Royale*, Playboy Enterprises, Woody Allen, February 1967.

P. Logically there should be a scene where Sir James and Moneypenny are escorted by the Guard Girls to the confinement area, where they are reunited with Mata Bond and Cooper.

Q. After escaping from the confinement area, Sir James, Mata, Moneypenny and Cooper all pass through a moving set, known as the fingerprint room because of the large continuous graphics covering its floor and walls, which simulate a giant fingerprint. Another production still confirms the shooting of this scene, featuring David Niven, Joanna Pettet, Barbara Bouchet and Terence Cooper, which failed to be included in the finished film. **Source:** *007 Magazine* No. 40, *Casino Royale*, Michael Richardson and Graham Rye, The James Bond 007 International Fan Club,

January 2002.

R. The Sunday 7 May 1967 edition of the American newspaper *The Gastonia Gazette* reported that the film's large-scale concluding melee was originally intended to occupy the entire final thirty minutes of the film, although there is no way of confirming this. Excluded from the wild brawl was more footage of the chimpanzee wearing a ginger toupee seen walking through the casino. **Source:** Opening titles. There is also a still photograph showing a missing scene where George Raft and the blonde David McCallum lookalike toast each other at the casino bar. **Source:** *Cinema Retro* Vol. 2 No. 6, *The Look of ... Mayhem*, Gareth Owen, Solo Publishing, September 2006. Further to this, additional images exist showing an unconscious Vesper Lynd lying against an overturned roulette table, amidst devastation. **Source:** *Playboy, The Girls of Casino Royale*, Playboy Enterprises, Woody Allen, February 1967. Another missing element involved a couple in a passionate embrace on the floor of the casino as general mayhem erupts all around them. **Source:** *Playboy, The Girls of Casino Royale*, Playboy Enterprises, Woody Allen, February 1967. Then, to confuse matters even further, a still exists showing cowboys emerging from an indoor swimming pool at the casino wearing scuba tanks. **Source:** *Cinema Retro* Vol. 2 No. 6, *The Look of ... Mayhem*, Gareth Owen, Solo Publishing, September 2006.

All of these tantalising clues only add to the mystery surrounding *Casino Royale* and what Feldman's three hour picture would have looked like in its original form. Unfortunately, after the passing of decades, it seems highly unlikely that Columbia Pictures/Sony Pictures Entertainment will ever reinstate the missing footage (which could in any case have been disposed of years ago) to create the ultimate *Casino Royale* release.

Appendix Three
Production Schedule

Joseph McGrath
Shepperton Studios
Second week in January to third week in February 1966
Main Cast: Peter Sellers, Ursula Andress, Orson Welles, Geoffrey Bayldon, John Wells, Jacky Bisset.

Robert Parrish
Shepperton Studios
Fourth week in February to fourth week in April 1966
Main Cast: Peter Sellers, Ursula Andress, Orson Welles, Duncan MaCrea, Colin Gordon, Chic Murray.

John Huston
Pinewood Studios
Second week in April to first week in June 1966
Main Cast: David Niven, Deborah Kerr, William Holden, Charles Boyer, Kurt Kazner, Tracy Reed.

Richard Talmadge
Shepperton Studios
Fourth week in May to second week in July 1966
Action scenes on the casino set.

Val Guest
MGM Studios
Third week in June to fourth week in September 1966
Main Cast: David Niven, Woody Allen, Barbara Bouchet,

APPENDIX THREE: PRODUCTION SCHEDULE

Jeanne Roland.
Guest splits his time between MGM Studios and Shepperton Studios.
Daliah Lavi joined this shoot from the second week in August.

Val Guest
Shepperton Studios
First week in July to fourth week in August 1966
Main Cast: David Niven, Ursula Andress, Woody Allen, Joanna Pettet, Terence Cooper, Barbara Bouchet.

Kenneth Hughes
MGM Studios
First week in August to first week in September 1966
Main cast: David Niven, Joanna Pettet, Bernard Cribbins, Derek Nimmo, Anna Quayle, Ronnie Corbett.

Val Guest
Shepperton Studios
Third week in September to second week in October 1966
Special effects shooting and pick-up shots.

Appendix Four
Recordings – UK Releases

Casino Royale tracks in **bold**

<u>7" Vinyl Singles</u>

ROLAND SHAW AND HIS ORCHESTRA
'The Look of Love'/'Have No Fear Mr Bond Is Here' (Decca F 12595, March 1967)

HERB ALPERT AND THE TIJUANA BRASS
'Casino Royale'/'Wall Street Rag' (A&M AMS 700, April 1967)

SHANI WALLIS
'The Look of Love'/'Let The Love Come Through' (London HL 10125, April 1967)

MIKE REDWAY
'Have No Fear Bond Is Here'/'My Poem For You' (Deram DM 124, April 1967)

DUSTY SPRINGFIED
'Give Me Time'/**'The Look of Love'** (Phillips BF 1577, May 1967)

BURT BACHARACH
'Bond Street'/'Alfie' (A&M AMS 702, May 1967)

THE HARRY ROCHE CONSTELLATION
'Casino Royale (Have No Fear Bond Is Here)'/'The Pad Of The

APPENDIX FOUR: RECORDINGS – UK RELEASES

Mountain King' (CBS 202653, July 1967)

CLAUDINE LONGET
'Good Day Sunshine'/**'The Look of Love'** (A&M AMS 708, September 1967)

THE FUNKY TRUMPET OF RAY DAVIES
'The Look of Love'/'Do You Love Me' (Fontana TF 867, September 1967)

VANILLA FUDGE
'Where Is My Mind'/**'The Look of Love'** (Atlantic 584 179, April 1968)

SERGIO MENDES & BRASIL '66
'With A Little Help From My Friends'/**'The Look of Love'** (A&M AMS 721, April 1968)

ANDY WILLIAMS
'The Look of Love'/'Our Last Goodbye' (CBS 3565, June 1968)

GLADYS KNIGHT AND THE PIPS
'The Look of Love'/'You're My Everything' (Tamla Motown TWG 844, February 1973)

7" EP

VARIOUS ARTISTS – THEMES FROM JAMES BOND FILMS
Includes **MERTENS BROTHERS STYLE**
'Casino Royale (Have No Fear Bond Is Here)' (CBS Special Products WEP 1126, 1967)

SOUNDTRACK ALBUM

Casino Royale (RCA SF 7874, stereo LP, June 1967)

Casino Royale (RCA RD 7874, mono LP, June 1967)

Casino Royale (Varese Sarabande, stereo LP, November 1990)

Casino Royale (Varese Sarabande, CD, November 1990)

Resources

Books

The Official Music Master Labels Catalogue, The Music Master Team, MBC Information Services, April 1991.

Websites

45Cat, retrieved September 2014.
Soundtrack Collector, retrieved September 2014.

Index

20th Century Fox 15-16, 19-20, 119
39 Steps, The 14
After the Fox 44, 93, 206
Agent Mimi/Lady Fiona 90, 102, 105, 109, 127, 153, 197, 213, 216
Allen, Woody 26-27, 33-35, 38, 41, 47-51, 53, 56-57, 60-61, 96, 99-100, 102, 107, 112, 121-122, 125-128, 130, 132-133, 139, 141, 143-145, 147-148, 168-169, 171, 178, 187-188, 213, 224-225, 227-228
Alpert, Herb 167, 174-175, 229
Andress, Ursula 33-34, 52-53, 60-61, 66, 81, 85-86, 88, 92-93, 100, 117, 122, 124, 132, 146, 148, 160, 165, 169, 171, 188-189, 213, 217-218, 227-228
Andrews, Harry 107
Ardmore Studios 105, 110
Ashmore, Peter 140, 145, 214
Austin Powers in Goldmember 181
Austin Powers: International Man of Mystery 180-181
Austin Powers: The Spy Who Shagged Me 181
Avengers, The 58, 62, 68, 71, 80, 131, 134
Bacharach, Burt 43, 93, 110, 128, 141, 157, 161-167, 170, 177, 181, 184, 218-219, 229
Baker, Jennifer 70-71, 214
Baker, Stanley 52
Baker, Susan 70-71, 214
Bananas 145, 187
Baron, The 115, 132
Barry, John 112, 219
Bastedo, Alexandra 70, 93, 106, 213-214
Bayldon, Geoffrey 65, 214, 227
Beatles, The 50, 75
Beck, Roy 135, 139, 214
Belmondo, John Paul 148, 213

Bennett, Charles 14
Bird, John 65
Bisset, Jacky/Jacqueline 67-68, 71, 161, 189-190, 213-214, 227
Bluthal, John 74, 213
Bolt, Robert 102
Bond, Jimmy/Dr Noah 15, 99-100, 109, 122, 125-126, 128-129, 131, 136, 139-140, 143-145, 148-149, 187, 213-214, 223-224
Bond, Mata 45, 100, 123, 125, 127, 133-137, 143, 148-149, 151, 153-157, 170, 204, 213, 223-224
Bond, Sir James 46, 50, 52, 60, 86, 100-101, 103-104, 108-109, 113, 122-125, 127-129, 131-132, 134, 136-139, 146, 148-150, 153, 163, 202, 213, 221-224
Bonhams 110
Born Free 112, 219
Bouchet, Barbara 122-124, 127, 162, 169, 171, 173, 190-191, 213, 224, 227-228
Bowie, Les 135, 217
Boy and the Bridge, The 17-18
Boyer, Charles 101-103, 192, 213, 227
Brace, Peter 138, 214, 218
Brady, Jim 60, 214
Brahms, Penny 72, 214
Bresler, Jerry 82-83, 86, 95, 106, 160, 162, 169, 171, 178, 217
Brindley, Madge 72, 214
Broccoli, Albert R/Cubby 20, 22, 24, 32, 35-38, 53, 162
Bryce, Ivar 17-18, 24
Buxton, Frank 61, 127, 168
CBS 13, 17, 20, 146, 209, 230
Chitty, Erik 104, 214
Christian, Linda 14
Chuntz, Alan 60, 152, 214
Collins, Joan 47

Columbia Pictures   10, 22, 36-40, 43, 47, 63, 75, 85, 90-91, 96, 99, 106, 126, 133, 161-162, 169, 175-176, 178-180, 193, 207, 213, 221, 225
Combie, Jean   139, 214
Connery, Sean   10, 23-25, 27, 29, 32, 35-37, 41, 52, 104, 197
Cook, Peter   42, 199
Cooper   137-138, 140, 146-148, 224
Cooper, Terence   31-32, 37, 39, 44, 100, 109, 123-125, 127, 146, 168, 191-192, 213, 224, 228
Corbett, Ronnie   80, 143, 151, 155-156, 213, 228
Craig, Daniel   182
Craig, Maxwell   60, 128, 155, 214
Cribbins, Bernard   151, 154-155, 195, 213, 228
Crisp, Tracey   106, 171, 213
Cummings, Bill   138, 152, 214, 218
Cuneo, Ernest   18
Daily Cinema, The   36, 52-53, 58-59, 62, 70, 83, 85, 90, 99, 101, 108, 118, 134, 142-143, 152, 158, 170
Daily Express   16, 44, 47, 50, 103, 134, 158-159, 171
Daily Mail   126, 175
Daily Mirror   32, 71, 80-81, 118, 128, 131-132, 143, 162, 175-176, 223
Danger Man   19-20, 89, 101, 115, 165, 192
Darc, Mierille   113, 214
Dark, John   68, 84-85, 217
David, Hal   43, 93, 141, 161, 163, 165, 177, 218-219
Davis Junior, Sammy   117
Davis, Wendy   130, 214
Deadlier Than the Male   118
Department S   71
Detainer, The   123, 139, 144-145, 148, 150, 198, 213, 224
Diamonds Are Forever   17
Donner, Clive   33-34, 41
Dorme, Norman   131, 217

Dr. No   10, 20, 22-23, 29, 33, 35, 52-53, 132, 146, 153, 180, 188, 214
Duse, Anna   110, 217
Dyall, Valentine   129, 132, 136, 214
Edwards, Blake   38, 76, 203, 206-207
Ekland, Britt   28, 60, 68, 96, 207
Ellis, Anthony   14
Ellis, Antonia   153, 216
Eon Productions   10, 22-23, 30, 32, 35, 38, 40, 43, 50, 53, 62, 64, 94, 112, 130, 133, 140, 153, 157, 162, 180, 182, 224
Eye of the Devil   127
Famous Artists Productions   24, 36, 70, 83-84, 93, 97, 121, 123, 149, 192-193, 213
Feldman, Charles K   9-10, 15, 20-21, 23-27, 29-57, 59-60, 62, 65, 68-69, 73, 75-76, 79-82, 84-86, 90-92, 94, 97-103, 105, 107-108, 112-113, 117, 119, 121-127, 131, 133, 141-143, 145, 147-148, 151, 153-154, 158, 160-171, 175-176, 178-180, 182-184, 187-189, 192-193, 206, 217, 221, 225
Fenn, Bob   21
Ferris, Paul   132, 214
Film Night   51
Financial Times   175
Finch, Peter   20
Fleming, Ian   10, 13-19, 21-22, 24, 30-32, 44, 50, 52, 105, 111, 174, 180, 213
For Your Eyes Only   17
Forbes, Bryan   40, 75, 203
Force, Nigel   41, 45, 48, 52, 57
Forster, Jane   130, 169, 214
From Russia with Love   17, 21, 23, 157
Funeral in Berlin   118
Funny Girl   60
Gardiner, Veronica   72, 216
Garrison, Michael   15-16, 20
Gastonia Gazette   72, 225

Ghost Squad	118	ITC	19-20, 32, 89, 112, 129, 132, 194-195, 203
Godfrey, Bob	64, 72, 214		
Goldfinger	32, 35, 43, 140, 224	*Jigsaw*	23, 194
		Johnson, Nunnally	101-102
Gone with the Wind	16	Joint, Alf	138, 215
Gordon, Colin	92, 213, 227	Jonathan Cape Ltd	13
Grant, Cary	23, 26, 57	Jones, Tom	43, 167
Great McGonagall, The	75, 200, 207	Kasznar, Kurt	102-103, 213
		Kennedy, President John F	21
Grove, Stella	130, 146-147, 214	Kennerley, Juba	135, 215
		Kerr, Deborah	90, 101-103, 106, 108-109, 119, 127-128, 143, 197-198, 213, 227
Guest, Val	9, 22-23, 49-50, 53, 56, 59-60, 85, 97, 99, 102, 117, 119, 121, 123-127, 130-131, 133-134, 137-139, 141-143, 145-147, 150-151, 153, 160, 163, 168, 171, 176, 181, 193-195, 213, 227-228		
		King Kong	222
		Kiss Me Stupid	27-28
		Lavi, Daliah	123-124, 144-145, 147, 150, 171, 198-199, 213, 228
Haggerty, Fred	139, 214		
Hancock, Tony	57, 65		
Harrington, Victor	139, 215	Law, John	80, 82, 168, 213
Harris, Julie	86, 110, 131, 177, 217	Le Chiffre	14, 25, 29, 46, 64, 66, 69-70, 72, 79, 86-88, 109, 128, 132, 142, 151-152, 157-158, 160, 208, 213-214, 223
Harvey, Laurence	52, 171		
Haunted House of Horror, The	71		
Hawks, Howard	23	Le Grand	102, 110, 213
Hecht, Ben	16, 25-26, 28-30, 33, 152, 168, 213	Le Mesurier, John	110, 215
		Leech, George	140, 215, 218
Heller, Joseph	38	Lester, Richard	75
Hendry, Ian	62, 216, 222	Lewis, Fiona	72, 91, 169, 215
Herbert, Percy	106, 214	Licudi, Gabriella	106, 109, 213
Hitchcock, Alfred	14, 18	*Life*	21, 176
Holden, William	52, 102-103, 147, 192, 213, 227	*Live and Let Die*	14, 32, 111
		Longitude 78 West	18-19, 21, 24
Horner, Yvonne	130, 215	Loren, Sophia	41, 44, 98, 206
Hughes, Kenneth/Ken	22, 98, 143, 151-153, 171, 195-196, 213, 228	Lorre, Peter	14, 155
		Lowe, Heather	71, 87, 215
		Lynd, Vesper	14, 25, 29, 52, 60-61, 64, 67, 75, 85, 87-88, 99, 109, 132, 135, 137-139, 142, 164, 213, 222-223, 225
Huston, Anjelica	106, 171, 216		
Huston, John	49, 63, 84-85, 90-91, 93, 101-106, 108-109, 112-113, 117-119, 124, 127, 143, 146, 160, 168, 171, 196-197, 213, 221, 227		
		M/McTarry	20, 25, 84, 101-102, 104, 108-110, 213, 221, 223
Hutchinson, Harry	104, 215	*Macbeth*	46
Ibbotson, Anne	106, 216	MacLaine, Shirley	26-27, 44-47, 125
Inspector Clouseau	58, 63, 128, 134, 206-207	Macmillan Publishing Company	13-14
		Macrae, Duncan	61-62, 159, 214
Interpol Calling	20, 39		
Ipcress File, The	118	*Magic Christian, The*	75, 200, 207

Maher, Frank 138, 215
Man from U.N.C.L.E., The 142, 190
Man Who Knew Too Much, The
  14
Mankowitz, Wolf 22, 35, 41-45, 48, 55-56, 59, 67, 80, 100, 121, 124-126, 140, 142, 168, 178, 184, 213
Margaret, Princess 73-74
Maroc 7 71
Marx, Groucho 33, 63
MCA 18-19
McClory, Kevin 17-19, 21, 24, 32, 35, 180
McGoohan, Patrick 19-20, 89
McGrath, Joseph/Joe 42-44, 55-57, 59, 66-68, 70, 73-75, 79, 83, 98, 125, 164, 166, 178, 199-200, 213, 227
MGM Borehamwood Studios
  121, 127, 130, 134, 141, 143-144, 149, 151, 154, 156-157, 159, 218, 227-228
Milligan, Spike 51, 127, 200, 205, 207
Moneypenny 29, 122-123, 128-129, 136-137, 146, 148, 191, 213, 224
Moonraker 111
Moore, Dudley 42, 199
Moore, Roger 32, 130, 153, 201, 203
Morley, Robert 20, 84
Moss, Stirling 58-59, 117, 215
Munro, Caroline 130-131, 171, 200-201, 215
Murray, Chic 66, 86-88, 96, 128, 171, 214, 223, 227
Naked Truth, The 42
Nelson, Barry 14
New York Times 16, 176
Nimmo, Derek 151-152, 154, 213, 228

Niven, David 51-52, 59-60, 81, 84, 90-91, 100-103, 105-106, 108-111, 113, 117-119, 122-123, 125, 127-129, 132, 134-137, 140, 143, 146, 148-149, 151-152, 157-158, 160, 171, 173, 184, 198, 202-203, 213, 218, 224, 227-228
Not Only ... But Also 42, 199
O'Neill, Terry 117
O'Toole, Peter 27, 34, 52, 88, 99, 215
Observer, The 175
Orson Welles' Sketch Book, The 209
Parrish, Robert 76-77, 79-82, 85, 94-99, 203-204, 213, 227
Pettet, Joanna 100, 123, 134-135, 143, 151, 153-154, 169, 204-205, 213, 218, 224, 228
Pinewood Studios 101, 106, 111, 113, 117-119, 134, 162, 218, 227
Pink Panther, The 51, 54, 202-203, 206-207
Playboy 131, 133, 152, 169, 224-225
Plumb, Dido 135, 215
Plummer, Terry 140, 215, 218
Potier, Suki 71, 215
Powell, Joe 106, 138-139, 152, 157, 215, 218
Prisoner, The 128
Prowse, David/Dave 89, 96-97, 148-149, 215
Quayle, Anna 143, 151, 155, 213, 228
Quiller Memorandum, The 118
Rabaiotti, Louisa 130, 144, 215
Rabanne, Paco 130-131, 218
Raft, George 141-142, 213, 225
Randall and Hopkirk (Deceased)
  72
Randall, Frankie 57
Ransome 102, 110, 147, 213
Ratoff, Gregory 15-16, 20
Redway, Mike 164, 174, 182, 219, 229

Reed, Tracy   70-72, 82, 91, 106, 109, 171, 213, 215, 227
Reede, Rosemary   71, 215
Rennison, Jan   71, 215
Return of the Pink Panther, The   74, 207
Richard, Cliff   84, 194
Richardson, Cliff   135, 217
Rickard, Marilyn   130, 149, 169, 215
Rietty, Robert   138, 215
Riley, Penny   113-114, 214
Robertson, Cliff   76
Robinson, Doug   106, 152, 157, 215
Rocket to the Moon   150, 199
Roeg, Nicholas   117-118, 151, 217
Roland, Jeanne   129-130, 147, 149, 171, 214-215, 228
Rolling Stones, The   71
Rose, Mickey   61, 126, 168
Routh, Jonathan   87-88, 96, 128, 214, 223
Ryan, Pat   128, 135, 215
Saint, The   32, 115
Saltzman, Harry   20-22, 32, 35-37
Sampson, Susan   146, 215
Sayers, Michael   38-39, 45, 80, 168, 213
Scarface   16, 141
Scoular, Angela   106, 118, 171, 213
Sellers, Peter   27-28, 31, 33-34, 36, 39-46, 48, 50-61, 63, 65-70, 72-77, 80-83, 85-89, 91-100, 102-103, 117, 125-126, 132, 142, 164, 168, 171, 175, 183, 204-208, 213, 221-223, 227
Sellers-Mankowitz Productions   41-42
Semple Junior, Lorenzo   16
She   33, 188

Shepperton Studios   53-54, 56, 58-59, 61-62, 66, 68, 73-74, 76, 79-80, 82-83, 85, 88-90, 94-97, 99-101, 108, 117, 121, 126, 131, 134, 137, 141, 143, 150-151, 157-159, 183, 218, 227-228
Shepridge, John C   36, 217
Sheridan, Dani   91, 215-216
Sherrier, Julian   138, 215
Sheybal, Vladek   152, 157, 214
Shot in the Dark, A   58, 82, 154, 206
Sleeper   145, 187
Smernov   102, 110, 213
SMERSH   66, 87-88, 90-91, 104, 113-116, 124, 126, 128-131, 138-140, 148, 155, 223-224
Snowden, Lord   73
Southern, Terry   45, 168, 213
Spencer, Maude   36, 94, 217
Springfield, Dusty   166, 176, 181, 218, 229
Spy Who Loved Me, The   130, 153, 201
Squire, Anthony   112, 217
Stark, Graham   61, 76-77, 81-82, 94, 214
Stewart, Jean   91, 216-217
Stewart, Robert Banks   19-20
Streisand, Barbra   60, 98
Stringer, Michael   62, 155, 217
Stubbs, Una   58-59, 62, 217
Sun, The   81, 83, 175
Sunday People, The   175
Sunday Times, The   18, 63, 73, 175
Sutton, Vanessa   130, 144, 169, 216
Take the Money and Run   47-48, 107, 187
Talmadge, Richard   112-113, 117, 121, 126, 133, 137-139, 151, 158-159, 217, 227
Taylor, Elaine   106, 171, 213
Taylor, Larry   138, 157, 216
Tempo   42
That Riviera Touch   70
Thunderball   19, 21-22, 24-25, 32, 35, 37, 43, 94, 174, 180

Tremble, Evelyn   57-58, 60-65, 67, 69, 74, 79, 85-89, 92, 96-97, 99, 109, 114, 132, 142, 158, 160, 164, 213, 221-223
UFO   130
United Artists   10, 22-24, 33-35, 37, 40, 48, 62
Universal Pictures   47, 149, 209
Van Ost, Valerie   71, 216
Van Rantwyk, Greta   87, 106, 140, 216
Variety   20, 23-24, 26, 33, 35-40, 44-46, 48, 52-53, 57, 59-60, 79, 81, 90-91, 94, 99, 105, 107, 118-119, 133, 144, 150, 157, 161, 163, 176, 178
Warwick, Gina   71, 91, 216
Wattis, Richard   152, 214
Welles, Orson   32, 45-46, 50, 53, 55-56, 66-67, 69-76, 79-80, 82, 85, 91, 94-95, 103, 117, 168, 171, 183-184, 196, 207-210, 213, 223, 227
Wells, John   214, 227
West, Anita   71, 216
What's New Pussycat?   26, 33-36, 39, 41, 43, 47, 54, 57, 66, 69, 88, 107, 113, 157, 162, 167-168, 187-188, 193, 206, 219
What's Up Tiger Lily?   60
Where the Spies Are   127, 194, 203
White, Jennifer/Jenny   87, 114, 130, 216
Whittingham, Jack   19, 24-25
Whybrow, Roy   135, 217
Wild Wild West, The   15
Wilder, Billy   27-28, 30, 38
Williams, Richard   63, 168, 217-218, 222
Wright, Maggie   70, 216
Xanadu Productions   18-19, 24
You Asked For It   14-15
You Only Live Twice   37, 133-134, 162
Young, Terence   23
Zanuck, Darryl   15, 19

About the Author

Michael Richardson is a freelance writer specialising in cult television and film. He has previously been responsible for Telos Publishing's *Bowler Hats and Kinky Boots: The Unofficial and Unauthorised Guide to The Avengers*, a comprehensive reference guide to the televised adventures of John Steed and his various assistants during the '60s and *The New Avengers* in the '70s. He has had articles and features published in various magazines including *TV Zone*, *Book and Magazine Collector*, *Record Collector* and *007 Magazine*. Between 1999 and 2007, he both edited and was the main contributor to the cult television magazine *Action TV*. For many years he has had a fascination with Charles K Feldman's '60s James Bond spy spoof *Casino Royale* and exactly how this multimillion-dollar extravaganza was filmed and assembled from different storylines and plot elements.

TELOS PUBLISHING
Email: orders@telos.co.uk
Web: www.telos.co.uk

To order copies of any Telos books, please visit our website where there are full details of all titles and facilities for worldwide credit card online ordering, as well as occasional special offers.

Printed in Great Britain
by Amazon